EVANGELISM IN AMERICA

EVANGELISM IN AMERICA

From Tents to TV

William Packard

PARAGON HOUSE
New York

First edition, 1988

Published in the United States by

Paragon House Publishers
90 Fifth Avenue
New York, NY 10011

Library of Congress Cataloging-in-Publication Data
Packard, William.
Evangelism : from tents to TV.
Bibliography: p.
Includes index.
1. Evangelistic work—History. I. Title.
BV3770.P33   1988   269'.2'09   87-2230
ISBN 0-913729-73-6
1-55778-179-6 (pbk.)

Manufactured in the United States of America

Contents

Preface		*vii*
Introduction	EVANGELISM: DIVINE AND DANGEROUS	*1*
Chapter 1	MARTIN LUTHER AND THE PROTESTANT REFORMATION	*22*
Chapter 2	THE GROWTH OF PROTESTANT EVANGELISM	*34*
Chapter 3	PURITAN AMERICA AND THE GREAT AWAKENING	*43*
Chapter 4	THE SOCIAL GOSPEL	*56*
Chapter 5	AMERICAN FUNDAMENTALISM	*67*
Chapter 6	DWIGHT L. MOODY	*77*
Chapter 7	TWENTIETH CENTURY EVANGELISTS	*95*
Chapter 8	BLACK EVANGELISTS	*125*
Chapter 9	MARTIN LUTHER KING, JR.	*138*
Chapter 10	BILLY GRAHAM	*151*
Chapter 11	RADIO AND TELEVISION EVANGELISTS	*162*
Chapter 12	FOUR CONTEMPORARY EVANGELISTS	*181*
Chapter 13	JERRY FALWELL	*200*
Chapter 14	WHY IN AMERICA?	*215*
Chapter 15	WHAT THEOLOGY FOR OUR POST-MODERN ERA?	*228*
Afterword	TOWARDS A NEW EVANGELISM	*244*
Suggested Reading		*259*
Index		*265*

Preface

THERE IS HARDLY any area of human behavior that is so highly charged as this controversial subject of Evangelism in America. Americans have been exposed to such a systematic onslaught of Evangelists in the twentieth century that they are not sure what to make of all the prophesies and promises, all the frenzy and flapdoodle.

I know of no single book that tries to trace the origins and practices of Evangelism in America today, in order to offer the reader some coordinates to gauge the authenticity of this phenomenon.

I did not set out to fan the flames of any of the Evangelical positions that are set forth in this book: I have tried to give as objective an account of the subject as I am capable of, and I would be glad if the book were seen as a comprehensive evaluation of the widespread desperate need for faith and values in our civilization today.

My own opinions should be fairly evident: I see no reason to conceal my heartfelt admiration for the lives and teachings of certain persons who are represented in this book—Jesus of Nazareth, Augustine, Martin Luther, Blaise Pascal, Albert Schweitzer, Mahatma Gandhi, Marcus Garvey, Malcolm X, and Martin Luther King, Jr. I confess to having ambivalent feelings towards St. Paul, and a profound partiality to the writings of Alexis de Tocqueville, Friedrich Nietzsche, Fyodor Dostoyevski, Rainer Maria Rilke, Leo Tolstoy, Henry David Thoreau, Sigmund Freud, and H. L. Mencken. I find I concur with almost all of the judgments that Marjoe Gortner makes about the contemporary Evangelists, which are cited in this book.

The reader will find that my approach to the subject of Evangelism is far-ranging in nature, and my definition of the term "Evangelism" is a broad one. As for the Evangelists, historical and contemporary, who are represented in this book, I have not tried to mask my criticisms, and any reader who may disagree with the choices or approaches I have taken here is welcome to explore the vast literature in a subject where there are enough divergent opinions to suit any taste. There is a list of Suggested Reading in the back of this book.

There were several reasons why I wanted to write this book. First, the subject of Evangelism has concerned me all my life because I come from Evangelicals on both sides of my family: Pentecostal Baptists on one side, including Elizabeth Parsons Ware Packard, a brave lady who agitated for the reform of asylum commitment laws in the nineteenth century; and Dwight L. Moody on the other side, who was one of the most representative of all American Evangelists and whose Moody-Sankey Revivals did so much to set the stage for so many contemporary Evangelical Crusades.

The second reason I wanted to write this book is that for the last twenty years I have had the good fortune to edit a national poetry magazine, the *New York Quarterly*, and to teach poetry writing classes at New York University, as well as acting and playwriting classes at the H. B. Studio in Manhattan. All these activities of editing, teaching, and writing imply a transfer of value systems that may take place in creative situations, a subtle kind of psychological Evangelism which can be stultifying to all parties concerned unless one labors to remain conscious of the strong transference field. Evangelism, then, and the subtle techniques of unconscious persuasion, must become a lifelong fascination for anyone who is involved in any aspect of education and the arts.

And finally, I wanted to write this book out of an enormous curiosity I had to try to understand why our American society should be so peculiarly susceptible to this practice of Evangelism, and what the phenomenon may mean to ourselves and to our world.

There was an enormous amount of research and interviewing over several years that went into investigating the subject matter of this book. Wherever possible I have tried to use primary sources which gave the actual words and sermons of the Evangelists themselves, as well as historical documents and court records which would help fix their place in time. All Bible references are to the 1611 King James Version. The reader will observe that my book uses no footnotes or citation sources because I did not want it to be cluttered with scholarly apparatus: I mention each primary source as I give it.

I am grateful to the many individual contributors who gave so generously to the making of this book: to Inessa Balashova, Amy Galowitz, Laura Herbst, John D. Mitchell, Stuart Sheffer, Carroll Terrell, Barbara Singer Zalkan; to Zeta Dawson and Dion Pincus, who contributed invaluable comments on the section on Black Evangelists; and to the unidentified contributors of the Jehovah's Witness and Alcoholics Anonymous sections.

I am also grateful to two early influences: Douglas V. S. Steere, Rufus Jones Professor of Philosophy at Haverford College and translator of Kierkegaard, for his course "Classics of Religious Thought"; and Father Karl Tiedeman, Order of the Holy Cross, who was Prior of Mount Calvary Monastery in Santa Barbara, California, where I spent many months as a novitiate.

I am also grateful to Antonio de Nicolás, Professor of Philosophy at SUNY/Stony Brook, New York, for his enthusiastic encouragement of this project; to Seymour Kurtz for his reading of the book in manuscript form and his perspicacious suggestions on restructuring the materials; to Laura Greeney for her careful attention to detail and organization in the actual writing of the book.

And I am especially grateful to Ken Stuart for his lively appreciation of the importance of the subject area, and to Shelly Estrin for her loyal friendship and incisive insights into the material.

WILLIAM PACKARD
New York, NY

Introduction

EVANGELISM: DIVINE AND DANGEROUS

WHAT IS EVANGELISM?

For our purposes in this book, we can use as a working definition of Evangelism any type of conversionary activity that tries to effect an authentic change in someone from one state of thinking and feeling to another. My definition is a broad one, transcending the usual association of Evangelism with Fundamentalist religion. But the diverse Evangelisms explored in this book have one trait in common: they all attempt to convert.

Of course such things are never easy. For one person to be able to effect a lasting change in anyone, there has to be a good deal of accident, chicanery, flimflam, psychological transference, or outright miracle at work. The German poet Rainer Maria Rilke (1875–1926) cautions us there is never any simple way for one person to share his or her spiritual values or insights with another person. In his *Letters to a Young Poet*, Rilke writes:

> . . . for at bottom, and just in the deepest and most important things, we are unutterably alone, and for one person to be able to advise or even help another, a lot must happen, a lot must go well, a whole constellation of things must come right in order once to succeed.

Yet even so, a large part of our everyday conversation is given over to trying to make others share the same tastes and insights and value systems that we have. Transferences, seductions, and intellectual persuasions are going on all around us always, and this very primitive

1

form of Evangelism reaches into almost all areas of our awareness: it takes place in advertising, education, politics, economics, sexuality, and in the arts.

And in the world of Christian Evangelism, these strong transferences, seductions, and intellectual persuasions are big business today. Billy Graham, Oral Roberts, Pat Robertson, Robert Schuller, Jimmy Swaggart, Jerry Falwell, Jim Bakker—all these Evangelists believe in a powerful conversionary approach to religion, something that must "happen" inside an individual before he or she can be at peace with God. All of these Evangelists believe literally in the following statement in John Chapter 3:

> 3   Except a man be born again, he cannot see the kingdom of God.

And all these Evangelists also sincerely believe they themselves can somehow help in this conversionary experience with anyone they come across, by showing the most dramatic and effective way of being born again.

Of course this is nothing new. During the Middle Ages, Evangelical Christianity was so aggressive in its passion to proselytize souls that the Crusaders tried to convert the whole civilized world: "If you don't worship the same God that we worship, then we'll kill you." And militant Christian Evangelism took this proselytizing a step further during the Inquisition: "If you can't *prove* to us that you worship the same God that we worship, then we'll torture you mercilessly before we kill you."

Where does this passion to proselytize come from? When did human beings begin to feel they had to Evangelize their own value systems onto other human beings?

It may have been there in our psyche since the beginnings of time, but surely the seeds of radical Evangelism are peculiar to historical Christianity. In fact the word "Evangel" refers to "Ministers of the Church, who assisted the apostles in spreading the gospel or evangel, of our Lord Jesus Christ" (Scofield Bible). The word "Evangel" comes from the Greek word *euangelion*, which is the opening word of the Gospel of Mark, and it means "glad tidings." And this spreading of glad tidings is meant to lead to a conversion of some sort, the experience of being "born again" to a state of grace, an indwelling of godhead within oneself, and a change of one's old life by putting on a new life that is characterized by an inexhaustible spiritual growth. Usually such a conversion involves a "repentance" of some sort, from the Greek word *metanoia* which means "to have another mind, to change one's mind."

Of course in the history of Christianity there have always been outsiders who were skeptical of this whole idea of "conversion" with its revelations of received dogma and doctrine. The German poet Goethe (1749–1832) expresses acid doubt about conversionary experience, as cited in Ludwig Lewisohn's *Goethe: The Story of a Man*:

> You accept the Gospel, as it stands, as divine truth. Well, no audible voice from heaven would convince me that a woman bears a child without a man, and that a dead man arises from the grave. I regard all these as blasphemies against God and his revelation of Himself in nature.

And if one were able to take a completely objective view of religion, perhaps these ideas of "conversion" and "repentance" and "revelation" would not play such a central role in the story of the human spirit. William James in *The Varieties of Religious Experience* makes an attempt at such an objective definition of religion:

> Were one asked to characterize the life of religion in the broadest and most general terms possible, one might say that it consists of the belief that there is an unseen order, and that our supreme good lies in harmoniously adjusting ourselves thereto.

That's objective enough to suit any taste, and it doesn't require any special "conversion" or "rebirth" to appreciate the validity of religion in the real world. It follows, then, that Evangelism is not necessarily a part of religion in any root meaning of the word.

And of course there are also conversionary experiences that happen completely outside the realm of religion: in art, for example, where the individual artist must experience a change inside himself before he can create anything worthwhile. The French poet Arthur Rimbaud (1854–1891) described just such a conversionary change that has to take place inside the soul of a poet:

> The poet makes himself a seer by a long, prodigious, and rational disordering of the senses. Every form of love, of suffering, of madness; he searches himself, he consumes all the poisons in him, and keeps

only their quintessences. This is an unspeakable torture during which he needs all his faith and superhuman strength and during which he becomes the great patient, the criminal, the great accursed—and the great learned one!—among men. For he arrives at the *unknown*! Because he has cultivated his own soul—which was rich to begin with—more than any other man! He reaches the unknown and even if, crazed, he ends up losing the understanding of his visions, at least he has seen them!

Surely the conversionary change which Rimbaud is describing does not have much to do with religion, and the "unknown" he posits as the goal of this conversion does not have much to do with the Judeo-Christian God. It has more to do with pursuing pure *poesis* and the worship of art for art's sake, which we will spend some time considering in the Afterword of this book.

But if the conversionary experience is not necessarily essential to the practice of religion, and if we can find examples of conversion that take place outside religion in completely alien realms, then we are right to wonder why there has always been such a strong emphasis on conversionary experience in historical Christianity. As we said, the seeds of radical Evangelism seem to be peculiar to Christianity, and to find out why and how this is so we will have to go back and examine the particular circumstances of the life and teachings of Jesus.

Jesus (the name was originally Yeshu'a, or "our Joshua," "the help of Yahveh") was born into one of the most turbulent periods of human history. The Romans were occupying Jerusalem, and many Jews were eagerly awaiting the coming of a Messiah. There were bizarre religious practices taking place: magic and witchcraft, possessions and exorcisms, miracles and prophesies, and hundreds of "thaumaturgists" or wonder-workers traveling from town to town performing instant cures and feats of sorcery. There were also ascetic sects and cults such as the Essenes, or "bathers," who lived a Buddhist-like life-style, and the Nazarenes who rejected Temple worship and denied the binding character of Mosaic Law.

The birth of the Christ child was foretold to Herod, who dispatched "wise men" as spies to find out where this new King of the Jews might be found. But when these wise men defected, Herod ordered the Massacre of the Innocents: the firstborn of all Jews were slaughtered indiscriminately to prevent the survival of the Christ child whose birth had been foretold.

After Jesus was born in Bethlehem, he was taken into Egypt, and we know very little of his childhood and education until he was twelve years old and teaching the scribes and rabbis in the Temple. He disappeared again, and the next time we see Jesus he has come into the presence of John the Baptist.

This John the Baptist was the first exemplary Evangelist: itinerant and eloquent, with a fanatic air and a sense of authentic frenzy, "his raiment of camel's hair and a leathern girdle about his loins, and his meat was locusts and wild honey"—he came "preaching in the wilderness," teaching the multitudes "Repent ye: for the kingdom of heaven is at hand." John called people to be baptized in the River Jordan, and he also denounced the Pharisees and Sadducees for their smug righteousness in thinking their parochial works of circumcision and the Law would earn them a place in the kingdom of heaven.

When John baptized Jesus, Matthew reports that the heavens opened and a voice was heard saying, "This is my beloved Son, in whom I am well pleased." Later when John was imprisoned and beheaded by Herod, Jesus apparently took up John's work and began preaching the same message John had preached: first, one had to repent; second, the kingdom of heaven was at hand. In all likelihood the multitude that followed Jesus and heard his message was the same multitude that had followed John, and most of the disciples of Jesus, including Peter, were very probably original followers of John the Baptist.

Who was this Jesus, and what did he actually teach?

Jesus the man probably wore a light tunic under his cloak, walked on leather sandals, and had a cloth headdress that fell over his shoulders to shield him from the heat of the sun. He attended banquets in the homes of wealthy men, he lived with publicans and sinners, and he moved among the untouchables—things which did not endear him to the Rabbis or the Pharisees.

The teachings of Jesus that recur in all four gospels are simple, straightforward, plain statements that ring intuitively true: the kingdom of heaven is within oneself; one should not judge others; one must leave one's family in order truly to love God. These statements all seem easy enough but of course they are the most difficult goals to achieve in one's own lifetime: to sense an indwelling divinity, to withhold judgment, and to make a complete severance from one's primal family.

What concerns us here is whether Jesus meant to create a basis for modern Evangelism, by telling people to go out and proselytize others.

Some people might like to believe the whole thing was a colossal mistake or misunderstanding, that Jesus may have said something figurative which was misinterpreted by his disciples.

But in the three places in the New Testament where Jesus gives the Apostolic Charge, there can be no mistake or misunderstanding about his clear intention to send Evangelists out in his own name to preach the gospel. And unless one argues that these three sections are interpolations and therefore spurious, one is left with the inescapable conclusion that Jesus did indeed intend for Evangelists to "teach all nations" and that the practice of Evangelism is therefore an inextricable part of Christian faith and experience.

The first account of the Apostolic Charge is in Matthew Chapter 10, which is a description of Jesus calling his disciples together and giving them power to heal by faith:

> 1   And when he had called unto him his twelve disciples, he gave them power against unclean spirits, to cast them out, and to heal all manner of sickness and all manner of disease.

There follows a listing of the names of these disciples, and then there is the specific charge for these disciples to become Evangelists:

> 7   And as ye go, preach, saying, The Kingdom of heaven is at hand.
> 8   Heal the sick, cleanse the lepers, raise the dead, cast out devils: freely ye have received, freely give.

Jesus then advises the disciples on how to live the Evangelical life:

> 9   Provide neither gold, nor silver, nor brass in your purses,
> 10   Nor scrip for your journey, neither two coats, neither shoes, nor yet staves: for the workman is worthy of his meat.

Jesus then gives specific instructions on what to do if people are unwilling to hear what these Evangelists have to say:

> 14   And whosoever shall not receive you, nor hear your words, when ye depart out of that house or city, shake off the dust of your feet.

Jesus leaves no doubt that these Evangelists will be entering into great danger:

16   Behold, I send you forth as sheep in the midst of wolves: be ye therefore wise as serpents, and harmless as doves.

This clearly is an Apostolic Charge which Jesus had thought out very carefully: what the Evangelists should preach, those places they should go, the response they should make if they are not listened to, and an awareness of the dangers they will be facing.

The other two Apostolic Charges in the New Testament are similar in form and intention. In Matthew Chapter 28, the resurrected Jesus again tells the disciples to become Evangelists, but this time there is no restriction that they should preach only to the lost sheep of Israel and stay away from Gentiles and Samaritans. Jesus tells them now to preach his gospel to all people:

18   And Jesus came and spake unto them, saying, All power is given unto me in heaven and earth.

19   Go ye therefore, and teach all nations, baptizing them in the name of the Father, and of the Son, and of the Holy Ghost.

20   Teach them to observe all things whatsoever I have commanded you: and, lo, I am with you alway, even unto the end of the world. Amen.

The third version of the Apostolic Charge is in the gospel of Mark and is more fanciful, giving instructions on demonology, speaking in tongues, and laying on of hands. C. I. Scofield writes in the *Oxford Bible* that the test is "highly doubtful, the verses are not found in the two most ancient manuscripts, the Sinaitic and Vatican, and others have it in an altered form." Here is the Charge, from Chapter 16:

15   And he said unto them, Go ye into all the world, and preach the gospel to every creature.

16   He that believeth and is baptized shall be saved; but he that believeth not shall be damned.

17   And these signs shall follow them that believe; In my name shall they cast out devils; they shall speak with new tongues;

18   They shall take up serpents; and if they drink any deadly thing, it shall not hurt them; they shall lay hands on the sick, and they shall recover.

As we said, unless we are prepared to reject all three of these reports of the Apostolic Charge, then we are left with the inescapable conclusion that Jesus did intend for there to be an ongoing Evangelism in all parts of the world, preaching his gospel and instilling in people an apocalyptic consciousness which expected the coming of the kingdom of heaven on earth.

But there's a complication here: while Jesus clearly gave the Apostolic Charge to his disciples in the above passages, elsewhere in the gospels Jesus seemed to be extremely skeptical as to the whole practice of Evangelism. Thus in the Sermon on the Mount, Jesus questioned whether anyone could ever be so free from sin and self-deception as to transmit any significant spiritual message to another human being: Matthew Chapter 7,

> 3 And why beholdest thou the mote that is in thy brother's eye, but considerest not the beam that is in thine own eye?
> 4 Or how wilt thou say to thy brother, Let me pull out the mote out of thine eye; and, behold, a beam is in thine own eye?
> 5 Thou hypocrite, first cast out the beam out of thine own eye; and then shalt thou see clearly to cast out the mote out of thy brother's eye.

This single passage, if taken literally, would blow the whistle on almost all the Evangelists who have ever practiced. And that raises another very interesting question: how can we ever tell which Evangelists we should take seriously?

Jesus gave an answer to that question also, in that same Sermon on the Mount, when he warned that many Evangelists would come after him and most of them would be frauds and charlatans. Jesus gave a very sensible gauge to determine which Evangelists ought to be taken seriously. Matthew Chapter 7,

> 15 Beware of false prophets, which come to you in sheep's clothing, but inwardly they are ravening wolves.
> 16 Ye shall know them by their fruits. Do men gather grapes of thorns, or figs of thistles?

"Ye shall know them by their fruits"—look to see what these Evangelists achieve in the world, before you take them very seriously. But as we shall see later on in this book, we have to be careful to distinguish what these true "fruits" of Evangelism really are: not the false fruits of superficial appurtenances and paraphernalia which some Evangelists use to promote themselves, self-publication and testimonials and computerized color-coded mailings and Arbitron ratings. These are not "fruits" in any true sense of the word, but are mere artificial flora that can be easily manufactured to meet the trendy needs of the marketplace.

The true fruits of Evangelism are the lasting evidences of a major spiritual presence which has left a clear legacy from a person's life work that changes the social and intellectual life of one's time. These true fruits bear witness that these Evangelists heeded the command of Jesus set down in the first letter of James Chapter 1:

> 22 But be ye doers of the word, and not hearers only, deceiving your own selves.

These are the measures and gauges of worthwhile Evangelism which Jesus left as a test to avoid being taken in by false prophets, and the test is as valid for us today as it was when it was first given two thousand years ago.

Whether Jesus did or did not intend for his disciples to go out and Evangelize the rest of the world, the whole matter becomes moot from a historical point of view because of something that happened at the very beginning of early Christianity. The Christian church had hardly established itself as an irksome upstart sect when there occurred one of the most dramatic and spectacular conversions that has ever been recorded, and this conversion has gone a long way towards fixing the permanent character of Christianity as a conversionary Evangelical religion.

It was only a few years after the trial and crucifixion of Jesus that Saul of Tarsus, a Roman citizen and Pharisee and tentmaker by trade, became active in the persecution and prosecution of early Christians. This Saul took part in the stoning of Stephen, the first Christian martyr (Acts 8:1), and he was also passionately eager to harass the other early Christians. These events are described in Acts, written by Luke, in Chapter 9:

> 1 And Saul, yet breathing out threatenings and slaughter against the disciples of the Lord, went unto the high priest,
>
> 2 And desired of him letters to Damascus to the synagogues, that if he found any of this way, whether they were men or women, he might bring them bound unto Jerusalem.

And having received his new orders to go seek out more early Christians to take prisoner, Saul began on his latest assignment when he experienced his dramatic conversion as it is described in that same Chapter 9:

> 3   And as he journeyed, he came near Damascus: and suddenly there shined round about him a light from heaven:
>
> 4   And he fell to the earth, and heard a voice saying unto him, Saul, Saul, why persecutest thou me?
>
> 5   And he said, Who art thou, Lord? And the Lord said, I am Jesus whom thou persecutest: it is hard for thee to kick against the pricks.
>
> 6   And he trembling and astonished said, Lord, what wilt thou have me to do? And the Lord said unto him, Arise, and go into the city, and it shall be told thee what thou must do.
>
> 7   And the men which journeyed with him stood speechless, hearing a voice, but seeing no man.
>
> 8   And Saul arose from the earth; and when his eyes were opened, he saw no man: but they led him by the hand, and brought him into Damascus.
>
> 9   And he was three days without sight, and neither did he eat nor drink.

This conversion was so cataclysmic that when Saul had his sight restored, he was baptized a Christian and changed his name to Paul. Then he went off and spent two years in Arabia, and when he returned he had a full understanding of the teaching of Jesus as he expounds it in the letters to Galatians and Romans. During Paul's Evangelistic career he endured eight floggings and one stoning and three shipwrecks before he was finally beheaded in Rome—but not before writing his great letters to the seven Gentile churches: Romans, Corinthians, Galatians, Ephesians, Philippians, Colossians, and Thessalonians. Not only did these letters help shape the future course of Christian thought, but they also underscored the Apostolic Charge of Jesus, as Paul encouraged all who read his letters to go and preach the gospel to others.

Two themes bear special notice in these letters of Paul. The first is the utter helplessness of man without God's grace, as in Romans Chapter 7:

> 19   For the good that I would, I do not; but the evil which I would not, that I do.

And the second theme is the total confidence Paul has in a coming Apocalypse with the accompanying change of bodily form, as in 1 Corinthians Chapter 15:

51 Behold, I shew you a mystery; We shall not all sleep, but we shall all be changed,

52 In a moment, in the twinkling of an eye, at the last trump; for the trumpet shall sound, and the dead shall be raised incorruptible, and we shall be changed.

These two themes—man's utter helplessness without the grace of God, and the imminent end of the world with our mysterious transfiguration—have become two of the strongest legacies of Christian theology, thanks to the interpolation of Paul. In fact over one half of the New Testament is letters: by Paul, Peter, James, John, and Jude. And these Epistles not only serve as commentary of what Jesus really meant in his teaching, but they also advance their own interpretation of other matters that Jesus never even touched on. No wonder Bible scholars have pointed out that these letters are the chief stumbling blocks of Christianity, since they so often seem to be at variance with the letter and the spirit of what Jesus was actually teaching. The resentment extends to lay readers of the Bible: thus the English poet John Keats (1795–1821) wrote in 1819 to George and Georgiana Keats: "It is to be lamented that the history of [Jesus] was written and revised by Men interested in the pious frauds of Religion. Yet through all this I see His splendour."

George Bernard Shaw made a more acerbic criticism in his Preface to the play *Androcles and the Lion*:

No sooner had Jesus knocked over the dragon of superstition than Paul boldly set it on its legs again in the name of Jesus . . . There has really never been a more monstrous imposition perpetrated than the imposition of the limitations of Paul's soul upon the soul of Jesus.

But whether one agrees with Paul's theological interpretation of the teachings of Jesus, it is the fact of Paul's spectacular conversion that has fixed for all time the Evangelical nature of Christian experience.

In spite of the writings of Paul, the early Christian church was a notorious hotbed of wild ideas, orgiastic communes, and ecstatic revelations. James Frazer reports a few of the early theological eccentricities of Christian thought in his book *The Golden Bough*:

> In the second century Montanus the Phrygian claimed to be the incarnate Trinity, uniting in his single person God the Father, God the Son, and God the Holy Ghost. Nor is this an isolated case, the exorbitant pretension of a single ill-balanced mind. From the earliest times down to the present day many sects have believed that Christ, nay God himself, is incarnate in every fully initiated Christian, and they have carried this belief to its logical conclusion by adoring each other. Tertullian records that this was done by his fellow-Christians at Carthage in the second century; the disciples of St. Columbia worshipped him as an embodiment of Christ; and in the eighth century Elipandus of Toledo spoke of Christ as "a god among gods", meaning that all believers were gods just as truly as Jesus himself.

Clearly there was a real need for someone to lay the foundations of a solid orthodox Christian theology, and St. Augustine (354–430) was the man to do that: trained in classical rhetoric and thoroughly versed in classical authors such as Plato and Plotinus and Virgil, Augustine had studied with Ambrose and had a firm grasp of basic Christian doctrines. But there was something else that recommended Augustine to become the first important Doctor of Faith of the Christian era.

In one of those curious accidents of history, Augustine, like Paul, had also had a spectacular and dramatic conversionary experience. To be sure, this had nothing to do with the teachings of Jesus: it was a total coincidence that Paul the Christian-baiter and Augustine the libertine were both converted into two of the most powerful personalities that early Christianity produced. This was all that was needed to establish historical Christianity as an Evangelical and conversionary religion.

Augustine's *Confessions*, published in A.D. 400, was the first modern autobiography in the sense that Augustine was the first author who thought it was important to record his childhood memories and his sexual life as crucial elements in the formation of his psychic character. Whereas Socrates had taught "Know thyself," Augustine taught "Confess thyself" so one could emerge as an experiential, childlike, remembering, and conscious soul, acknowledging its deepest longing for God.

The *Confessions* begins with a statement of man's never-ending need for God: "For Thou madest us for Thyself, and our hearts are restless until they rest in Thee."

Born in North Africa, Augustine's first experience away from home was at Carthage and it was a disaster of worldliness and lust:

> To Carthage then I came, where there sang all around me in my ears a cauldron of unholy loves. I loved not yet, yet I loved to love, and out of a deep-seated want I hated myself for wanting not. I sought what I might love, in love with loving, and safety I hated, and a way without snares . . .

Augustine's conversion took place in A.D. 386 and he describes it in detail. He was still stubbornly resisting and trying to delay:

> "How long? How long? Tomorrow and tomorrow? Why not now? Why not is there this hour an end to my uncleanness?"
>
> So was I speaking and weeping in the most bitter contrition of my heart, when, lo! I heard from neighboring house a voice, as of boy or girl, I know not, chanting and oft repeating, "Take up and read. Take up and read." (*Tolle et lege! Tolle et lege!*)

Augustine picked up his Bible and opened it at random, letting his eyes fall on the first words that appeared on the page. This practice of stichomancy or chance opening of a holy book and reading the first words one happens on, is neither unusual nor is it confined to Christian practice: it occurs in almost all major religions and is a kind of *I Ching* of Evangelism. In this case, Augustine's eyes fell on the following passage from Romans Chapter 13:

> 13 . . . not in rioting and drunkenness, not in chambering and wantonness, not in strife and envying.
> 14 But put ye on the Lord Jesus Christ, and make not provision for the flesh, to fulfill the lusts thereof.

Immediately Augustine knew a conversionary change had taken place inside of him, and all his years and years of stubborn delay were at an end. He was at one with himself and God at last, and he had only one regret about his conversion: "Too late loved I thee . . ."

After A.D. 400, the Visigoths began an invasion of Italy and in A.D. 410, the Fall of Rome shook the civilized world: barbaric hordes began to plunder the Vatican and rape the Christian women and desecrate the altars, and non-Christians living in Rome blamed the catastrophe on Christianity for its denial of the pagan gods. Augustine was so distressed at these events that he began to write *The City of God*, which was to be his major contribution to Christian theology.

The City of God (*civitas Dei*) was distinguished from the City of this world (*civitas terrena*) by its existence in reality, whereas our own world exists only in shadow-play and charades. Augustine had obviously been strongly influenced by Plato and Plotinus and the Neoplatonists in his youth, as this description of our own world as nothing but shadow-play is like something out of Book VII of Plato's *Republic*.

Also while he was a young man in Milan, Ambrose had encouraged Augustine to read the Bible figuratively and not literally, according to the precept of Paul in 2 Corinthians Chapter 3:

6 . . . for the letter killeth, but the spirit giveth life.

With these underlying assumptions of the non-reality of this world and the figurative interpretation of scripture, Augustine quite naturally based his theology on the supremacy of faith over reason. Where Socrates would have sought for understanding so he could know what to believe, Augustine reversed the approach and summarized his thought in three words: "*Credo quia intelligo,*" I believe in order to understand.

This theology of total faith was, in effect, the beginning of the formal Christian era insofar as Augustine had initiated the approach which would dominate Medieval thought for the next thousand years. And in so doing, Augustine confronted almost all the major dilemmas of Christian apologetics. He debated Fortunatus, the Manichean Bishop who contended good and evil were co-existent realities, and Augustine not only won the debate by insisting that evil has no real existence, he also succeeded in having the Catholic Church declare Manicheanism a heresy. Augustine also contended with the English monk Pelagius who held there was no original sin and hence man could earn his own salvation through his works and did not need the saving grace of God; in A.D. 415, Augustine sent a warning to Jerome of the dangers of Pelagianism, and at the Council of Ephesus in A.D. 431, at the instigation of Augustine, the Church declared Pelagianism a heresy.

Augustine was also concerned to reconcile free will with the foreknowledge of God, in *De Libero Arbitro* (On Free Will). And Augustine's lasting concern with the nature of time and memory fills hundreds of pages in the *Confessions* and *The City of God*. Towards the end of his life, Augustine summarized the teachings of Jesus as follows: *"Dilige et quod vis fac."* ("Love God and do what you want.")

This may seem too permissive as a theology, but Augustine's reasoning was that if one really loved God, one could not possibly do anything that would be out of accord with God's will.

As Augustine kept on with his writing, the barbaric invasions kept on, and in A.D. 429, an army of 80,000 Vandals under Genseric crossed the Straits of Gibraltar and swept across North Africa to begin a fourteen month siege of the city of Hippo where Augustine was Bishop. Augustine died in A.D. 430, the same year these Vandals succeeded in capturing and burning Hippo. But Augustine had provided the new religion of Christianity with its first systematic theology, and Augustinian thought would dominate Christian faith and practice for the next thousand years as it continued to spread over the rest of the known world.

There began a curious period of world history, the so-called Dark Ages, roughly from A.D. 400 to 1000, when there was no significant advance in religious or cultural history. In A.D. 438, Christianity became the official religion of the Roman Empire, but there followed such a retrograde state that, to quote W. P. Ker, "All was Gothic, all was Dark." Samuel Eliot Morison describes this period as "A hollow in which many great, beautiful, and heroic things were done and created, but in which knowledge, as we understand it, and as Aristotle understood it, had no place."

Pope followed pope in orderly succession, Church Council followed Church Council, but except for isolated events of warfare and individual heroism, nothing of real cultural significance occurred.

But elsewhere in the world, events began transpiring that would force Christianity back to its Evangelical origins. The prophet Mahomet was born in Mecca in A.D. 570, and in A.D. 610 he recorded a conversionary vision he had while he was alone in a cave:

> While I was asleep under a silk cover the angel Gabriel appeared and said "Read!"—I said "I do not read." He pressed me with silk covers so tight I thought I would die, then he said "READ!" So I read aloud and he left, and I awoke and the words were written in my heart. And I left the cave and went halfway up the mountain and I heard a voice from heaven say "O MAHOMET YOU ARE THE MESSENGER

OF ALLAH, AND I AM GABRIEL." I looked up and there was Gabriel
in the form of a man with feet set on the edge of the sky . . .

Following this experience, Mahomet proclaimed himself a prophet
in A.D. 611 and founded the Muslim religion, or Islam, which sought
to restore the monotheism of Adam and Noah and Abraham. Mahomet
died in A.D. 632, the Koran was recorded in A.D. 634, and Islam began
to increase so rapidly it became a major challenge to Christianity: one
hundred years after the death of Mahomet in A.D. 732, Moslem war-
riors fought the Christian armies at the Battle of Tours. The Christians
won the battle, and for one day the fate of the entire world was in the
balance: as Gibbon writes, "The Koran would have taken the place of
the Bible if the Moslems had not been beaten at Tours."

The year following Tours, A.D. 733, at Poitiers, foot soldiers of
Charles Martel held off a furious attack of Arab horsemen who had
overrun the south of France, and in A.D. 778 Charlemagne was am-
bushed at Roncevaux and one single man, Roland, held the pass, as
is told in *Chanson de Roland*. A few centuries later, Lady Godiva rode
naked through the noonday streets of Coventry in England in 1060 to
protest a tax her husband Leofric had levied on the people. And in
the single most important event of the entire era, William the Con-
queror won the Battle of Hastings in 1066 and became William I of
England, completing the Norman conquest.

During these Dark Ages of cultural stalemate, a whole body of heroic
folklore grew up that eventually became the legends of Medieval chivalry, and this folklore would have significant consequences for Christian Evangelism. The stories of King Arthur and his Knights of the
Round Table were compiled by Chrétien de Troyes, but as these fables
took form the knight-errant's mission, originally seen as the defense
of one's lands and family and the honor of one's Lady, became more
and more linked with a search for the Holy Grail. This Grail was
supposed to have been the plate on which Christ broke bread at his
Last Supper, and the Lance that accompanied the Grail was supposed
to be the spear which Longinus used to pierce the side of Christ on
the cross. Lancelot was allowed to see the Grail in a vision but was
not allowed to approach it, and fell in a swoon immediately afterwards.
Later Percival replaced Lancelot as the archetypal Knight, just as the
Grail had replaced the Lady as the true object of the King's mission,
and just as the Crusades eventually replaced courtly love as the chief
agon of chivalry.

By this time pilgrimage to the Holy Land had become an important part of religious life: small bands of penitents journeyed to Canterbury, or to Rome, but most of all, to Jerusalem. The nature of such pilgrimage was not always as cheerful and easygoing as Chaucer would have us believe: in 1064, some 7,000 pilgrims were waylaid by Turks and harassed by Caliph Hakim, and in 1070 the Turks took Jerusalem itself and pilgrims began bringing back stories of vile cruelties and unbelievable tortures and persecutions.

In response to these reports of infidel atrocities, Pope Urban II in 1095 declared the First Crusade to retake Jerusalem, and he promised remission of all penance for anyone who went on this Crusade:

> From the confines of Jerusalem and from Constantinople a grievous report has gone forth that an accursed race, wholly alienated from God, has violently invaded the lands of these Christians, and has depopulated them by pillage and fire. They have led away a part of the captives into their own country and a part of them have been killed by cruel tortures. They have destroyed the sacred altars and have defiled them with all manner of uncleanness . . .

It was the beginning of one of the most monstrously misguided and colossal acts of militant Evangelism in human history, but at the time everyone in Christendom thought it was necessary and appropriate. One can search history books in vain for any Western voice that spoke out and opposed the Crusades, at the time they were happening. To the contrary, Bernard of Clairvaux declared this First Crusade "a splendid bargain" for Christians:

> Do not miss this opportunity. Take the sign of the cross. At once you will have indulgence for all the sins which you confess with a contrite heart. It does not cost you much to buy and if you wear it with humility you will find that it is worth the kingdom of heaven.

And thousands of knights, squires, journeymen, mercenaries, merchants, and adventurers did jump at the opportunity, and in 1099 the First Crusade stormed Jerusalem and slaughtered the Turkish garrison there, fired the mosque and synagogues for good measure, and massacred over 40,000 people. All in the name of the teachings of Jesus.

Following is an overview of all the Crusades that followed, with their results:

1095   Pope Urban II proclaims the First Crusade.
1099   First Crusade successfully storms Jerusalem.
1101   Second Crusade is slaughtered on way to Jerusalem.
1189   Third Crusade is led by Richard the Lion-Hearted, conquers
       Cyprus.
1202   Fourth Crusade never reaches the Holy Land.
1212   Children's Crusade: 50,000 children are killed or sold into
       slavery.
1217   Fifth Crusade against the sultanate of Egypt fails.
1223   Sixth Crusade recovers Jerusalem from the Moslems.
1291   End of Crusades.

As more and more of these Crusades were organized to rescue the
Holy Land from the infidels, a sense of worldly cynicism and futility
began to creep into the enterprises. Richard Barber observes in *The
Reign of Chivalry*:

> In a sense, the crusading ideal was something which could be used
> effectively only once, when there was a clear objective and before the
> realities of everyday politics could intrude. The men of the First Crusade
> had a clear objective and almost no idea of the difficulties involved;
> the leaders of the Second Crusade, on the other hand, came to have
> all too clear an idea of the difficulties and little idea of their objectives.

It is an interesting irony of history that there was a reverse Evangelism at work during these Crusades: while the Crusader Knights
carried with them a token Christianity to implant in the Holy Land,
many of them brought back Muslim ideas which later infiltrated Western thought. One such idea was the use of Arabic numerals which
greatly facilitated the development of Western mathematics and sci-
ences, which would be unthinkable using Roman numerals: try multiplying LXVI and CDII and see how far you can get.

A second major Evangelism the Crusaders brought back with them
was the forgotten philosophy of Aristotle. The reclamation of the works
of this great classical philosopher whom Dante called "the master of
those who know" came as a profound shock to Medieval religionists.
Unlike Plato, Aristotle had placed knowledge over faith, and this presented such a challenge to Christian theology that monasteries all over
Europe began to sponsor Scholastics like Thomas Aquinas (1225–
1274) who labored to produce *Summa Theologia* which could displace

the suddenly outdated Platonism of Augustine and try to reconcile the scientific knowledge of Aristotle with the teachings of Jesus.

And the third major Evangelism the Crusaders brought back with them were the unimaginable cruelties they had gone to Jerusalem to extirpate. Because the Crusaders had not been successful in overcoming the infidel atrocities of the Turks, the Catholic Church incorporated these cruelties in an institution of its own called the Inquisition. Proclaimed just after the last Crusade in 1227 by Pope Gregory IX, this Inquisition was set up to combat heresy and schism and it was not only a religious court: the Inquisition had the full force of temporal power behind it also, for the simple reason that any lapse from faith was seen as civil treason against the state.

The Inquisition ran for some twenty years as an ordeal of verbal examination but quite obviously did not get the results the Inquisitors were after, and so in 1247 Pope Innocent IV approved the use of torture to elicit confessions of heresy. Henceforth the examiners were empowered to use the rack and the screw, flogging and burning and starving in solitary confinement, as well as the more exotic cruelties the Crusaders had stormed Jerusalem to put an end to.

Over the next three hundred years the Inquisition compiled a monstrous record of persecutions, of which the following atrocities are a fair sampling:

1239   Robert the Dominican sends 180 prisoners to the stake in a single day, including one bishop who was accused of being too merciful towards heretics.

1304   Clement V orders the Inquisition to move against the Apostolic Brethren of Parma because they rejected the supremacy of the Pope, so thousands of citizens of Parma were slaughtered in a general siege.

1431   Joan of Arc is sentenced at Rouen as a heretic and she is burned at the stake as a witch.

1485   41 women are burned as witches at Como.

1498   The trial and torture and execution of Savonarola in Florence.

1510   140 persons are burned at Brescia.

1514   300 persons are burned at Como.

1518   70 persons are burned at Brescia.

If the Crusades were monstrously misguided and colossal acts of militant Evangelism, aimed at overthrowing what Pope Urban II de-

scribed as "an accursed race, wholly alienated from God," the Inquisition was a reenactment of the "cruel tortures" these infidels were
supposed to be practicing in the Holy Land—only now the curse and
the atrocities had come back to roost on home soil, within the very
corpus of Christendom. It would not be the first time that Evangelism
would reverse itself with a vengeance and reenact those very crimes it
was devoted to overthrowing.

What can one say of this first millennium of Christian thought and
practice? How did the teachings of Jesus give rise to such militant
Evangelism? And how could the cross be made the emblem of armed
Knights at full gallop bearing down on hapless victims, crushing skulls
with pikes and truncheons all over bloody cobblestones? And what
caused Christendom to turn inwards on itself, tormenting its own
lapsed church members in stinking, filthy dungeons before burning
them alive in public squares?

Not all the speculation or reconstruction in the world can reconcile
the beauty of Christ's Sermon on the Mount in Matthew, Chapters
5–7, with the oppressive mandates issued from the Christian See during
the course of its first thousand years, and Christians themselves initiated
more exquisite and monstrous persecutions than any pagan or infidel
ever devised for Jerusalem pilgrims or the Roman Colosseum.

There is this to be said for the Romans: they never lied to themselves
about their sadism. They freely acknowledged that they thought it was
terrific fun to toss helpless Christians to starving lions as a holiday
frolic, and they openly admitted that they loved to sit and watch a
large bear tear a Christian woman to shreds. But Christians themselves
did equally terrible things to heretics and infidels and alleged witches,
and they lied to themselves about what they were doing: they pretended
it was holy piety and righteousness that drove them to use intricate
torture devices such as the strappado which dislocates shoulders and
then tears whole arms out of their sockets.

The hypocrisy of Christian Evangelism towards the horrors it was
perpetrating seems delusional and hallucinatory. It reminds one of
what Lucretius wrote in *De Rerum Natura*: *"Tantum religio potuit
suadere majorem."* ("So great are the evils to which religion has led
men.")

Evangelism during the first thousand years of Christianity was a
powerful instrument for light and life, and a vessel for the conversion
and renewal of authentic free spirits like Augustine, who emerges as
one of the great intelligences of all time. But Evangelism was also a

ludicrous and destructive force in the world, indulging itself in all manner of abominable sillinesses such as the Crusades and the Inquisition.

In a word, Evangelism manifested itself as *chthonic*, of God and the devil at one and the same time: both divinely inspired and demonically dangerous.

Chapter 1

MARTIN LUTHER AND THE PROTESTANT REFORMATION

LONG BEFORE THE BIRTH of Martin Luther (1483–1546), there were other voices crying out against the abuses and corruptions of the Medieval Catholic Church. Because these abuses were so flagrant and widespread among priests and nuns, bishops and Cardinals, almost all of whom took part in the round-robin of bribes and favors, even the Pope himself became hopelessly ensnared in the immoral charade of game-playing.

There were levels and levels of corruption: on the physical level, the Church owned vast real estate holdings that were not taxable by the State, and the Church also controlled wills and probate hearings on wills: so there were abundant opportunities for wheeling and dealing in almost all areas of contractual negotiation. Within its own ranks, the Church freely sold its offices: a Cardinal's hat could be bought for the right price, and the Borgia Pope purchased his Papacy outright. Add to this the irreverent revelry in most convents and monasteries where a never-ending rustle of robes and wimples took place behind cloistered doors. Everyone knew all about these things, but no Christian dared to speak about them openly.

On the spiritual level, probably the basest corruption of all was the sale of Indulgences under the pretext that the Church would forgive any sin for a certain fee: this practice turned the sacrament of confession into a mere travesty, and rendered the meaning of the Mass pointless if the perfect sacrifice of Christ had to be helped along with the additional sale of an Indulgence.

It was beginning to look as if Christendom had become a mockery of its own catechism, and its human representatives were so inextricably caught up in the corruption, there seemed to be no way the Church could ever reform itself from within.

But as we said, there were voices who were beginning to cry out against these abuses and corruptions of the Medieval Catholic Church. There were individual Reformers and Crusaders who balked at the hypocrisy and double-dealing of the Official Church. And there were the poets—chief among them Dante Alighieri (1265–1321), whose great *Commedia*, or *Divine Comedy*, described the complacency and backsliding of the Church, and Dante even placed certain Popes right in his *Inferno*. In Canto XXVII of the *Paradiso*, Dante portrayed St. Peter himself, glowing red with rage as he rails against the degradation of the Papacy:

> He that usurps on earth my place, my place, my place,
> which in the sight of the Son of God is empty,
> has made of my tomb a sewer of blood and filth,
> so that the apostate who fell from here above
> takes comfort there below . . .
>
> (tr. Ciardi)

The bitterness of Dante's attack on the Church was echoed by other leading humanist poets: Geoffrey Chaucer (1340–1400) in his *Canterbury Tales* portrayed the unscrupulous Pardoner who had just come from Rome with his wallet stuffed full of Indulgences to be sold for the remission of sins. In lines 696–704 of the Prologue, Chaucer describes how this Pardoner set about depriving the peasantry of their hard-earned money:

> He seyde, he hadde a gobet of the seyl
> That seynt Peter hadde, whan that he wente
> Up-on the see, til Jesu Crist him hente.
> He hadde a croys of Latoun, ful of stones,
> And in a glas he hadde pigges bones.
> But with thise relikes, whan that he fond
> A povre person dwelling up-on lond,
> Up-on a day he gat him more moneye
> Than that the person gat in monthes tweye.
>
> (He said, he had a fragment of the sail
> Saint Peter had when he sailed on the sea
> till Jesus Christ called him to ministry.

He had a metal cross chock full of stones,
and in a glass he carried dead pig bones.
But with these relics firmly in his hand,
when he found some poor person on his land,
he made more cash in one day's quick affair
than that poor person could make in two months there.)

(tr. Packard)

And Michelangelo Buonarroti (1475–1564), the great sculptor and painter, wrote of the corruption that was taking place in Rome during the height of the Italian Renaissance, in one of his masterful sonnets:

Here, to make swords and helmets, war devours
our chalices, and here Christ's blood is sold
by the pint, and cross and thorns are cast into mold
for shields and spears yet Christ's patience showers . . .

(tr. Tuisiani)

In addition to the poets, there were humanist thinkers like Rabelais (1495–1535) who were beginning to proclaim man should be free of his Medieval shackles to live as he wanted to live: as Rabelais wrote in archaic French, *"Fay ce que vouldras,"* do just what you want to do.

And there was also one of the fiercest Evangelists who ever lived: Girolamo Savonarola (1452–1498), a Dominican monk who actually set up a theocracy in Florence and openly defied the Borgia Pope Alexander VI, giving sermons from the pulpit of San Marcos monastery attacking the Pontiff's blatant immorality.

Savonarola blamed the Church's decay on the pernicious influence of pagan classics:

The only good things which we owe to Plato and Aristotle, is that they brought forward many arguments, which we can use against the heretics. Yet they and other philosophers are now in hell. An old woman knows more about faith than Plato. It would be good for religion if many books that seem useful were destroyed . . .

And destroy them he did: Savonarola set up a "Pyramid of Vanities" in the public square of Florence, on which he placed "obscene books and pictures" which probably included books by Ovid, Boccaccio, Petrarch, Catullus, Terence, Livy, Hesiod, Plautus, Xenophon, and some of the great paintings by Sandro Botticelli which were considered too lascivious to remain intact: Botticelli himself fell under Savonarola's spell and surrendered the paintings of his own free will. These and many other items of jewelry, clothing, art objects and other finery were consigned to the purifying flames of the bonfire as the beguiled Florentines stood by and watched.

But this theocracy was rapidly growing into an unbearable fascism: as Jacob Burckhardt writes in *The Civilization of the Renaissance in Italy*: "[Savonarola] did not shrink from the most vexatious interferences with the most prized freedom of Italian private life, using the espionage of servants on their masters as a means of carrying out his moral reform."

And, we should add, Savonarola also used children: he had his own Hitler Youth trained to go door to door, collecting whatever humanist books and pagan paintings and statues they could get their hands on.

Finally Alexander VI could no longer tolerate this open challenge to his Pontificate, and he excommunicated Savonarola. That made no difference to Savonarola; he kept on with his preaching against Alexander and his bonfires in the public square. As a last resort, Alexander had Savonarola arrested, tortured on the strappado, and hanged: and as a special indignity the public hangman took a stick and lifted the robes of the dead man to expose his private parts to the crowd below, before the body was taken down and burned. It was a signal to the Florentines that they were rid of their short-lived theocracy, and everyone was free to return to a life of licentiousness.

Humanist thinkers were also beginning to advance their intellectual arguments and satire against the Church, and these written attacks were more disquieting than any sermons which might be preached against the Church's immorality. Erasmus of Rotterdam (1466–1536) had traveled to England in 1499 to meet with Thomas More, and Erasmus had ample opportunity to observe the corruption and cynicism of the Roman Church. In 1509 Erasmus published his *Ecomium Moriae*, or *The Praise of Folly*, which stirred theologians to an uproar with its biting satire on the absurdities of Church teaching, its ridicule of the Pope and celibacy and other sacred tenets of Catholicism. Erasmus reserved his chief scorn for his fellow clergy:

> . . . whose brains are the rottenest, intellects the dullest, doctrines the thorniest, manners the brutalest, life the foulest, speech the spitefullest, hearts the blackest, that ever I encountered in the world.

The most obvious target for attack by the new humanists was the Catholic doctrine of transubstantiation, which held that the bread and wine of the Eucharist were actually changed into the body and blood of Christ during the Mass. After 1,000 years of the practice of the Mass, humanists questioned whether such a doctrine was necessary or even intended by the Gospels.

But again and again, the leading Reformers came back to the morals of the Church. John Wycliffe (1320–1384) attacked the Papacy as "Antichrist itself" and condemned the Church hierarchy, blasting a corrupt clergy:

> The third default of evil curates is, that they are angels of Satan to lead men to hell; for instead of truly teaching Christ's gospel, they are dumb, or else tell men's traditions . . . and for example of holy devotion, devout prayer, and works of mercy, they teach idleness, gluttony, drunkenness, and lechery, and maintaining of these sins, and many more . . .

Wycliffe went on to deny transubstantiation altogether, and asserted the right of every man to read the Bible for himself. The Church retaliated swiftly: in 1410 two hundred manuscripts of Wycliffe were burned, and at the Council of Constance in 1415, Wycliffe's work was condemned and his body dug up and his bones burned.

Jan Hus (1373–1415) was a Bohemian preacher who also agitated against Church teaching, and his work was also condemned at the Council of Constance and Hus himself was burned alive at the stake. Ulrich Zwingli (1484–1531), a Swiss theologian, rejected the Mass and denied transubstantiation as Wycliffe had done. Philip Melancthon (1497–1560), a humanist professor of Greek at the University of Wittenberg, was an immediate forerunner of Luther in his criticism of Church theology and his rejection of transubstantiation in the Mass.

An unexpected catalyst for change that helped these humanist thinkers spread their message was the printing press of 1454 and the subsequent translation and circulation of Bibles into all lands and languages, so that for the first time in history a curious Christian no longer needed to know Latin or consult a priest before he was allowed to search through scripture and find out what was actually there.

Another unexpected catalyst for change were the natural disasters of the period. The Black Death Plague of 1346–1348 reduced the population of Europe by half and was an embarrassment to Christian theology: how could a good God allow this to happen even in a fallen world? To make matters worse, those who cared for Plague victims invariably caught the Plague themselves, whereas those who abandoned the sick and withdrew to a safe haven as the ten men and women in Boccaccio's *Decameron* did, invariably remained healthy and could pass the time by telling risqué stories to each other. It simply didn't make any sense in the sort of ordered moral universe the Church had always insisted on.

But probably the strongest catalyst for change was the work of a modest Polish astronomer named Nicolas Copernicus (1473–1543), who challenged the geocentric view of the universe which had been first asserted by Ptolemy and tenaciously espoused by the traditional Church. Of course, early thinkers had questioned whether the earth was indeed the stationary center of the universe: Plato had his doubts about it in the *Dialogues*, and free thinkers from the Greeks onwards challenged Ptolemy in private. But it took the 1514 edition of *Nicolai Copernici de Hypothesibus Motuum Coelestium a se Constitutis Commentariolus*, the so-called "little commentary" of Copernicus, to declare: "The center of the earth is not the center of the universe, but only of gravity and of the lunar sphere." Copernicus went on to say: "All the planets revolve about the sun as their mid-point, and therefore the sun is the center of the universe."

It would be difficult for a modern reader to estimate the shock and disorientation these statements caused to the Medieval mind: to be told the earth was not the center of the universe was tantamount to saying man himself did not occupy the central place in God's architectural cosmos. Centuries of Church teaching and theology were suddenly undermined, and everything seemed to be falling to pieces with no way of putting it back together again.

And as if the various scientific revolutions were not bad enough in the eyes of the Church, there were also new ocean voyages taking place, and wide-eyed sailors brought back fabulous accounts of exotic new civilizations that had never been known before. This was enough to unnerve not only the Official Church but also lay persons as well. The discovery of America and the exploration of Asia not only upset most mapmakers, they also challenged the common man's traditional notions about the shape of the earth. Ferdinand Magellan (1480–1521) sailed five ships across the North Atlantic to South America and then crossed the Pacific Ocean to return to Seville in 1522, a circumnavigation of the globe that took three years and left no doubt in anyone's mind that the earth was round.

Clearly, the Medieval mind was ready to be challenged and overthrown, and the various astronomical and geographical revolutions were translated into a curious popular folklore: all over Germany there was a belief in witches and demons; charms and talismans were sold to soldiers to protect them from injury; and astrologers would cast anyone's horoscope for a few pieces of silver, and they would also sell almanacs to anyone who wanted to bypass the established faith and try reading the stars instead.

One folk legend in particular had a prophetic and frightening message: it told of one Doctor Faustus, who had sold his soul to the devil in order to achieve a magical freedom and power. This fabulous myth had a very special significance when one man actually did rise up and challenge the authority of the whole Roman Catholic Church, thus becoming Faustus incarnate.

This man was Martin Luther (1483–1546), son of Hans Luther, a simple peasant and miner who hated clerics with a passion.

Martin Luther was born in Eisleben and at the age of twenty-two he entered the Order of the Augustinian Eremites—a severe monastic rule that put Luther in a cold cell where he began an endless ritual of fasting, prayer, and scourging himself to get rid of whatever devils might be inhabiting his body. As Luther himself reported:

> I was a pious monk, and so strictly observed the rules of my order that . . . if ever a monk got into heaven by monkery, so should I also have gotten there . . . If it had lasted longer I should have tortured myself to death with watching, praying, reading, and other work.

In 1506 Luther took the vows of poverty, chastity, and obedience to become a tonsured Augustinian monk, and in 1508 he was a monastic instructor of logic and physics and theology at the University of Wittenberg, where he began to ponder the meaning of the verse in Romans Chapter 1:

> 17   The just shall live by faith.

This was an unnerving thought for Luther: if faith is the chief end of religion, then works were not so important, and ritual and sacrament and other outward forms might be mere hollow things. These thoughts preyed on his mind and made him begin to question some of the most precious tenets of Catholic theology, and just at this time a curious thing happened: a Dominican friar named Johann Tetzel came to Wittenberg and began selling plenary Indulgences to anyone who would contribute money towards the building of a new St. Peter's. Several of the sealed Papal letters offering forgiveness of sins in exchange for money came to Martin Luther's attention, and he was so incensed by them that he composed his ninety-five theses entitled *Disputatio pro Declaratione Virtutis Indulgentiarum*, or "A Disputation for the Clarification of the Power of Indulgences." Luther posted these ninety-five theses on the main door of the Castle Church of Wittenberg on October 31, 1517, knowing that a large crowd could be expected on the next day, November 1, which was All Saints' Day. Immediately after posting his challenge against Catholic Officialdom, Luther took a German translation down to the local printer and had copies printed so he could circulate them among the people.

There was a violent shock wave that went through Christendom as soon as Luther's views were understood: Luther was seen as a modern Faustus figure deliberately selling his soul to the devil. Pope Leo X, the excellent Medici Pope, summoned Luther to Rome in 1518 and tried to squash the Reformer in a private audience, but it was not possible. Luther clung to his heretical views: he insisted that every Christian was a priest by baptism, and that every Christian had the right to read the scriptures and to interpret them according to his own lights. Leo X concluded that Luther had to be dealt with officially, and he was therefore summoned to the Diet of Worms in 1521, where he was ordered to retract the heresies in his writings.

Thomas Carlyle tells the story of this confrontation in his book *On Heroes, Hero-Worship and the Heroic in History*:

> The Diet of Worms, Luther's appearance there on the 17th of April 1521, may be considered as the greatest scene in Modern European History; the point, indeed, from which the whole subsequent history of civilization takes its rise . . .
>
> Luther is to appear and answer for himself, whether he will recant or not. The world's pomp and power sits there on this hand: on that, stands up for God's Truth, one man, Hans Luther the poor miner's son.
>
> Friends had reminded him of Hus, advised him not to go; he would not be advised. A large company of friends rode out to meet him, with still more earnest warnings; he answered, "Were there as many Devils in Worms as there are roof-tiles, I would on."

Luther stood before that Diet of Worms and made an ingenious challenge to their challenge: "Confute me by proofs of Scripture, or else by plain just arguments: I cannot recant otherwise. For it is neither safe nor prudent to do aught against conscience. Here stand I; I can do no other: God assist me!"

Luther went on to assert that "The form of communion was not important, what mattered was the spirit in which it was received." He based his entire position on the principle "*sola scriptura*," the Bible is the only source and norm for all religious faith, not the Church: "My conscience is captive to the Word of God. I cannot and I will not recant anything, for to go against my conscience is neither right nor safe. God help me. Amen."

Predictably, the Diet of Worms concluded that Luther's views were heretical and charged that he had soiled marriage, disparaged confession, and denied the sacrament of communion. "He is pagan in his denial of free will," the Inquisitors wrote: "This devil in the habit of a monk has brought together ancient errors into one stinking puddle, and has invented new ones."

The Diet ordered Luther's books burned, and sentenced him to Wartburg prison where he spent ten months translating the New Testament into German. The sentence did not change Luther's views in the least; if anything, it simply reinforced them: he became more outspoken and went on to deny that marriage itself was even a sacrament, and he became more and more contemptuous of any rational basis of faith: "Reason is the greatest enemy that faith has . . . She is the Devil's greatest whore."

Luther held firmly to Romans 1:17, "The just shall live by faith," and he claimed that compared with the great power of faith, the works of men are nothing: "The dung of one's own merits, the filthy puddle of one's own righteousness . . ."

We can get some estimate of the impact of Luther's Evangelism from a modern commentator, William L. Shirer, in his book about the tragedy of modern Germany, *The Rise and Fall of the Third Reich*:

> Through his sermons and his magnificent translation of the Bible, Luther created the modern German language, aroused in the people not only a new Protestant vision of Christianity but a fervent German nationalism and taught them, at least in religion, the supremacy of the individual conscience . . .

It was the beginning of the Protestant Reformation, and the Christian faith would never be the same again.

The Catholic Church reacted swiftly to the Protestant Reformation: the Inquisition doubled its efforts to examine heresy and excommunicate dissidents, and in 1534 Ignatius de Loyola founded the Society of Jesus, or Jesuits, which became the main arm of the Counter-Reformation, to press the attack against Protestant Reformers. In 1559, the *Index Librorum Prohibitorium* was established and all suspect books were placed on this Index and their printers were either fined or censored. And in 1573, in one of the most extraordinary repressive measures, the Inquisition began summoning painters to appear before its courts: El Greco was examined and rebuked, and Veronese was criticized for a painting that had too many parrots and dwarfs in it and so was ordered to repaint the picture at his own expense.

But all these makeshift prohibitions were not effective against the momentum of the Protestant Reformation because once Luther began it in Germany, Evangelical fervor broke out in almost all other countries that were under Catholic authority. In Scotland, John Knox (1505–1572) declared the corruption there was greater than in any place in Europe; he called the Roman Church "the Synagogue of Satan" and its priests "bloody wolves." Knox worked tirelessly for reform, although the cost was high. He had to serve nineteen months as a galley slave for his activities, and then fled to Switzerland where he met with John Calvin. Returning home, Knox triumphed when Parliament passed the Confession of Faith in 1560, which separated the Scottish Church from the authority of the Pope, and Parliament also instituted Knox's reformed creed and ritual and outlawed the celebration of Catholic Mass on pain of flogging, exile, and death. Knox wrote the account of his struggle in *The History of the Reformation of Religion Within the Realm of Scotland*.

The other major figure of this Protestant Reformation who, like Luther, established new ideas and revolutionary forms of worship, was John Calvin (1509–1564). Born in Noyon, France, Calvin studied at the University of Paris where he advanced the doctrine of predestination: that the world is divided into the damned and the elect. To prove that his doctrine made practical sense, Calvin set up a theocracy in the peaceful city of Geneva, Switzerland, with the Bible as the sole arbiter of law, and with all civic and religious matters administered by a Presbytery. The religious experiment extended into all aspects of life such as education and business and the distinction of social classes. It was this model for Christian living that Knox witnessed when he visited Geneva, and Knox reported that Calvin had devised "the most perfect school of Christ that ever was on earth since the days of the Apostles."

The immediate practical and political consequences of the Protestant Reformation came in more and more open confrontations between Church and State—as in Henry VIII's divorce from Catherine of Aragon on the pretext of her inability to provide a male heir. Cardinal Wolsey, following traditional Catholic practice, set out to obtain for Henry an annulment of the marriage, but the Pope declined to grant it. When he learned of this, Henry had his own Parliament legislate the Act of Supremacy announcing Henry's independence from the Roman Catholic Church in all matters of faith and morals. In 1533 Henry married Anne Boleyn, who was already four months pregnant with the future Queen Elizabeth. The Pope disallowed Henry's new marriage, so Henry retaliated by persuading Parliament to pass the Act of Succession in 1534, declaring his marriage to Anne Boleyn valid and requiring every Englishman to take an oath to the King affirming that Henry was in effect the new arbiter of faith and morals. Almost all Englishmen agreed to take this oath except for Thomas More, who stood by his sworn faith as a Christian and a Catholic. More was arrested, sent to the Tower and put on trial in 1535, judged guilty of treason, and subsequently beheaded, and his head was fixed on an iron spire atop London Bridge. This was a curious reverse martyrdom, with a Roman Catholic being victimized by the new Evangelical Protestant Reformation.

There were more long-range consequences of the Reformation: almost a hundred years later the scientist Giordano Bruno was burned at the stake in 1600, and in 1633 the Italian astronomer and physicist Galileo Galilei (1564–1616) was called before the Inquisition for having atheistic opinions. Galileo had indeed been making revolutionary discoveries: that unequal weights drop with equal velocity (a theory he proved true by dropping objects from the leaning tower of Pisa); that the planet Jupiter has satellites; and that the Copernican theory that the earth moves around the sun is true. It is some evidence of the desperation of the Counter-Reformation that it would persecute physical scientists almost midway into the seventeenth century, for views that almost everyone at that time was beginning to realize had to be accurate.

But the Inquisition persisted, and asked Galileo whether his views on physical science had destroyed his faith in God. Galileo answered by reaching down and picking up a straw from the floor of the court, and he said: "If there were nothing else in nature to teach me the existence of a Deity, then this straw would suffice."

Nonetheless, Galileo was forced on pain of death to recant his views of heavenly motion and deny that the earth moved. He did so, but under his breath he whispered: *"Eppur si muove."* ("Even so, it still moves.")

More than anything that Luther or Calvin or Knox could ever allege against Catholicism, these events of the Counter-Reformation showed that Roman Catholicism was still clinging stubbornly to its Medieval view of the world, and the Church was going to go on being just as refractory and intransigent on all other matters of faith and morals.

But at least Martin Luther had opened the door to the Protestant Reformation, and no one would ever be able to shut that door again.

Chapter 2

THE GROWTH OF PROTESTANT EVANGELISM

AFTER MARTIN LUTHER'S declaration of independence from the Medieval Church, modern Evangelical Protestantism began to multiply in radical new forms and doctrines. It was like the spectacular explosion of some huge supernova that sends nebulae and luminosities in reckless eccentricity across the night sky. From horizon to horizon, there did not seem to be enough space to accommodate the different configurations of this new freedom-seeking revolutionary spirit.

The Protestant Reformation became a proliferation of new creeds and beliefs, new sects and cults, new movements and denominations, as difficult to contemplate as they are to chronicle. New churches and new forms of conversionary experience and new types of radical Evangelism began to crop up within each country in western Europe and within the new American colonies. And in many ways this proliferation of new forms is still going on around us today.

But in the period immediately following Martin Luther, it was a bewildering spectacle to behold. With the virtual overthrow of almost all traditional dogmas and doctrines, there was a sudden need for something that most people rarely find time to think about. This desperate need, this immediate necessity, was for a new theology. For it's one thing to overthrow all the old traditional forms, but it's quite another thing to come up with an adequate basis for new forms.

As soon as men decided they could not live under the old Catholic theology, they began to devise new theologies based on whatever predispositions or faculties seemed to be the most propitious and appropriate. Chief among these was a faith in the rational powers of the human mind, and this gave rise to what has been called the Age of

34

Reason. It seemed innocent enough on the surface, and it also gave rise to a new natural religion known as Deism, which was a curious form of free thought that characterized so much of seventeenth and eighteenth century thought.

René Descartes (1596–1650), a French mathematician and philosopher who lived the major part of his life in Holland and Sweden, was the chief architect of the Age of Reason with his book *Le Discour de la Méthode*, in which he asserted the central tenet of Cartesian philosophy: "*Cogito, ergo sum,*" "I think, therefore I am." Descartes believed that reason and reason alone was the only reality of man which validated his existence here on earth. After centuries of reason being subordinate to the claims of faith, man was ready to proclaim his faith in reason.

Cartesian thought had some implications which were even more revolutionary for the modern world. Because the French language uses the same word "ésprit" for both mind and spirit, Descartes' assertion of reason was a subtle despiritualization of the physical universe. Cartesian philosophy drew a sharp distinction between mind and body, spirit and matter, and therefore man became, in the words of Gilbert Ryle, "a ghost in a machine"—disembodied reason somehow entrapped in a corporeal mechanism.

Of course this was blasphemy to Medieval Scholastic notions that God or Spirit inhabited the whole known universe. But for Descartes, everything in nature existed in space and matter and motion, all of which had to obey ineluctable and mechanistic and mathematical laws. Clearly the stage was being set for the tremendous perilous adventure of modern physics and astronomy, but at the awful expense of the loss of God in the world around us.

If Descartes was the philosopher of human reason, Immanuel Kant (1724–1804) was the Evangelist of Critical Thinking. Kant spent his entire life in the city of Königsberg, Prussia, where he was professor of logic and metaphysics at the University there and where he developed his Critical Philosophy. In his major works *The Critique of Pure Reason* (1781), *The Critique of Practical Reason* (1788), and *The Critique of Judgment* (1790), Kant claimed that reason could not solve the basic problems of reason itself, so it remained a paradoxical riddle to us. As Kant writes in the opening page of *The Critique of Pure Reason*:

Human reason has this peculiar fate that in one species of its knowledge it is burdened by questions which as prescribed by the very nature of reason itself, it is not able to ignore, but which, as transcending all its powers, it is also not able to answer.

Among the "unanswerable questions" which human reason is not able to ignore or resolve are the problems of freedom, causality, immortality, and God. In fact, Kant argues that religion and morality are completely outside the realm of reason and all we can ever hope to do is live our lives *als ob*—"as if" we were free, "as if" it were a casual universe, "as if" there were a God, and "as if" the soul were immortal:

> As follows from these considerations, the ideal of the supreme being is nothing but a *regulative principle* of reason, which directs us to look upon all connections in the world *as if* it originated from an all-sufficient necessary cause.

It may seem as if the whole thing were circular, and Kant's reason has returned to the bosom of faith to find its legitimacy. And from a purely philosophical point of view that's true, but it did not deter the Age of Reason from pursuing its advocacy of reason in all things religious and moral and political.

As a consequence of this Age of Reason, a curious substitute religion began to take shape. Known as Deism, it was a belief in a Supreme Being who was the origin of all existence, by-passing all traditional Christian forms and historical revelations. During the seventeenth and eighteenth centuries, Deism attracted some of the most brilliant free-thinkers, including Ethan Allen (1738–1789), Revolutionary leader of the Green Mountain Boys of Vermont and New Hampshire who captured Fort Ticonderoga with a small band of followers and called for the surrender of the British outpost with the words, "In the name of the great Jehovah and the Continental Congress!" After the American Revolution, Ethan Allen published a tract in 1784 entitled *Reason: The Only Oracle of Man, or A Compendious System of Natural Religion.* This tract denied the Bible was the word of God, and asserted Deism as the only tenable theology.

The American political activist Thomas Paine (1737–1809) was also a Deist. Paine's most significant contribution to history was his pamphleteering before and during the American Revolution: *Common Sense,* issued in 1776, was a chronicle of events that led up to the Revolution, and *The Crisis* (1776–1783) was a series of pamphlets that urged resistance against England. These essays were so effective in arousing the colonists against England that George Washington credited Paine with the success of the American Revolution. After the colonists had secured their independence, Paine traveled to France during the French Revolution and published *The Rights of Man* (1791), and in 1795 Paine published *The Age of Reason*, "thoughts on religion" written in Paris during the height of the Revolutionary Terror. Paine himself narrowly escaped the guillotine, since he was one of the few members of the Convention who openly opposed the execution of Louis XVI.

Thomas Paine's Deism can be seen in his simple statement, "My own mind is my own church." Paine's only test of the authenticity of anyone's religion is a man's moral character:

> It is impossible to calculate the moral mischief, if I may so express it, that mental lying has produced in society. When a man has so far corrupted and prostituted the chastity of his mind as to subscribe his professional belief to things he does not believe, he has prepared himself for the commission of every other crime.

Another political activist who espoused Deism was Thomas Jefferson (1743–1826), drafter of the *Declaration of Independence*, third United States President for two terms, and founder of the University of Virginia. Jefferson also drafted the Virginia Statute of Religious Liberty in 1786, in which he asserted that the exercise of religion is a natural right, often impinged on by overly zealous legislators and rulers. Jefferson insisted equally on the right *not* to worship, if that was the will of the individual: "No man shall be compelled to frequent or support any religious worship, place or ministry whatsoever."

Jefferson's Deism led him to urge others to examine any religious question as skeptically as possible. As he wrote to Peter Carr in a letter from Paris, 1787:

> Question with boldness even the existence of a God; because, if there be one, he must more approve of the homage of reason, than that of blindfolded fear. You will naturally examine first, the religion of your own country. Read the Bible, then, as you would read Livy or Tacitus . . .
>
> For example, in the book of Joshua, we are told, the sun stood still several hours. Were we to read that fact in Livy or Tacitus, we should

class it with their showers of blood, speaking of statues, beasts, &c. But it is said, that the writer of that book was inspired. Examine, therefore, candidly, what evidence there is of his having been inspired . . .

Do not be frightened from this inquiry by any fear of its consequences. If it ends in a belief that there is no God, you will find incitements to virtue in the comfort and pleasantness you feel in its exercise, and the love of others which it will procure you. If you find reason to believe there is a God, a consciousness that you are acting under his eye, and that he approves you, will be a vast additional incitement; if that there be a future state, the hope of a happy existence in that increases the appetite to deserve it; if that Jesus was also a God, you will be comforted by a belief of his aid and love . . .

Your own reason is the only oracle given you by Heaven, and you are answerable, not for the rightness, but the uprightness of the decision . . .

Thomas Jefferson seems to echo Thomas Paine and Ethan Allen in his insistence that reason is our only oracle, and he seems to echo Immanuel Kant in his assertion that we have to live "as if" various articles of faith were true. But these are all common doctrines of Deism.

In the midst of this Age of Reason and Deism, there was an equally strong reaction against it and a call for a return to the claims of pure faith. Blaise Pascal (1623–1662), a French mathematician and physicist who made a systematic study of probability and odds in gambling, grew up at Port-Royal under Jansenist training and believed, with them, that human nature was incapable of good without the grace of faith. Pascal lived a short life, dying at the age of thirty-nine, having had one mystical experience in 1654 and thereafter carrying a paper with the single word "FIRE," sewn into the inner lining of the coat he wore. It is claimed that Pascal had memorized the entire Bible, word for word, before his death—a claim which, if true, would be one of the most monumental feats of human memory ever recorded.

Pascal wrote the *Provincial Letters* (1656–57), which were arguments against the Jesuits who were persecuting the Jansenists at Port-Royal. His major work, *Pensées* or *Thoughts*, was a collection of fragmentary phrases and outlines towards an apologia for Christianity, published posthumously in 1670. The depth and insight of these *Pensées* make them one of the classics of religious thought. They begin with an assessment of man's place in the universe:

72 Man's disproportion . . . The whole visible world is only an im-
    perceptible atom in the ample bosom of nature. No idea approaches
    it . . . What is a man in the infinite? But to show him another
    prodigy equally astonishing, let him examine the most delicate
    things he knows . . . I will let him see therein a new abyss . . .
    For, in fact, what is man in nature? A Nothing in comparison
    with the Infinite, an All in comparison with the Nothing, a mean
    between nothing and everything . . . Let us, then, take our com-
    pass; we are something, and we are not everything. The nature of
    our existence hides from us the knowledge of first beginnings which
    are born of the Nothing; and the littleness of our being conceals
    from us the sight of the Infinite . . .

Pascal remarks that most of the mischief of this world comes from
man's innate restlessness: "I have discovered that all the unhappiness
of men arises from one single fact, that they cannot stay quietly in
their own chamber." (139) He goes on to present an image of our
pitiful human plight:

199 Let us imagine a number of men in chains and all condemned
    to death, where some are killed each day in the sight of the others,
    and those who remain see their own fate in that of their fellows
    and await their turn, looking at each other sorrowfully and without
    hope. It is an image of the condition of men.

And in one of the most haunting lines of the *Pensées*, Pascal describes
the estrangement we feel when we confront the cosmos: *"Le silence
éternel de ces espaces infinis m'effraie."* ("The eternal silence of these
infinite spaces terrifies me.") (206)

Pascal's basic premise in the *Pensées* is that the truth about God
cannot be approached through human reason, as the Deists believe:
"If there is a God, He is infinitely incomprehensible, since, having
neither parts nor limits, He has no affinity to us." (233) Therefore
Pascal offers us a proposal: since God cannot be approached through
reason, we must make an irrational gamble on His existence. This
may strike us as ludicrous because it seems to make God into some
sort of Cosmic oddsmaker—but Pascal is quite serious. After all, in
his mathematical work he had made a systematic study of gambling
and so he knew what he was talking about:

A game is being played at the extremity of this infinite distance where
heads or tails will turn up. What will you wager? According to reason,
you can do neither the one thing nor the other; according to reason,
you can defend neither of the propositions . . .

This is no idle speculation for Pascal—the choice of heads or tails is
an inescapable necessity: "Yes, but you must wager. It is not optional.
You are embarked."

At this point, midway through these *Pensées*, Pascal steps aside from
his argument and disclaims any vanity or self-congratulation in the
writing of his book:

> If this discourse pleases you and seems impressive, know that it is made
> by a man who has knelt, both before and after it, in prayer to that
> Being, infinite and without parts, before Whom he lays all he has, for
> you also to lay before Him all you have for your own good and for His
> glory, that so strength may be given to lowliness.

He returns then to his attack on Descartes and the Cartesian enthrone-
ment of reason: "The last proceeding of reason is to recognize that
there is an infinity of things which are beyond it . . ." (267) One of
the infinity of things which are beyond reason is our childhood, and
Pascal urges us to try to reclaim the memory of those fearful early
years: "*La sagesse nous envoie à l'enfance*." ("Wisdom sends us to
childhood.") (271) Pascal insists that reason is of no help at all in our
irrational gamble of faith: "There is nothing so conformable to reason
as this disavowal of reason." (272)

In one of the great statements of the *Pensées*, Pascal contrasts the
wisdom of the heart with the ignorance of reason: "*Le coeur a ses
raisons, que la raison ne connait point*." ("The heart has its reasons,
which reason knows nothing about.") (277) He argues the mind cannot
do what the heart has to experience: "The knowledge of God is very
far from the love of him." (280) As for the human condition, Pascal
asserts that there is a conspicuous vacuity inside of us which we cannot
fill by ourselves: " . . . the infinite abyss can only be filled by an
infinite and immutable object, that is to say, only by God Himself."
(425) It does no good to study theology or try to prove the existence
of God by reason, as Descartes and the Jesuits do:

> 534   The metaphysical proofs of God are so remote from the reasoning
>   of men, and so complicated, that they make little impression;

and if they should be of service to some, it would be only during
the moment that they see such demonstration; but an hour afterwards they fear they have been mistaken.

Finally, Pascal turns his attention to the true object of faith, which
is the mystery of Jesus: "Jesus will be in agony even to the end of the
world." (553) There is hope, as Pascal recreates the voice of Jesus
speaking to our human condition: "Console thyself, thou wouldst not
seek me, if thou hadst not found me . . ." And in one of the final
entries of these *Pensées*, Pascal echoes the Jansenist doctrine of the
Elect: "We understand nothing of the works of God, if we do not take
it as a principle that He has willed to blind some and enlighten others."
     Put in the very simplest terms, Pascal in the *Pensées* is arguing for
a return to the claims of a childlike intuition which has always understood the primacy of faith in a world we cannot hope to know or
control. And for all their fragmentary nature, these *Pensées* are a
powerful document of Christian apologetics: they offer a strong re-
pudiation of the philosophical underpinnings of the Age of Reason,
as initiated by Descartes and (much later) by Kant. Faith in God and
one's own personal salvation is not a matter of human reason, nor is
it something one has to live "as if" in a state of permanent irresolution.
As Pascal argues, we are embarked and we must make a choice.
     Furthermore, these *Pensées* of Pascal also offer a strong repudiation
of later Deistic freethinking such as Ethan Allen, Thomas Paine, and
Thomas Jefferson engaged in. The *Pensées* make it plain that the only
sensible grounds for any authentic wager of faith lie in the life and
teachings of Jesus.
     The implications of these *Pensées* for modern religious thought are
quite clear: Pascal had successfully taken on the most sophisticated
alternative philosophies and theologies based on human reason and
he had shown that they were not viable options for our human condition. Only the risk of a genuine faith can save us from the awful
spectre of our ongoing sojourn in a hostile or meaningless universe.
     Following Martin Luther's decisive break from the Medieval Church,
modern Protestant thought began to create new theologies in a desperate attempt to justify the myriad sects, cults, and denominations
that were springing up all over the world. Deism emerged as the
strongest alternative to the traditional orthodox Catholicism of the
Middle Ages, and it happened to coincide with the founding of the
American Constitutional Republic. "We hold these truths to be self
evident" is a Deistic trust in the principles of human reason, just as

"In God we trust" is an assertion of Deistic faith. The God of the founding fathers of America was a Deistic God, which is not necessarily associated with the Judeo-Christian God.

This will have important implications for Evangelism in America because there never was a very specific Christian theology behind the Constitutional framework of the United States. Therefore all the various Protestant sects, cults, and denominations have had to work out their own theologies according to their own needs and natures. *E Pluribus Unum* is as good a description of modern American Protestantism as it is of anything else in our Republic.

Chapter 3

PURITAN AMERICA AND
THE GREAT AWAKENING

PURITANISM BEGAN as an Evangelical reaction against the empty forms and rituals associated with Catholicism and the Church of England, and Puritans were committed to restoring the zeal and purity of the earliest Christian Church of the first centuries. As such, the chief feature of Puritanism was its sincerity—Samuel Eliot Morison writes in the *Oxford History of the American People*:

> Puritanism was essentially and primarily a religious movement; attempts to prove it to have been a mask for politics or money-making are false as well as unhistorical. In the broadest sense Puritanism was a passion for righteousness; the desire to know and do God's will.

The first Puritans were, in this sense, purists: they wanted to strip religion of all its outward ornaments and get down to sacred fundamentals. And of all the purist sects of Protestantism which had their origin in Puritanism, no movement was more devoted to stripping away outer forms and rituals than the Quakers.

George Fox (1624–1691) explained the word "Quaker" as a name given to himself and his followers who "Tremble at the word of the Lord." Fox heeded the still small voice within himself, and from this voice he derived his idea of a new religion that eschewed all outward forms in dress and worship, even down to the detail of not wearing buttons or lapels on one's coat.

At Quaker "meetings," members sit in silence until one is moved

by his "inner light" to stand and share a concern with his brethren.
Macaulay writes:

> George Fox (the Quaker) raised a tempest of derision by proclaiming
> that it was a violation of Christian sincerity to designate a single person
> by a plural pronoun, and that it was idolatrous homage to Janus and
> Woden to talk about January and Wednesday.

Hence the Quaker usage of "thee" and "thou" in direct address,
and the designation of "first month" and "fourth day" to indicate
calendar dates.

George Fox was a man of frail health who suffered from an acute
nervous condition, and he related in his *Journal* how he first received
a call to preach to Lichfield:

> Then I walked on about a mile, and as soon as I was got within the
> city, the word of the Lord came to me again, saying: Cry, 'Woe to the
> bloody city of Lichfield!' So I went up and down the streets, crying with
> a loud voice, Woe to the bloody city of Lichfield!

This may strike us as eccentric, but of course it was what Jonah
was punished for *not* doing to Nineveh. Before we consign Fox and
his Quakerism to the annals of quaintness, we should pay attention
to what William James says in his *Varieties of Religious Experience*:

> The Quaker religion which [Fox] founded is something which it is
> impossible to overpraise. In a day of shams, it was a religion of veracity
> rooted in spiritual inwardness, and a return to something more like the
> original gospel than man had ever known in England.

The Quakers eventually emigrated to America to escape persecution,
and early Evangelists like John Woolman (1720–1772) recorded in his
Journals his earnest concern against slavery, and how he traveled from
town to town to confront slave-holders face to face so he could try to
persuade them to listen to the light of their own conscience and release
their slaves to freedom.

A contemporary of George Fox was John Bunyan (1628–1688), who
was arrested in November 1660 for preaching without a license and
refusing to comply with the law, and Bunyan was kept in prison for
twelve years until Charles II declared a general Indulgence. Bunyan

used his time in prison to write nine books, principally *Grace Abounding to the Chief of Sinners* (1666), and on his release from prison he began to write *The Pilgrim's Progress*, which was published in 1678. This latter book depicts a dream of Bunyan's in which Christian, with a burden on his back, reads in a book that the city where he and his family live will be consumed with fire. On the advice of Evangelist, Christian flees from the City of Destruction after having failed to persuade his wife and children to accompany him. Thereafter Bunyan describes Christian's pilgrimage through the Slough of Despond, the Valley of Humiliation, and Vanity Fair where he meets Mr. Worldly Wiseman. It is one of the most compelling allegories ever written, emblematical of our soul's journey through life, and it is probably the Protestant equivalent of the great *Commedia* of Dante during the Medieval era.

Perhaps the most important of Puritan apologists was the English poet John Milton (1608–1674), whose epic poems *Paradise Lost* and *Paradise Regained* retold the story of the Fall of Man in the Garden of Eden, and the Coming of Christ to redeem humankind. In Milton's early life he visited Galileo in prison and was well aware of the cruelties and injustice of the Catholic Inquisition. In 1641, Milton wrote a pamphlet against the episcopacy, and in 1643 he wrote a pamphlet on the doctrine and discipline of divorce which caused him considerable notoriety. Although afflicted with blindness, Milton served as Latin secretary to Oliver Cromwell during the Puritan Revolution in England (1642–1660), and Milton continuously asserted the right of Puritans to pursue their religious freedom. After the Restoration of Charles II, Milton was arrested and questioned, but released.

The Restoration in England brought increasing persecution to the Puritans, and many of them chose to emigrate from England and other parts of Europe to the new colonies of America. These Puritans found an ideal sanctuary for their radical faith in New England where they were free to set up whatever churches and practices they desired. Of course, there were occasional collisions of personality and principle: after Roger Williams had a dispute with Cotton Mather, Williams founded Rhode Island as the only colony that would be completely free of any official religious denomination. As Roger Williams commented, "Forced worship stinks in God's nostrils."

John Endicott settled Salem in 1628 and he tried to establish a theocracy there in the same way Savonarola had set up a theocracy in Florence and John Calvin had administered a theocracy in Geneva.

Endicott had the advantage of founding his Church-State on completely new soil, so he could initiate whatever institutions and laws he deemed necessary for a godly civil authority.

Harvard University was founded in 1636, and in 1639 the first book off the new University Press was the Holy Bible translated into Algonquin by the Reverend John Eliot of Roxbury, who devised Roman letters for the phonetic Algonquin language. Reverend Eliot, John Cotton, and Richard Bourne used this Algonquin Bible to Evangelize among the Native American Indians, taught them to read and write their own language, and set up a series of "Praying Indian Towns" along northern Connecticut, with twenty more Indian towns around Cape Cod. There were about 2,500 converted Indians living in these Indian Prayer Towns, engaged in farming and trading with the white colonists.

Another book from the new Press was Cotton Mather's *Memorable Providences Relating to Witchcraft and Possessions* (1685), which described a case of witchcraft that Mather had litigated in Boston in which an aged woman was executed. Mather's book contained lurid descriptions of the symptoms of demon possession, and this book fell into the hands of some young girls living in the settlement of Salem. Apparently bored with sitting on cold pews and listening to dull sermons, these girls began practicing the symptoms of demon possession until they were so expert at their charade that they were able to hoax the whole community into believing that Tituba, a good-natured woman who was half-Indian and half-Negro, had put a hex on them. Tituba was whipped and threatened with death, so the poor woman made a false confession and implicated two goodwives of Salem as her confederates, and before anyone knew what was happening the witch-hunt was on.

These Salem Witch Trials were a paroxysm of righteousness in which the Puritans set up a special court to try the two women accused of being witches; others were implicated, and before long select judges from out of town were hearing "spectral evidence" and confessions of how Salem women had had sex with the devil, how they danced naked at witches' sabbaths, and how they went on midnight broomstick rides.

One can get some sense of the bizarre proceedings by reading a section of the transcript of the trial of Bridget Bishop of Salem, June 2, 1692:

13.   One thing that made against the Prisoner was, her being evidently convicted of *gross lying in the Court*, several times, while she was making

her plea; but besides this, a Jury of Women found a preternatural Teat upon her Body; but upon a second search, within 3 or 4 hours, there was no such thing to be seen . . .

This sort of voodoo evidence may strike the modern reader as being so patently absurd it could not possibly hold up in any court of law, but we must remember that a theocracy not only controls ecclesiastical law, it controls civil and criminal law as well—so these Salem courts were, in effect, an extension of the Puritan religion. And we must also remember the peculiar mind-set of these early Puritans: they did truly believe they were performing an essential Evangelical task. William Stoughton, the chief justice of the court that condemned the Salem witches, spoke of the awesome charge he felt had been laid on his jurisdiction: "We must look upon our selves as under a solemn divine Probation; it hath been and it is a Probation-time, even to this whole people . . . This hath been and is a time and season of eminent trial to us."

Notice the wording: it is an eminent trial *to us*. No matter that fourteen women and five men were hanged as witches and Giles Corey was pressed to death for refusing to plead either guilty or not guilty. The chief justice of the court insisted it was the Puritans themselves who were on trial, not the defendants.

Later in that same year 1692, the Massachusetts Governor dissolved the special court and ordered the jails opened to release some 150 prisoners who were still awaiting trial as witches. Only one of the nine judges who were involved in the Salem trials, Samuel Sewell, later admitted the error of the proceedings publicly. But by that time it was too late to save the twenty people who had been so shamefully humiliated and executed.

It was a devastating experience in American history, as Arthur Miller writes in the notes to his play *The Crucible*: "The witch-hunt was a perverse manifestation of the panic which set in among all classes when the balance began to turn toward a greater individual freedom."

The American poet Wallace Stevens has a poem "The Blue Buildings in the Summer Air" which captures something of the desperate empty zeal that gave rise to these witch hunts:

> Cotton Mather died when I was a boy. The books
> He read, all day, all night and all the nights,
> Had got him nowhere. There was always the doubt,
> That made him preach the louder, long for a church

In which his voice would roll its cadences,
After the sermons, to quiet that mouse in the wall . . .

As if these Salem Witch Trials weren't bad enough, by the middle of the eighteenth century New England witnessed another major outbreak of Evangelistic zeal. In 1734, Jonathan Edwards preached a sermon in Northampton, Massachusetts, entitled "Sinners in the Hands of an Angry God." It was a harrowing sermon, depicting the human condition as nightmarish in the extreme:

Natural men are held in the hand of God, over the pit of hell . . . The devil is waiting for them, hell is gaping for them, the flames gather and flash about them, and would fain lay hold on them, and swallow them up; the fire pent up in their own hearts is struggling to break out . . . You have nothing to stand upon, nor any thing to take hold of; there is nothing between you and hell but air.

Shortly after delivering this sermon in Northampton, Joanthan Edwards published it in a pamphlet entitled "A Faithful Narrative of the Surprising Work of God in the Conversion of Many Hundred Souls in Northampton, 1736." The sermon and its subsequent publication were all that was needed to begin the Great Awakening.

This Great Awakening movement was occasioned by itinerant lay preachers who held "hellfire and brimstone" Revival meetings throughout the colonies: an Evangelical preacher would become so frenzied he would approach hysteria, and his congregation would respond with weeping and screaming and writhing in an ecstasy of salvation. Some of these stumping Evangelists even went so far as to enact Christ's agonies from the pulpit.

The first stirrings of this movement are attributed to Revivals held by Theodorus Frelinghuysen, a minister of the Dutch Reformed Church in New Jersey, in 1719. Over the next few years the Awakening reached its emotional peak in New England under the forceful leadership of Jonathan Edwards. Gilbert Tennent, an Irish-born Presbyterian Evangelist who often denounced the elders of his own church, carried the movement to the Middle Colonies from Philadelphia. Samuel Davies fanned Evangelical flames in Virginia, to the dismay of the established Anglicans.

George Whitefield, an English minister who had read Jonathan Edwards' "Sinners in the Hands of an Angry God" while he was in

Georgia, was inspired to Evangelical fervor throughout the South and into New England, exciting huge Revival meetings to fever pitch. In seven American visits after 1738, Whitefield roamed the colonies from Maine to Georgia, casting a strong spell of Calvinist oratory over the populace. The response was so overwhelming in New Haven that classes at Yale had to be suspended when students poured out to watch Whitefield dance and roar and make violent gestures in the air from his pulpit.

By 1750 the Great Awakening had created such turmoil that it threatened the existence of many established churches. And although the movement gradually began to subside, it left bitter doctrinal schisms within denominations in its wake, pitting traditionalists against those who wanted a less formal religion that would be based on the testimony of their own personal experience. The Great Awakening also left three new Ivy League colleges behind as a consequence of the controversy and enthusiasm that had been stirred up: Dartmouth, Brown, and Princeton. Jonathan Edwards lived out the last days of his life as President of Princeton University.

A Second Awakening began in Kentucky in 1797 when James McGready, who had been driven from his first pastorate in North Carolina for being too intemperate in his damnation of local sinners, started preaching before Camp Meetings of frontiersmen. This was an entirely new form of open air Revival Meeting which began in Logan County, Kentucky in 1800, when frontier people came together with picnic baskets, pitched tents, and sleeping bags in an open field so they could hear McGready and other Revivalists preach fiery sermons by torchlight far into the night. It gave rise to the popular Revival song,

> We're tenting tonight
> on the old camp grounds . . .

One of the most colorful descriptions of a Camp Meeting ever written was by Mark Twain in his novel *Huckleberry Finn*. In Chapter Twenty, Huck and the Duke and the Dauphin leave the Mississippi River and travel to a one-horse town called Parkville where they find "Everybody that warn't too young or too sick or too old was gone to camp-meeting, about two mile back in the woods." After precipitating some mischief in town, these rascals set off for the site of the Camp Meeting, and Huck tells in his own words what they found there:

We got there in about half an hour fairly dripping, for it was a most awful hot day. There was as much as a thousand people there from twenty mile around. The woods was full of teams and wagons, hitched everywhere, feeding out of the wagon-troughs and stomping to keep off the flies. There was sheds made out of poles and roofed over with branches, where they had lemonade and gingerbread to sell, and piles of watermelons and green corn and such-like truck.

The preaching was going on under the same kinds of sheds, only they was bigger and held crowds of people. The benches was made out of outside slabs of logs, with holes bored in the round side to drive sticks into for legs. They didn't have no backs. The preachers had high platforms to stand on at one end of the sheds. The women had on sun-bonnets; and some had linsey-woolsey frocks, some gingham ones, and a few of the young ones had on calico. Some of the young men was bare-footed, and some of the children didn't have on any clothes but just a tow-linen shirt. Some of the old women was knitting, and some of the young folks was courting on the sly.

The first shed we come to the preacher was lining out a hymn. He lined out two lines, everybody sung it, and it was kind of grand to hear it, there was so many of them and they done it in such a rousing way; then he lined out two more for them to sing—and so on. The people woke up more and more, and sung louder and louder; and towards the end some begun to groan, and some begun to shout. Then the preacher begun to preach, and begun in earnest, too; and went weaving first to one side of the platform and then the other, and then a-leaning down over the front of it, with his arms and his body going all the time, and shouting his words out with all his might; and every now and then he would hold up his Bible and spread it open, and kind of pass it around this way and that, shouting, "It's the brazen serpent in the wilderness! Look upon it and live!" And the people would shout out, "Glory— A-a-a-*men!*" And so he went on, and the people groaning and crying and saying amen:

"Oh, come to the mourner's bench! come, black with sin! (*amen!*) come, sick and sore! (*amen!*) come, lame and halt and blind! (*amen!*) come, pore and needy, sunk in shame (*a-a-men!*) come, all that's worn and soiled and suffering!—come with a broken spirit! come with a contrite heart! come in your rags and sin and dirt! the waters that cleanse is free, the door of heaven stands open—oh, enter in and be at rest!" (*a-a-men! glory, glory hallelujah!*)

And so on. You couldn't make out what the preacher said any more,

on account of the shouting and crying. Folks got up everywheres in
the crowd, and worked their way just by main strength to the mourners'
bench, with the tears running down their faces; and when all the mourners had got up there to the front benches in a crowd, they sung and
shouted and flung themselves down on the straw, just crazy and wild.

Mark Twain was writing about Camp Meetings that were becoming
increasingly active through the nineteenth century, and these im-
promptu Revival services continued with even more fervor and abandon into the twentieth century. A contemporary American playwright,
Stuart Sheffer, describes a Tent Revival he went to when he was seven
or eight, on the outskirts of Knoxville, Tennessee. The time would be
in the 1960s:

> It wasn't until the revival actually began that I realized how different
> these people were from the people who made up my middle-class world.
> What they lacked in money, education and "manners" they more than
> made up for in commitment and raw emotion. They didn't just sit back
> and listen to a service as if it were a lecture on the Dewey Decimal
> System like the people in all the churches I had gone to before, both
> Disciple of Christ and Baptist. If the people here felt like shouting out
> in the middle of a sermon, they shouted out, and instead of being
> quieted down like they would have been in every church I had ever
> been to, they were encouraged by the congregation. To a young boy
> discouraged from doing anything beyond judicious whispering in church,
> this was an incredibly exhilarating experience. I found myself watching
> the congregation instead of the Evangelist, constantly waiting for some-
> one else to find himself filled with the spirit of the Lord and start shout-
> ing . . .

Both the Huck Finn and Stuart Sheffer accounts of Camp and Tent
Revival Meetings give us an interesting insight into one important
factor of mass Evangelism: there seems to be a conspicuous release of
libido at these rough frontier gatherings, and it's significant that this
is the first thing the young Huck Finn and Stuart Sheffer pick up on.
These impressionable young men are seeing grown-ups carry on as
they never saw them carry on before, utterly free of any inhibitions or
social constraints, and with the full approval of the Lord these grown-
ups are shouting out loud and taking part in the wild contagious
Dionysian goings-on. It's a little like a child's witnessing the orgiastic

swooning of bobby-soxers over Frank Sinatra when he first played the Palace, or the frenzy that swept through middle-aged women when Elvis Presley began gyrating his hips and thighs onstage. Of course for the people being affected by these strong trigger mechanisms, the libidinal release will seem to be absolute evidence of an authentic rapture. To a child witnessing it from the outside, however, it will seem to be slightly foolish and not a little dangerous.

And of course the borderline fringe element was especially in evidence during this period. James Frazer in *The Golden Bough* recounts one such maverick Evangelist who suddenly popped up as the incarnate Second Coming, and how this man was roundly dealt with:

> About the year 1830 there appeared, in one of the States of the American Union bordering on Kentucky, an impostor who declared that he was the Son of God, the Saviour of mankind, and that he had reappeared on earth to recall the impious, the unbelieving, and sinners to their duty. He protested that if they did not mend their ways within a certain time, he would give the signal, and in a moment the world would crumble to ruins. These extravagant pretensions were received with favour even by persons of wealth and position in society. At last a German humbly besought the new Messiah to announce the dreadful catastrophe to his fellow-countrymen in the German language, as they did not understand English, and it seemed a pity that they should be damned merely on that account. The would-be Saviour in reply confessed with great candour that he did not know German. "What!" retorted the German, "you the Son of God, and don't speak all languages, and don't even know German? Come, come, you are a knave, a hypocrite, and a madman. Bedlam is the place for you." The spectators laughed, and went away ashamed of their credulity.

Partly through such fanatical activities as Camp Meetings and Tent Revivals and itinerant Evangelists who were free to preach all manner of madness, Protestantism increased the membership of its individual churches during the first half of the nineteenth century in a remarkable way: Methodists, for example, multiplied their numbers sevenfold, and Baptists threefold.

Another phenomenon of this time was the circuit rider, who was a frontier Evangelist on horseback who rode from town to town in rural America and spread the Word. Francis Asbury was a Methodist missionary from England who became a circuit rider up and down the Atlantic colonies, logging over 300,000 miles on horseback. Asbury became the first Bishop of the Methodist Episcopal Church in the United States, and he in turn ordained some 3,000 circuit riders to continue his work. Another circuit rider, Peter Cartwright, rode the Middle West, becoming so well known for his lively Revival sermons that in 1846 he ran against Abe Lincoln for Congress in Illinois (he lost by a landslide).

In the early nineteenth century the most outstanding pre-Civil War Evangelists were Timothy Dwight, who was the grandson of Jonathan Edwards, and eventually became President of Yale University; Charles Finney; and Lyman Beecher.

Charles Finney was trained in the law but after his conversion in 1821 he devoted the rest of his life to his calling as a preacher and Evangelist—he was characterized as a "briary, disputatious, sockdolagizing pioneer lawyer." Devoting himself to a ten-year Crusade through the Eastern states, Finney converted thousands with his plain style and simple message: "free and full salvation." In 1851, Charles Finney began his tenure as President of Oberlin College in Ohio.

Lyman Beecher was a Presbyterian Evangelist who could bring tears to the eyes of his congregation when he described the evils of slavery, just as easily as he could turn his listeners into an anti-Catholic mob intent on arson. In 1831, Beecher's Boston parishioners became so inflamed after listening to the Evangelist's charges about a Papist plot that they dispersed from the church and put the torch on a nearby convent. Beecher had thirteen children who all shared their father's powerful command of the English language, including Harriet Beecher Stowe, whose *Uncle Tom's Cabin* did so much to bring about the American Civil War, and her brother Henry Ward Beecher, who became a religious author and journalist. Lyman Beecher was tried for heresy in 1835 by his fellow Presbyterians, but was acquitted.

The only way for us to get some sane gauge of what all this hellfire and brimstone Evangelism in America may mean to us, is to contrast it with the Evangelism which was taking place in England during this same period. Both John Wesley (1703–1791) and his brother Charles Wesley (1707–1788) were born of Puritan ancestry but their later experiences led them to a much broader base of Protestant inquiry. The so-called "Methodist Society" was founded at Oxford in 1729 for the promotion of piety and morality, and the whole doctrine of Methodism that John Wesley is credited with developing began as an impassioned reaction against the apathy of the Church of England in all matters of faith and morals.

In 1735, the year after Jonathan Edwards delivered his fiery "Sinners in the Hands of an Angry God" in Northampton, Massachusetts, John Wesley was in the colony of Georgia observing firsthand the conditions of slavery and plantation ownership. When Wesley returned to England, he came under the influence of the Moravians, an eighteenth century Protestant sect founded in Saxony that held strongly to the views of Jan Hus, who had been burned alive in 1415 for his protest against the Catholic practice of Mass and other Church teachings.

Secure now in his understanding of the appropriate grounding for Protestant theology, Wesley installed himself in a church in Bristol and over the course of his long ministry there he preached over 40,000 sermons. And what is most significant for the future of Evangelism, Wesley also published over twenty-three collections of hymn books. Undoubtedly this instinct of John Wesley to fuse sacred music with preaching led modern Evangelists to program so many rousing and emotional hymns for their Crusades and Revival services. John's younger brother Charles was the chief contributor to these Methodist hymn books, and Charles Wesley is credited with composing the words for hundreds of Protestant hymns which are still current, including such staples as "Hark, The Herald Angels Sing," "Christ The Lord Is Risen Today," "Love Divine, All Love Excelling," and "Ye Servants of God, Your Master Proclaim."

America, on the other hand, was committed to a far different kind of Evangelism during this period: more frenzied, more fanatical. The difference between John Wesley and Jonathan Edwards is the difference between night and day. Wesley was informed, literate, and thoroughly grounded on a solid theology he had worked out for himself. Jonathan Edwards was nightmarish, forceful, and utterly haunted by the spectre of the Salem Witch Trials that had preceded him. The awful legacy of Puritanism is something few Protestant Evangelists have been able to escape, and it was enough to prompt H. L. Mencken to give his sardonic definition: "Puritanism: the haunting fear that someone, somewhere, may be happy."

The American poet Robert Lowell recreates the grotesque obsessiveness of this era in his poem "Mr. Edwards and the Spider":

> I saw the spiders marching through the air,
> Swimming from tree to tree that mildewed day
>   In latter August when the hay
>   Came creaking to the barn. But where
>   The wind is westerly,

Where gnarled November makes the spiders fly
Into the apparitions of the sky,
They purpose nothing but their ease and die
Urgently beating east to sunrise and the sea;

What are we in the hands of the great God? . . .

Chapter 4

THE SOCIAL GOSPEL

THE NINETEENTH CENTURY witnessed the rise of the Industrial Revolution with its use of the steam engine, power loom, spinning frame, laying of railroads and construction of steamboats for navigation of inland waterways. Centuries of civilization that had depended on human toil were swept aside in favor of these new machines which seemed to multiply exponentially the labor that used to be obtained from peasants and beasts of burden.

And yet ironically these same revolutionary machines created new conditions of work that were even more onerous and insupportable than had ever prevailed in the most despotic of slave states. Sweatshops and loft factories began to exploit women and children in tedious and soul-stifling circumstances until the social fabric was ready to fall apart.

To make matters worse, as commerce and business flourished through the use of these new modes of transportation and machine power, the sudden windfall wealth of robber baron power brokers seemed to confirm the concepts of laissez-faire and free enterprise which Adam Smith had outlined in his *Enquiry into the Nature and Causes of the Wealth of Nations* (1776). Adam Smith anticipated the Evolutionary theories of Charles Darwin in *The Origin of Species* (1859), in which Darwin asserted the "natural selection in consequence of the struggle for existence" among all living things, which resulted in "the survival of the fittest."

"The survival of the fittest"—this was not an easy time for religion to keep pace with the rapidly changing social and economic realities and the abuses of a swiftly industrialized civilization. Indeed, for a

time religion seemed to be at a total loss to know how to cope with
the cost in human suffering. And just as in the Medieval period when
poets like Dante and Chaucer and Michelangelo were more vocal than
priests and Reformers in crying out against the corruptions of the
Church, so now in the nineteenth century the Romantic movement
began partly as a reaction against the inhuman circumstances created
by this Industrial Revolution and its crippling alienation of man from
his natural environment. Thus Charles Dickens did more to portray
atrocious social conditions in a novel like *Oliver Twist* than any Cru-
sading Reformer could, and William Blake's poem "London" pinpointed the ugliness and horror of the modern industrialized city better
than any Evangelist could:

> I wander thro' each chartered street,
> Near where the charter'd Thames does flow,
> And mark in every face I meet
> Marks of weakness, marks of woe.
>
> In every cry of every Man,
> In every infant's cry of fear,
> In every voice, in every ban,
> The mind forg'd manacles I hear.
>
> How the Chimney-sweeper's cry
> Every black'ning Church appalls;
> And the hapless Soldier's sigh
> Runs in blood down Palace walls.
>
> But most thro' midnight streets I hear
> How the youthful Harlot's curse
> Blasts the new born infant's tear,
> And blights with plagues the Marriage hearse.

In America during this period, the Industrial Revolution gave rise
to the idea of free enterprise run amuck with robber barons exploiting
the amorality of capitalism to their own ends. Andrew Carnegie in
steel, Henry Ford in assembly line automobiles, John D. Rockefeller
in oil, Henry Clay Fricke in railroads, John Jacob Astor in fur trade,
and J. Pierpont Morgan in finances—all these industrial leaders had
no scruples about perpetrating the most despicable acts of extortion
and aggrandizement in order to perpetuate their own empires.

The use of brute force and terrorist tactics in union-busting; the employment of Chinese coolies to lay the transcontinental railroad; shooting trappers in the beaver trade so they would not have to be paid—we don't need to assign particular crimes to particular persons; it's common knowledge that all the above named individuals committed wicked practices that became so onerous that Teddy Roosevelt eventually had to break up their ruthless monopolies through the stringent enforcement of antitrust laws.

But this cynical side of American industrialism should not blind us to the fact that there were genuine Evangelists of endless invention and pragmatism who typified an authentic genius for originality and technology. Benjamin Franklin (1706–1790) was a canny Pennsylvanian with his Franklin stove, his thrifty savings bank, and his extraordinary demonstration of electricity by flying a kite in the middle of a thunderstorm. Franklin was one of the original drafters of the Declaration of Independence and an ambassador to France, and he was also one of the signers of the American Constitution in 1787. From almanacs to printing presses to newspapers, Franklin exemplified the American knack for creating the right thing at the right time. A man of universal interests and appetites, he founded the American Philosophical Society and the academy which later became the University of Pennsylvania.

Another American who demonstrated endless invention was Thomas Alva Edison (1847–1931), whose quiet life produced so many ingenious things that have become a part of our modern life: the components of the Bell telephone; the incandescent electric lamp; the kinetoscopic camera for taking motion pictures; and innumerable devices for the storage and transmission of that same electricity which Franklin had demonstrated a hundred years earlier with his kite. Without the work of Benjamin Franklin and Thomas Edison, modern American Evangelists would not be able to send their messages over television, nor would the average person have stereo sets, computer chips, word processors, or all the information retrieval systems that keep track of every aspect of a citizen's life.

The problem for modern Protestantism was twofold: how to provide a theology that would accommodate itself to the new advances in science and technology that were taking place, and how to provide the basis for social reform that was needed to relieve the suffering that industrialization had brought on the world.

In America, the answer to the theological problem came from the Transcendentalist movement in New England, and the answer to the sociological problem came from many brave Reformers who embraced the Social Gospel.

Ralph Waldo Emerson (1803–1882) in his lectures and essays developed a strong individualist philosophy that placed a serene optimism in the power of each person to work out his own appropriate way. It was exactly what American Protestantism needed to counter its rigid Puritan heritage and give courage to individuals who felt overwhelmed by the massive industrial incursion into their private lives.

Emerson had resigned his cloth from the Unitarian Church because he was unwilling to administer the Lord's Supper, and for the rest of his life he lived in Concord, Massachusetts, writing essays and traveling to give lectures on a whole range of humanist subjects. Emerson's main theme was that human nature itself was divine, and with the simplicity of the Sermon on the Mount he developed a theory that there are sublime laws of compensation which function without our awareness, and each individual can grasp the truth without the intercession of any church or priest. One senses here a hint of Pelagianism and Deism with all their seductions and limitations, but Emerson had a way of making it sound Christlike and inevitable.

Emerson advanced his unconventional theory of spiritual laws to the graduating class at Harvard Divinity School in 1838, where he stated:

> These laws execute themselves. They are out of time, out of space, and not subject to circumstance; Thus, in the soul of man there is a justice whose retributions are instant and entire. He who does a mean deed is by the action itself contracted. He who puts off impurity thereby puts on purity. If a man is at heart just, then in so far is he God; the safety of God, the immortality of God, the majesty of God, do enter into that man with justice. If a man dissemble, deceive, he deceives himself, and goes out of acquaintance with his own being.

In Emerson's major essay "Self-Reliance," he develops an Evangelism of extreme individuality. Following are some excerpts:

> To believe in your own thought, to believe that what is true for you in your private heart is true for all men, that is genius.

> Society everywhere is in conspiracy against the manhood of every one of its members. Society is a joint-stock company, in which the members agree, for the better securing of his bread to each shareholder, to sur-

render the liberty of the eater. The virtue in most request is conformity. Self-reliance is its aversion. It loves not realities and creators, but names and customs.

Whoso would be a man, must be a nonconformist.

A foolish consistency is the hobgoblin of little minds, adored by little statesmen and philosophers and divines. With consistency a great soul has simply nothing to do.

"Ah, so you shall be sure to be misunderstood."—Is it so bad then to be misunderstood? Pythagoras was misunderstood, and Socrates, and Jesus, and Luther, and Copernicus, and Galileo, and Newton, and every pure and wise spirit that ever took flesh. To be great is to be misunderstood.

Prayer is the contemplation of the facts of life from the highest point of view. It is the soliloquy of a beholding and jubilant soul. It is the spirit of God pronouncing his works good.

Insist on yourself; never imitate.

Nothing can bring you peace but yourself. Nothing can bring you peace but the triumph of principles.

Like Jesus, Emerson located the kingdom of heaven inside ourselves, and he urged us to allow the spiritual laws to have their way with us, without our judgmental interference.

This was radical Evangelism indeed, and at least three of Emerson's contemporaries began to reflect its spirit in their own work. The young Herman Melville (1819–1891) in *White-Jacket* (1850), a book immediately preceding his great *Moby Dick* (1851), wrote an account of life on a naval frigate in which he recorded his Evangelical sense of America as the Promised Land:

We Americans are the peculiar, chosen people—the Israel of our time; we bear the ark of the liberties of the world . . . God has predestined, mankind expects, great things from our race; and great things we feel in our souls. The rest of the nations must soon be in our rear . . . Long enough have we been sceptics with regard to ourselves, and doubted whether, indeed, the political Messiah had come. But he has come in *us.*

Another contemporary of Emerson, Henry David Thoreau (1817–1862), published his *Walden* in 1854 and set down how he had put Emerson's Transcendental principles into action:

I went to the woods because I wished to live deliberately, to front only the essential facts of life, and see if I could not learn what it had to teach, and not, when I came to die, discover that I had not lived. I did not wish to live what was not life, living is so dear; nor did I wish to practice resignation, unless it was quite necessary. I wanted to live deep and suck out all the marrow of life, to live so sturdily and Spartan-like as to put to rout all that was not life, to cut a broad swath and shave close, to drive life into a corner, and reduce it to its lowest terms, and, if it proved to be mean, why then to get the whole and genuine meanness of it, and publish its meanness to the world; or if it were sublime, to know it by experience, and be able to give a true account of it in my next excursion. For most men, it appears to me, are in a strange uncertainty about it, whether it is of the devil or of God, and have *somewhat hastily* concluded that it is the chief end of man here to "glorify God and enjoy him forever."

A third contemporary of Emerson, Walt Whitman (1819–1892), knew the minute he read Emerson's essays that he had found what he had been looking for over the years to tie his experience together and begin writing *Leaves of Grass.* As Whitman put it quite simply: "I was simmering, simmering, and Emerson brought me to a boil."

In harmony with Emerson's faith in individual initiative, major Evangelical Reform movements began to take place on purely social levels. In 1848 in Seneca Falls, New York, the Woman's Rights Movement was begun in America by Elizabeth C. Stanton and Lucretia Mott and Lucy Stone, but it was Susan B. Anthony (1820–1906) who fired the imagination of the movement. As Susan B. Anthony wrote during the campaign for divorce law reform in 1860:

Cautious, careful people always casting about to preserve their reputations and social standing, never can bring about a reform. Those who are really in earnest must be willing to be anything or nothing in the world's estimation.

The Revolution was the woman's suffrage newspaper which advocated "equal pay for equal work," and it insisted women had to have equal power "in the making, shaping, and controlling of the circumstances of life." In 1873, during her trial for committing the crime of voting, Susan B. Anthony testified: "Woman must not depend upon the protection of man, but must be taught to protect herself." Chiefly because of the heroic persistence of Susan B. Anthony, this Woman's Rights Movement culminated in the ratification of the nineteenth amendment to the Constitution in 1920, giving women the right to vote.

There were other social reform movements that were Evangelical in character: the Women's Christian Temperance Union may conjure up the image of Carrie Nation taking an axe to smash bars in local pubs, but the Movement itself was more a lobbying group founded in 1874 to seek legislation against the consumption of alcohol. In 1883 the W.C.T.U. became a worldwide movement through the efforts of Frances Willard, and it went on to conduct research into the abuses of tobacco and narcotics.

Jane Addams, the founder of Hull House which espoused the cause of homeless people, wrote of the need for public subsidy of welfare cases in *Twenty Years at Hull House* in 1910: "Private beneficence is totally inadequate to deal with the vast numbers of the city's disinherited."

Another Evangelical Reformer, Dorothea Dix, began a Crusade at the age of thirty-three for humane treatment of the mentally ill. Commitment to most asylums at that time meant inmates were "chained, naked, beaten with rods and lashed into obedience." In 1843, Dorothea Dix appeared before the Massachusetts legislature, then traveled around the United States lobbying for reform, and finally persuaded Congress to establish St. Elizabeth's Hospital in Washington, D.C.

As a result of the efforts of Dorothea Dix, nine Southern States established legitimate hospitals for the mentally ill, and Dorothea Dix left America to go to Europe where she had audiences with Queen Victoria and the Pope. When she returned to America during the Civil War, she was appointed Superintendent of the Union Army Nurses, overseeing some 3,000 volunteer women who tried to heal the wounded of that war where Union forces had over 90,000 killed in action or dying from wounds and diseases claiming twice that number, mostly typhoid and dysentery, and pulmonary diseases such as tuberculosis.

Still, the legislation governing commitment of those adjudged to be mentally ill was scandalously defective. In 1860, Elizabeth Parsons Ware Packard was committed to a state insane asylum by her Calvinist minister husband in Illinois, where the law stated any husband could commit his wife without a court order. Elizabeth Packard records the awful event:

> Early on the morning of the 18th of June 1860, as I arose from my bed, preparing to take my morning bath, I saw my husband approaching my door with two physicians, both members of his church and our Bible-class—and a stranger gentleman, Sheriff Burgess.
>
> Fearing exposure, I hastily locked my door, and proceeded with the greatest dispatch to dress myself. But before I had hardly commenced, my husband forced an entrance into my room through the window with an axe! And I, for shelter and protection against an exposure in a state of entire nudity, sprang into bed, just in time to receive my unexpected guests.
>
> The trio approached my bed, and each doctor felt my pulse, and without asking a single question both pronounced me insane! Of course, my pulse was bounding at the time from excessive fright; and I ask, what lady of refinement and fine and tender sensibilities would not have a quickened pulse by such an untimely, unexpected, unmanly, and even outrageous entrance into her private sleeping room?

Elizabeth Packard was committed to an asylum, where she made a plaintive protest against her diagnosis:

> I don't know why it is, Doctor, it may be merely a foolish pride which prompts the feeling, but I can't help feeling an instinctive aversion to being called insane. There seems to be a kind of disparagement of intellect attending this idea, which seems to stain the purity and darken the lustre of the reputation forever after.

After her release from the Illinois asylum, Elizabeth Packard traveled around the countryside and appeared before state legislatures to tell her story and agitate for a change in commitment laws. She was successful in making the legislatures of Illinois and several other states adopt a more stringent test of psychiatric insanity before allowing anyone to be committed to a state asylum.

There were other radical Evangelical movements in this century: Joseph Smith published *The Book of Mormon* at Palmyra, New York, in 1830, and this book later converted Brigham Young on his westward push across America from Nebraska. Brigham Young had taken 142 men, three women, and two children with him in his search for the Promised Land, and when Young first saw the valley of the Great Salt Lake in Utah on July 24, 1847, he shouted "This is the place!" Young set up a Mormon theocracy in Utah not unlike Endicott's Salem theocracy, although the Mormons held more experimental views on marriage and did not exclude the practice of polygamy. In 1878, the United States Supreme Court rejected the claim of a Mormon named Reynolds who claimed polygamy was protected by the First Amendment "freedom of worship" clause.

In one of the more bizarre adventures of modern Evangelism, William Miller (1782–1849) predicted the Millennium or Second Coming of Jesus would take place on October 22, 1843, and thousands of loyal followers assembled on rooftops and hills and haystacks to witness this spectacle from the skies. However, by the end of the day when nothing had happened, the multitude began to drift off, and eventually these people split off into two separate groups: the Seventh Day Adventists and the Jehovah's Witnesses.

Other Evangelical movements included the Shakers who were formed under Mother Ann Lee at New Lebanon, New York; and John H. Noyes, who created the Oneida Community. Reverend Sylvester Graham, who railed against the deficiencies of white bread, invented the cracker which bears his name to this day. And there was also renewed interest in astrology and the occult: Emanuel Swedenborg taught his followers "As above, so below"; Franz Mesmer, the first serious practitioner of hypnotism, developed a technique of inducing trance states through concentration which was to have important uses in the fields of psychology and psychoanalysis, but his followers misused it for performing ersatz seances and simulating possession.

The Rosicrucian movement was reputed to be an ancient society, first established in 1484 by Christian Rosenkreuz, but it conducted its mysteries behind such a veil of secrecy that no one could research what was actually going on within the cult. By the time it surfaced in 1614, the Rosicrucian Order claimed it had magical powers of alchemy, the ability to prolong human life, and other occult methods of controlling the four elements. The modern version of Rosicrucianism, which Max Heindel is credited with founding, kept some of the aura of secrecy and occult mystery to its Society but concerned itself more with moral and religious reforms in the secular world.

The Social Gospel was the most important movement of the late nineteenth century, as it tried to correct the social and economic abuses of industrial society in America through the principles of applied Christianity for better working conditions in labor, abolition of child labor, better housing for the poor, and a living wage for all people. In short, the Social Gospel tried to effect the claims of Christianity within the capitalist system.

Washington Gladden, a Congregational minister, believed that an economic system which was based solely on competition was "anti-social and anti-Christian" and he argued for reform, including the right of workers to organize trade unions. Gladden rose to national prominence when he chastised his fellow Congregationalists for accepting "tainted money"—a $100,000 gift from John D. Rockefeller.

Josiah Strong, a clergyman and author, coined the phrase "safety first," and insisted the Church must concern itself with human welfare here on earth. He wrote *Our Country* (1885), which became an international best seller.

Charles M. Sheldon, another clergyman and author, wrote more than thirty religious novels in which he popularized the Social Gospel. *In His Steps* (1896), the story of people who patterned their lives after Jesus, sold millions of copies worldwide.

Other Protestant ministers, however, despaired of ever realizing any significant reform within the capitalist system, and these clerics sought to establish a cooperative economic system, a sort of Christian Socialism based on the teachings of Jesus.

Walter Rauschenbush, a Baptist minister in New York's "Hell's Kitchen" was so appalled by slum conditions that he stated "he could hear human virtue cracking and crashing all around." His effective parish work among the poor led him towards a more radical Christianity.

Lyman Abbott left his law practice in 1859 to become a Congregationalist minister, and as editor of *The Christian Union* he turned this leading Christian journal into the voice of liberal theology and social and economic criticism.

The legacy of all these Social Gospel movements is a stronger consciousness in modern liberal Protestant clergymen and women. But by the end of the nineteenth century, Evangelical Protestantism was still proliferating into cults and sects and myriad movements and denominations.

There was also a growing sense of sadness—the realization that, for all the Evangelical fury of Revival and Social Reform, something valuable in religion had somehow been lost. Matthew Arnold captures this note of sadness in a world that is about to enter the uncertainties of the modern era, in his poem "Dover Beach":

> The Sea of Faith
> Was once, too, at the full, and round earth's shore
> Lay like the folds of a bright girdle furled.
> But now I only hear
> Its melancholy, long, withdrawing roar,
> Retreating, to the breath
> Of the night-wind, down the vast edges drear
> And naked shingles of the world . . .

Chapter 5

AMERICAN FUNDAMENTALISM

As the Social Gospel became more widespread in America, Protestant conservatives began to react with increasing alarm at the emergence of so much liberal and laissez-faire theology and practice. This reaction took the form of American Fundamentalism.

The doctrine of Fundamentalism grew out of a number of crises in historical Christianity: there was the new higher Bible criticism, which threatened to undermine the basis of all Christian belief; there was the rapid development of modern scientific thought, particularly the Evolutionary theories of Charles Darwin; there was the high incidence of immigration into the United States, especially Jews and Catholics who brought with them disquieting and alien forms of worship; and finally, there was the post-Industrial era which made modern urban life and morality so complex and problematical.

The reactionary Protestant response to these strong social and intellectual forces took the form of a rigid return to the essential tenets of Christian faith. It was a little like a Supreme Court justice's strict constructionist approach to the American Constitution: going by the jot and the tittle of the letter of the law as it was set down by the Founding Fathers, with an absolutely uncompromising attitude towards any liberal or figurative interpretation that would try to accommodate the document to historical changes in circumstance or mores.

Christian Fundamentalism is just such an uncompromising return to scripture as it was originally set down by the Prophets of God, with no regard to how individual conscience or consciousness may seek to interpret it in light of changing realities or social structures.

The specific articles of this Fundamentalist teaching were laid down in a series of tracts that were published 1910–1912 as "The Fundamentals," which listed the following points of indisputable Protestant Christian faith:

1. belief in the deity of Jesus Christ
2. belief in the virgin birth
3. belief in the resurrection of Jesus
4. belief in the Second Coming of Christ
5. belief in the inerrancy of the Holy Bible

It is this last tenet—the unwavering belief that the Bible is literally true, word for word, verse for verse, chapter for chapter—which has come to characterize all later Fundamentalist thought. There can be no "interpretive" or "figurative" approach to the Bible: one has to accept every part of scripture as God's immutable Word and therefore unerringly and actually true.

Therefore, according to Fundamentalist teaching, one has to believe there was a real Flood that actually wiped out every living thing except for those species that Noah herded onto his Ark (Genesis 6:9–11); there really was a day in which the sun actually stood still in the middle of the sky while Joshua avenged himself upon his enemies (Joshua 10: 12–14); and there was a real fish that actually swallowed Jonah and kept him alive until he made up his mind to go and preach to Nineveh (Jonah 1:17).

It is the belief in the Second Coming of Christ that gives Fundamentalism its peculiarly apocalyptic eschatology: Fundamentalists believe this world is utterly damned and only the imminent return of Jesus Christ can save anyone; furthermore, Fundamentalists believe this Second Coming is about to take place very soon. All we can do, therefore, is prepare for it through conversion, repentance, and renewed commitment to the teachings of Jesus.

Finally, the belief in the literal and unerring truth of the Bible means that Fundamentalists must challenge any scientific discoveries which seem to contradict the Word of God: particularly, Fundamentalists must oppose the theory of Evolution wherever it rears its head, since Evolution's description of the gradual development of life over millions of years on earth goes against the account of the Creation of the world in only six days, as set forth in Genesis Chapter 2, verses 2–4.

A spin-off of all these Fundamentalist tenets is an ongoing attack on liberals and so-called "secular humanists" who may teach either Evolution or other forms of scientism or a merely figurative approach to the Bible. Fundamentalists insist it is these "modernists" who have infected our public school systems and our mass media with their godless version of the truth, thereby hastening the moral decay of our age.

Two further definitions: in addition to these Fundamentalist tenets listed above, there are those who also believe that the events of Pentecost ("fifty" days before the anniversary of the Resurrection of Jesus) are a gift of God that can be freely received today. The Book of Acts Chapter 2 describes what these events of Pentecost were:

2 And suddenly there came a sound from heaven as of a rushing mighty wind, and it filled all the house where they were sitting.
3 And there appeared unto them cloven tongues like as of fire, and it sat upon each of them.
4 And they were all filled with the Holy Ghost, and began to speak with other tongues, as the Spirit gave them utterance.

Pentecostals therefore are Fundamentalists who believe in "glossolalia" or speaking in tongues when the Holy Ghost is upon them. The practice is also common among Quakers, Shakers, and Mormons.

Finally, Charismatics are Evangelicals who usually believe all the aforementioned tenets of Fundamentalism, sometimes including speaking in tongues, and they also believe in the practice of faith healing by the laying on of hands.

It is possible, then, to have a wide spectrum of different types within the Fundamentalist catechism. Jerry Falwell, for example, is a strict Fundamentalist, but he is not a Pentecostal or a Charismatic. Jimmy Swaggart is a Fundamentalist Pentecostal. Oral Roberts is a Fundamentalist Charismatic. Jim Bakker is a Fundamentalist Pentecostal Charismatic. And so it goes: one can make up one's own scorecard for other contemporary American Evangelists.

As a political movement, Fundamentalism first showed itself in America in 1925 at the Scopes Trial in Dayton, Tennessee. Fundamentalists successfully pressed the indictment of a high school biology teacher who had violated the state's anti-evolution statute.

This "Monkey Trial" was more than the mere prosecution of a man named John Scopes: it was, in fact, the first major crossroads of mainstream American religious assumptions, a confrontation between strict Fundamentalist thought on the one hand, and liberal modernism on the other.

The prosecutor was William Jennings Bryan, a renowned orator and former Secretary of State under President Woodrow Wilson. Bryan was an uncompromising champion of the new orthodox Fundamentalist tenets, and at the beginning of the trial Bryan tried to characterize the entire proceedings as an attack on Christianity itself:

> The purpose is to cast ridicule on everybody who believes in the Bible, and I am perfectly willing that the world shall know that these gentlemen have no other purpose than ridiculing every Christian who believes in the Bible.

For the defense, attorney Clarence Darrow gave a sharp retort to Bryan's charge as to the significance of the trial: "We have the purpose of preventing bigots and ignoramuses from controlling the education of the United States and you know it, and that is all."

Clarence Darrow described himself as a modernist, a pro-evolutionary spokesman and an agnostic: "I do not consider it an insult, but rather a compliment, to be called an agnostic. I do not pretend to know where many ignorant men are sure—that is all agnosticism means."

H. L. Mencken was covering the Scopes Trial for the *Baltimore Sun* and *Mercury* magazine, and he wrote acerbic reports on "the old conflict between science and religion": "It was hot weather when they tried the infidel Scopes at Dayton, Tennessee, but I went down there very willingly, for I was eager to see something of evangelical Christianity as a going concern . . ."

Mencken got to see an example of Southern Baptist Evangelism in a Revival Meeting nearby, and he reported it with gusto and savage delight:

> Words spouting from his lips like bullets from a machine-gun—appeals to God to pull the penitent back out of Hell, defiances of the demons of the air, a vast impassioned jargon of apocalyptic texts. Suddenly he rose to his feet, threw back his head and began to speak in the tongues—blub-blub-blub, gurgle-gurgle-gurgle. His voice rose to a higher register. The climax was a shrill, inarticulate squawk, like that of a man throttled. He fell headlong across the pyramid of supplicants . . .

Mencken was equally savage in his description of what was taking place during the Scopes Trial:

The Scopes Trial had brought them in from all directions. There was a friar wearing a sandwich sign announcing that he was the Bible champion of the world. There was a Seventh Day Adventist arguing that Clarence Darrow was the beast with seven heads and ten horns described in Revelation XIII, and that the end of the world was at hand. There was an evangelist made up like Andy Gump, with the news that atheists in Cincinnati were preparing to descend upon Dayton, hang the eminent Judge Raulston, and burn the town. There was an ancient who maintained that no Catholic could be a Christian. There was the eloquent Dr. T. T. Martin, of Blue Mountain, Miss., come to town with a truck-load of torches and hymn-books to put Darwin in his place. There was a singing brother bellowing apocalyptic hymns. There was William Jennings Bryan, followed everywhere by a gaping crowd. Dayton was having a roaring time. It was better than a circus. But the note of devotion was simply not there; the Daytonians, after listening a while, would slip away to Robinson's drug-store to regale themselves with Coca-Cola, or to the lobby of the Aqua Hotel, where the learned Raulston sat in state, judicially picking his teeth. The real religion was not present. It began at the bridge over the town creek, where the road makes off for the hills.

Mencken could be acid in his analysis of what this Scopes trial meant for the future of religion in America:

. . . The Christian church, as a going concern, is quite safe from danger in the United States, despite the rapid growth of agnosticism. The theology it merchants is full of childish and disgusting absurdities; practically all the other religions of civilized and semi-civilized man are more plausible.

The Christians of the Apostolic Age were almost exactly like the modern Holy Rollers—men quite without taste or imagination, whoopers and shouters, low vulgarians, cads.

That Protestantism in this great Christian realm is down with a wasting disease must be obvious to every amateur of ghostly pathology. One half of it is moving, with slowly accelerating speed, in the direction of the Harlot of the Seven Hills: the other is sliding down into voodooism.

William Jennings Bryan and the Fundamentalists won the Scopes Trial, and Bryan died five days later. John Scopes was adjudged guilty of breaking the Tennessee anti-evolution statute, he was ordered to pay a sizable fine and court costs, and the Creationist prohibition against teaching the theory of Charles Darwin remained in force in the state of Tennessee.

But in a larger sense Bryan had lost the real argument of the trial: Bryan's Fundamentalist position had been embarrassed in court by Clarence Darrow's rational arguments, and Bryan's Evangelical oratory had been pilloried in the free press by H. L. Mencken's caustic prose. As historian Henry Steele Commager comments:

> For all his eloquence [Bryan] was unable to demonstrate the connectedness between fundamentalism and morality, or explain the relevance of fundamentalism to the complex problems of the twentieth century or infuse the fundamentalist cause with vitality or dignity.

With the nominal victory of the Scopes Trial behind them, Fundamentalists began to realize they could assert their position politically if they organized and trained themselves to work within the Constitutional framework. And so three years later, in the Presidential election of 1928, the incumbent Republican Herbert Hoover faced the Democratic candidate Al Smith, who happened to be an Irish Catholic: and Fundamentalists in America were ready to join battle. They began a vicious whispering campaign across the country, implying that any Catholic in the White House would be a pawn of the Pope and would turn the United States into a vestibule of the Vatican.

No matter that Al Smith had served four terms as Governor of New York with no major violation of Church/State separation; no matter that Smith had worked his way up from "the sidewalks of New York" through Tammany, and that he had been nominated at the 1928 Democratic Convention by no less a personage than Franklin D. Roosevelt, who characterized Al Smith as "The Happy Warrior." Fundamentalists still did everything in their power to strike terror into the hearts of American voters, using scare tactics and innuendo about the horrors of Roman Catholicism and giving absolutely no regard to Al Smith's record of proven merit. The fact that Al Smith was a "wet" on the Prohibition issue didn't help his image with Fundamentalists, either: Al Smith lost the election, and Fundamentalists realized another victory of applied political influence.

With these initiatives behind them, Fundamentalists turned their attention to the founding of educational institutions which could provide centers for the teaching and dissemination of Fundamentalist doctrine. Dwight L. Moody had already founded the Moody Bible Institute in Chicago in 1889, and this organization had been continuously supplying Fundamentalist groups with scriptural literature on the various official Christian positions on faith and morals. Now Fundamentalists created additional outposts of indoctrination such as Bob Jones University in Greenville, South Carolina, and later Evangelists would found such strict Fundamentalist schools as Oral Roberts University, Liberty University, and Jimmy Swaggart Bible College as part of their ongoing legacy.

But it was not only "modernists," "liberals," and "secular humanists" who posed a menace to Protestant Fundamentalism. Behind these labels there lurked a far worse threat to Christianity which has grown in intensity during our time: the international Communist conspiracy, which challenges the very existence of religion itself. The "Red Scare" holds more danger for religionists of whatever persuasion than it does for any political activists, since any Marxist regime would immediately work to obfuscate the freedom to worship in all forms whatsoever. And it is this realization of an authentic Communist menace in our time which fires almost all contemporary American Fundamentalist Evangelists and makes them even more tenacious in their insistence on the inerrancy of the Bible and the imminence of the Second Coming of Jesus.

Recent conferences and conventions confirm that Fundamentalism is very much a strong social and political force in America. In June 1986, in Atlanta, Georgia, the annual meeting of the Southern Baptist Convention revealed this one Church alone has 14.4 million members and is therefore the nation's largest Protestant body, second in membership only to the Roman Catholic Church in America. The 45,000 Church delegates to the Convention reaffirmed their absolute belief in the inerrancy of the Bible: Paul Pressler, a judge serving in the Houston Court of Appeals, made it very plain what the gathering was all about: "There is one issue and one issue alone. It is whether we want our institutions to stand on the fact that the Bible is God's word without any mistake or error in it."

Nancy Ackerman, a teacher of Sociology of Religion at Emory University, was quoted in the *New York Times*:

> We're finding that the fundamentalists are madder, they're more discontented, more alienated and by virtue of that discontent have a little more momentum behind their efforts at the political convention. What fundamentalism offers is a very orderly world, a set of answers, a clear sense of right and wrong, a clear sense of who should be in authority. And that's very attractive in a world that looks very disorderly, where nobody knows what's right or wrong.

The irony here is that these modern Fundamentalists are coming up with a stricter catechism than that Medieval Catholicism which Martin Luther originally broke away from. And more and more, the sense of freedom and individuality, which Luther fought so hard to encourage, is being replaced by a kind of iron rigidity and uniformity which Luther himself despised.

Meanwhile militant right wing Fundamentalist groups kept pressing their attack on books, music, magazines, television programs, movies, and the public education system. In July 1986, in Greenville, Tennessee, a group of mothers sued to protect their children from textbooks in the public schools which explored themes and thoughts which these mothers claimed were anti-Christian. The suit, they said, was a test of religious freedom and a challenge to secular humanism.

The textbooks in question in this 1986 Tennessee trial were mostly a reading series put out by Holt, Rinehart and Winston, which encouraged students to use their own imagination and engage in such innovative adventures as thought transference and mental telepathy. One mother argued these things were supernatural attributes which only God could have: "Our children's imaginations have to be bounded," she testified from the witness stand, and she said she objected to any book that suggested her children use "the magic eye inside your head" because it was, in her words, "encouraging an occult practice."

Other objections of these mothers centered on male/female role reversals in the home, pacifism, and situational ethics. The textbooks were defended by lawyers from a Washington law firm which donated its time and talent to the case at the urging of the anti-Fundamentalist group, People For the American Way, founded by television producer Norman Lear to monitor the Religious Right. The plaintiff mothers were represented by a conservative law group funded by television Evangelist Pat Robertson.

There were also many ultra-Fundamentalist sects and cults cropping up across the country. Ronald Enroth of Westmont College in Santa Barbara, California, reported:

These organizations claim they alone are plugged in to the Almighty; they practice elitism, authoritarian control that almost always dips into the personal lives of members, and they try to lead them away, isolate them from the rest of society.

What distinguishes these Fundamentalist sects from more traditional Church groups is the greater degree of power the leaders hold. Reginald Alev, Executive Director of Citizens For Freedom, describes these ultra-Fundamentalist sects as growing at a faster rate than older groups like the Unification Church or the Hare Krishna movement. These new Fundamentalist sects feature "intimate spiritual connecting" which involves dancing, hugging, and kissing during Church services, shouting and speaking in tongues, and in some extreme cases leader-conducted adultery and killing of demon-possessed children. One group, the Community Chapel and Bible Training Center, claimed its pastor, Donald Lee Barnett, encouraged parishioners to "Dance before the Lord" by choosing spouses of other members of the congregation for their "spiritual connection" and then fondling, gazing into each other's eyes, holding hands, and spending an inordinate amount of time with each other.

This background of Fundamentalism as a reaction against strong historical forces is indicative of a very powerful social and political reality in America. Fundamentalism was certainly instrumental in securing the Presidential elections of Ronald Reagan in both 1980 and 1984, and heaven knows Ronald Reagan himself did everything he could think of to court this crucial Fundamentalist constituency. In one of his speeches at a 1971 fund-raising dinner, Ronald Reagan seemed to be espousing the apocalyptic doctrine of mainline Fundamentalist thought:

Everything is falling into place. It can't be too long now. Ezekiel says that fire and brimstone will be rained upon the enemies of God's people. That must mean that they'll be destroyed by nuclear weapons. They exist now, and they never did in the past.

Ezekiel tells us that Gog, the nation that will lead all of the other powers of darkness against Israel, will come out of the North. Biblical scholars have been saying for generations that Gog must be Russia.

What other powerful nation is to the north of Israel? None. But it didn't seem to make sense before the Russian revolution, when Russia was a Christian country. Now it does, now that Russia has become communistic and atheistic, now that Russia has set itself against God. Now it fits the description of Gog perfectly.

It's all there: the inerrancy of Biblical prophesy, the implied Second Coming of Jesus, the Red Scare of the international Communist conspiracy—even a subtle political plug for the modern state of Israel. Fundamentalists thought this kind of thing was wonderful, and elected Ronald Reagan by one of the greatest electoral votes in the whole of American history. And then they began examining the voting records of liberal and left-wing political figures, so they could begin systematic campaigns to overthrow these enemies of the New Christian Right at the next local and state elections.

Fundamentalism, then, is not only a theological doctrine that underlies most contemporary Evangelists in America—it is also a powerful political instrument that has as its stated objective the creation of a theocracy of Church/State control of the American way of life.

Chapter 6

DWIGHT L. MOODY

THE FIRST of the individual American Evangelists we will look at in this book also happens to be the most representative of all Evangelists: a man whose Crusades and Revival services have been used as model programs by so many of today's leading contemporary American Evangelists. As will be seen, his dramatic preaching style and his emphasis on zeal rather than theology would be mimicked by future Evangelists.

One author calls this man "an immense, magnificent agency for bringing men to God"—a man who was commanding and Zeus-like in the pulpit, "possibly the single mightiest colossus in the annals of all revivalism—Dwight L. Moody, a thick and stumpy man with the mossy look of that time's dense-whiskered political eminences like Hayes and Garfield."

Dwight Lyman Moody (1837–1899) found himself face to face with a bewildering modern world where millions of simple country people were forced to migrate to oversized and cynical industrial cities—a modern world where capitalist robber barons like Andrew Carnegie, John Wanamaker, J. P. Morgan, and Cyrus McCormick practiced a distorted Calvinism to transform their money-making into a sacral activity—a modern world where P. T. Barnum, master circus impresario and entrepreneur, was not above using a good dose of hokum and humbug to put together his Greatest Show on Earth.

Moody's genius was that he himself was a simple country person who brought these same oversized and cynical cities to his Revival services where he preached the urgency of conversion. He helped finance his Evangelical ministry by enlisting the wholehearted support of capitalist robber barons like the aforementioned Carnegie, Wana-maker, Morgan, and McCormick—and his own great Crusades were every bit as spellbinding as anything that P. T. Barnum ever put together.

D. L. Moody embodied all the foibles and fabulous aspirations of his age, and he was a fierce tornado unleashed on the unsuspecting countryside. As one contemporary, Duffus, reported:

> In his rage to save souls he traveled more than a million miles, addressed more than a hundred million people, and personally prayed and pleaded with seven hundred and fifty thousand sinners. All in all, it is very probable, as his admirers claim, that he reduced the population of hell by a million souls.

Dwight L. Moody was born in East Northfield, Massachusetts, in 1837, of Anglo-Saxon stock, Unitarian in his first Church affiliation, and he grew up in the quiet beauty of the Pioneer Valley of the Connecticut River. Called Quinnetuk by the earliest Indians, "Long River with Waves," this waterway flowed south from Vermont through green pasturelands and clear air around the small communities of Gill, Bernardston, and Warwick where Moody's ancestors had lived for some two hundred years plying the family trade of masonry, brick-making, and laying stone foundations for chimneys and houses.

Dwight's father Edwin died suddenly at the age of forty-one, leaving his widow with crushing debts and seven children—Isaiah, Cornelia, George, Edwin, Dwight, Luther, and Warren—and the young widow was pregnant with twins, Sam and Lizzie. It was a calamitous time for the large family, and after creditors had stripped their house bare of almost all furniture and possessions, they all had to pitch in to earn whatever money they could to keep from starving.

One day in the spring of 1854, young Dwight was splitting logs on a nearby mountain with his brothers, when something prompted him to throw down his axe and announce: "I'm tired of this! I'm not going to stay around here any longer, I'm going to the city!"

Dwight left East Northfield and went to Boston to go into the shoe business, and later he traveled to Chicago where he got a job in his cousin Holton's shoe store. It was there that Edward Kimball, a Sunday School teacher, took an interest in the young boy from Massachusetts. Kimball reported: "I can truly say that I have seen few persons whose minds were spiritually darker when he came into my Sunday-School class, or one who seemed more unlikely to become a Christian."

But Kimball persisted in his concern for the young boy, and one day he went by Holton's store and found Dwight in the back, wrapping shoes. Kimball sat down opposite him and began talking to him about Christ's love for him. Dwight listened, and immediately thereafter he knelt and accepted Christ as his personal Savior.

Moody himself reported the effect that his conversion had on him:

> The morning I was converted I went outdoors and fell in love with everything. I never loved the bright sun shining over the earth so much before. And when I heard the birds singing their sweet songs, I fell in love with the birds. Everything was different.

As soon as Moody was converted, he began converting others. He formed his own Sunday School in Chicago, and he recruited the local toughs to serve as "Moody's Bodyguard" and help him in his work, bringing in other young people to learn about Christ's love. Moody became so zealous at his new vocation that people came to know of him by reputation:

> "Are you a Christian?"
> "That's none of your business!"
> "Oh yes it is!"
> "Then you must be D. L. Moody!"

When the Civil War broke out, Moody gave up his business for full-time Evangelical missionary work among the Union soldiers in 1861, and in 1862 he married Emma Revell. His dedication to Evangelism was continuously increasing, and during a Crusade in England in 1867, sitting and listening to a sermon in Bristol, England, Moody heard the preacher say:

> The world has yet to see what God will do with and for and through and in and by the man who is fully and wholly consecrated to Him.

And as Moody sat there in his pew he thought: "I will try my utmost to be that man." By this time Moody had been holding Revival meetings for many years, and one evening in 1870 he was so impressed with the way a layman helped organize the singing that he went up to Ira Sankey after the meeting and had this exchange with him:

Moody: Where do you live?

Sankey: In Newcastle, Pennsylvania.
Moody: Are you married?
Sankey: Yes.
Moody: How many children have you?
Sankey: One.
Moody: Where are you in business?
Sankey: A revenue officer.
Moody: Well, you'll have to give that up. You are the man I have been
          looking for this last eight years. You must give up your business
          in Newcastle and come to Chicago. I want you to help me with
          my work.

It was like Christ's call of Peter, and it was just as effective: Sankey did as Moody asked, and the Revival team of Moody and Sankey began its historic work. Ira Sankey played on the organ and sang gospel hymns at every service where Moody preached his Evangelical message.

Ira Sankey did more than this: he created his own repertory of gospel hymns, sometimes with miraculous spontaneity. Once at a meeting Moody turned to Sankey and asked him to sing something. Sankey had nothing prepared, but then he remembered he had clipped a poem from a local newspaper that day, with the thought of someday setting it to music. Sankey drew the clipping out of his pocket and he began improvising music to the poem as he began to sing it. He claims that he heard a voice inside him saying: "Sing the hymn and make the tune as you go along—and note by note, the music was given to me clear through to the end of the tune." This was to become one of the great gospel hymns, "The Ninety And The Nine."

As a preacher, Dwight Moody tended to be stubborn about taking any ideas from others. He had been goaded by friends to go hear the celebrated boy preacher Henry Moorehouse in Dublin, but Moody demurred: "He was a beardless boy—he didn't look more than seventeen and I said to myself, 'He can't preach.' " When Moody returned to America, Moorehouse wrote him saying he was also coming on a preaching tour of America and he would be happy to come to Chicago and preach for Moody if he wanted. Moody wrote off a cold note: "If you come West, call on me." Moorehouse did exactly that, and Moody reluctantly scheduled him to preach on an evening when Moody would be out of town. Moorehouse preached that evening, and the one sermon grew into a series of sermons, and when Moody returned one of his friends told him he really ought to go and hear that young preacher: "He tells the worst sinners that God loves them." Moody replied curtly: "Then he's wrong." The friend said, "I think you will agree with him when you hear him."

Moody went to hear Moorehouse, who was preaching variations on the same sermon, based on a verse from John Chapter 3:

> 16 For God so loved the world, that he gave his only begotten Son, that whosoever believeth in him should not perish, but have everlasting life.

Moorehouse preached with such persuasiveness on the reality of God's love that Dwight Moody just sat there in his pew without being able to believe his own ears. He commented later: "I never knew up to that time that God loved us so much. This heart of mine began to thaw out; I could not keep back the tears. It was like news from a far country: I just drank it in."

Moody was in Chicago during the Great Chicago Fire of 1871; it destroyed his Farwell Hall and the Illinois Street Church. Finally when word came that he had to abandon his own home, there were only a few minutes to decide what to take along with him. Moody rescued his two children and some silverware, but his wife wanted him to take the portrait Healy had painted of him in 1867. Moody balked:

> Take my own picture! Well, that would be amusing! Suppose I am met on the street by friends in the same plight as ourselves, and they say: "Hello Moody, glad you have escaped; what's that you have saved and cling to so affectionately?" Wouldn't it sound well to reply: "Oh I've got my portrait!"

Moody's wife prevailed and the portrait was knocked out of its heavy frame and taken with them as they escaped the flames that were beginning to burn down the block.

Both these anecdotes tell how Moody was talked out of a strong predisposition he had, and they give us some insight into his remarkable character: the man was all Yankee instinct, and unless he was gently blocked or nudged in a different direction, he invariably followed his gut hunches in all things. And because he was born with uncommon good sense about most things, he was usually right in his instincts, as witness his calling of Ira Sankey to join him in his ministry. Moody trusted his own instincts to such a degree that he cultivated a know-nothing attitude towards religious matters—he had a subtle contempt for any book learning aside from the Bible: "I would rather have zeal without knowledge; and there is a good deal of knowledge without zeal."

For Moody, faith consisted of a trust in a blind obedience to the will of God: "If I believed that God wanted me to jump out of that window, I would jump."

Needless to say, this kind of Evangelical trust in the inner promptings of God presupposes an extraordinary sanity—otherwise one is in very real trouble. Furthermore, Moody never seemed to have the slightest interest in pursuing religious ideas beyond the immediate conversion of others. He had absolutely no curiosity about any world views beyond what his Fundamentalist training provided him; nor did he have any concern about trying to reconcile the claims of science with the claims of religion. Like many modern and contemporary Evangelists, he was entirely self-taught and the Bible was the beginning and end of his education. It was natural for him to leave the appalling social and economic problems that were created by the Industrial Revolution for others to work out: Moody's only calling was to preach and convert.

Nor did Moody seem to be at all bothered about such a single-minded adaptation to the complexities of the real world: he once commented to a woman who said she objected to his theology, "My theology! I didn't know I had any. I wish you would tell me what my theology is."

He was, in short, a complete innocent who trusted totally in his own instincts to tell him God's will for his own life. And this simplistic reduction of complexities of the modern world to gut hunches and an inborn sanity probably goes a long way towards accounting for Moody's enormous appeal: how many people in his congregation secretly envied such a seemingly carefree acceptance of things as they are, or an indomitable belief that things could be changed if one simply accepted Jesus Christ as one's personal Savior?

Moody's chief genius was in his preaching, and the best way we can get a sense of what he was able to achieve in the pulpit is to look at one of his most powerful sermons of this period. It is called "Excuse Giving," and it is based on the following verses from Luke Chapter 14:

16 Then said he unto him, A certain man made a great supper, and
     bade many;

17 And sent his servant at supper time to say to them that were bidden, Come; for all things are now ready.

18 And they all with one consent began to make excuse. The first said unto him, I have bought a piece of ground, and I must needs go and see it: I pray thee to have me excused.

19 And another said, I have bought five yoke of oxen, and I go to prove them: I pray thee have me excused.

20 And another said, I have married a wife, and therefore I cannot come.

Moody's sermon on this text begins:

Tonight I have an invitation for you to a feast, not an ordinary but a royal feast . . . Now I challenge you. If any of you men have a better excuse get up and give it. These excuses look very absurd when you come to look at them, but your own wouldn't look any better.

He was aware of the usual excuses that were commonly given to avoid answering his call:

One of the popular excuses now is this old book. You talk to a man now, especially a young man, and he says, "I cannot become a Christian because there are so many things in that old book that I cannot understand." Well I want to say in the first place you don't know anything about it. There are very few men who have read the Bible any way . . . As for the mysteries in that book I am glad they are there . . . If I could take that book up and understand it all it would be pretty good proof that it did not come from God.

He knew he was beginning to hit close to home, and he almost exulted in stirring up some mischief in a few of the souls that were sitting out there: "Throw a stone among a group of dogs and the dog that gets hit goes off yelping every time."

Moody then goes into a series of advance refutations, singling out individuals all over the hall: ". . . there is a Scotsman over there, he says, 'Mr. Moody's excuses don't touch me at all. I don't know as I am one of the elect.' Now you have nothing more to do with the doctrine of election than the government of China." He kept picking out other individuals around the hall:

Now there is a young man up in the gallery who says, "Mr. Moody
don't touch my difficulty, I tell you the reason I don't become a Christian. You want me to put on one of those long faces, look right straight
up and down and have no more pleasure until I get to heaven . . . ?"
Now I believe that the biggest lie ever uttered in hell is that the devil
is an easy master and God a hard one . . . I have tried both masters,
and I want to say now my God is not a hard master.

Moody called on the whole congregation to back him up in this claim:
"I would like to have those men who have found God is not a hard
master to ring out "no" tonight. (*Shouts of no*). Do you think we are
lying? Don't we know?"

Then Moody returned to speaking directly to individuals sitting in
the hall:

There is a man down there in the middle of the hall who says that if
he is ever converted he won't be converted in a meeting like this; too
much excitement; if he is really honest and he doesn't want to be
converted here because there is so much interest, I will find him some
church that doesn't believe in revivals, where everything is cold and
dead; if there is too much excitement here go to a graveyard and be
converted; there is no excitement there. It is only an excuse . . .

Moody even singled out individuals who were secretly glad that Moody
was singling out other individuals: "Here is a man at my right in the
balcony who says: 'I am glad Moody is giving it to them tonight. I
have been watching some men tonight and I have seen him hit them,
but he hasn't hit me. I have got a good excuse . . .' " Moody's most
scathing attack was on those members of the congregation who feared
the ridicule of their peers:

I tell you what they would say—"Up to hear Moody last night, eh?
Did Moody catch you? did you get converted? did you get pious? did
you get religion?" and you would say, "No, sir, I don't believe in
him—big humbug, I wasn't there." . . . I pity in my heart a man who
may be laughed out of a principle, a man who will let a saloon keeper
or a gambler or a harlot keep him from what is right. God have mercy
on such a man.

Moody's summary of all the excuses that might be given is finished,
and now he composes a formal reply to the invitation:

TO THE KING OF KINGS, TO THE LORD OF GLORY:
I received a pressing invitation from one of your ministers to be
present at the marriage supper of your only begotten Son; I pray thee
to have me excused.

Moody offered this cowardly refusal to his congregation, and he challenged anyone to step forward and set his name to the document:
"Who would sign that? I don't believe there is a man in this house
that could be hired to do it."

There was dead silence in the hall as Moody waited to see if anyone
would stand and step forward to sign the refusal. It was a brilliant
reversal of the usual Evangelist's call because this time Moody was
asking people to come forward to *refuse* the call: and of course, no
one dared to do it.

Moody then took a moment to remind his congregation of the
seriousness of this invitation:

> . . . inside of fifteen minutes many a man that is almost holding his
> breath now, listening to things that pertain to his eternal destiny will
> be in the street, some cracking jokes about the preaching and turning
> the whole thing into a jest. I beg of you tonight, do not make light of
> this invitation . . .
>
> I can imagine some of you saying: "My father and mother were godly
> people, they are in glory now; I may be pretty wild, but I never got so
> wild as to make light of religious things." You do make light of it if
> you go out without answering this invitation.

Finally, after allowing the suspence to build to fever pitch, Moody
rewrote his formal reply to God's invitation and offered it to the congregation again:

> Let us see if we can all sign this:
> TO THE KING OF KINGS, TO THE LORD OF GLORY:
> While sitting in a religious meeting, I received a pressing invitation
> from one of your servants to be present at the marriage supper of your
> only begotten Son. I hasten to reply: By the grace of God I will be
> there.

After the gauntlet of individual challenges all over the hall, and
after reversing the usual Evangelist's call and challenging anyone to

step forward and formally refuse the invitation, Moody now called on the congregation to come forward to the front as public testimony of their willingness to accept Christ as Savior.

After reviewing such a remarkable sermon, we can understand why so many tens of thousands of Moody's listeners did feel compelled to stand and answer his call. The sermon is a masterpiece of analyzing and overcoming the resistance of his congregation, in much the same way that a master hypnotist might seek to lower the resistance of a subject in order to induce a desired trance state.

And if one wants to get some insight into why this particular sermon works as well as it does—beyond the confrontational direct address to the congregation that is so relentless, and the skillful use of advance re-futations and reversals and all the other classical oratory devices that are being used so subtly—the reader is invited to go back over the sermon excerpts and examine the plain style Anglo-Saxon diction that is being used. The word choice throughout the entire sermon is so uncommonly simple and unaffected, it seems to breathe an honesty and sincerity that would win over any audience. Plain speech like this cannot be feigned, or at least it very strongly suggests that it could not possibly be insincere. It is the same type of plain style diction that Moody's great contemporary Abraham Lincoln used in his "Gettysburg Address."

After their successful Evangelical work in America, Moody and Sankey took their Revival Meetings to the British Isles in 1873 through 1875, and they scored major successes in Glasgow, Dublin, Manchester, Birmingham, and finally in London, where 17,000 people were admitted to the huge Agricultural Hall for the opening service, and as many persons had to be turned away. There were a total of 285 meetings held in London, with an estimated attendance of some 2,580,000 persons. It was one of the largest Crusades in the history of the British Isles.

During this period, Moody gave interviews with a curious press and local ministers on how to run successful Revival Meetings:

Question: How can we get more life into our prayer meetings?
Moody: Get more life into yourselves first!
Question: What should be a man's posture when praying?
Moody: I don't know. I don't think it makes any difference if his heart only bows before God. There are times, I believe, when a man should be on his face. We should be very charitable to those who don't do as we do. That is of man, not of God.

Question: What is the best book on revivals?
Moody: The Bible!
Question: Why don't you preach more about baptism?
Moody: That is none of your business!

One writer commented during this period: "Mr. Moody was humble. If he were here now, he would not allow a word said in his praise; he shrank from public commendation and felt grieved at whatever savored of adulation."

Moody scored an intriguing victory at Oxford University, where everyone declined to listen to him because the ecclesiastics scorned to receive the Word from a "dissenter," and the skeptics scorned the message itself. Moody was not to be outwitted by such a doctrinal gambit: with unaccountable Yankee cunning, he called a prayer meeting the next day for all the mothers of the students at Oxford. Once the mothers had heard Moody's message, the following day their sons began coming to his meetings by the hundreds. Moody had beaten the clerics and the skeptics at their own game, through the use of pure gut hunch and determination.

While he was in London, Moody gave a sermon in which he told of Elijah's ascension into heaven: Moody described how Elisha looked up into the skies to see Elijah, and Moody concentrated his own focus so persuasively in the air, several Parliamentarian orators in the congregation stood up in their seats and turned around and looked upwards, to see what Moody was looking at. But Moody kept on with his sermon:

I see Elisha digging the sand out of his eyes, and he happened to see something in the air, and he looked up and there was Elijah. And he shouted, "My father, my father, the chariot of Israel, and the horsemen thereof!" And he rent his clothes. Men, rend your mantle. You are nothing, get down in the dust. And he took up the mantle of Elijah and smote the waters and passed over. Man, take God at his word. "Blessed are they that hunger and thirst after righteousness, for they shall be filled."

Moody's Crusades were not all easy going: some of the press got so vicious it tried to ridicule Moody right off the Revival platform. One English paper wrote:

Judged by the low standard of an American ranter, Mr. Moody is a third-rate star . . . Mr. Moody, with a jocular familiarity which painfully jarred our sense of the reverential, translated freely passages of the Bible into the American vernacular. The grand, simple stories of Holy Writ were thus parodied and burlesqued.

Another, from *Tabernacle Sketches*:

Oh, the way that man does mangle the English tongue! The daily slaughter of syntax at the Tabernacle is dreadful. His enunciations may be pious but his pronunciations are decidedly off color. It is enough to make Noah Webster turn over in his grave and weep to think that he lived in vain.

Another, from the *London Saturday Review*:

As for Mr. Moody, he is simply a ranter of the most vulgar type . . . It is possible that his low fun and screechy ejaculations may be found stimulating by the ignorant and foolish; but it is difficult to conceive how any person of the slightest culture or refinement can fail to be pained and shocked.

One observer gave a haunting portrait of Moody's physical presence when he was not on the platform:

When he is at rest, no person could well seem more uninteresting or vacant. His face is neither pleasant nor attractive, his eye dead and heavy, his figure short and thick-set, his bodily presence weak and his speech contemptible.

And one critic from within Moody's own movement commented on how Moody tended to discard people when he no longer had any use for them:

When he dropped men it was as if they were "hot coals" and it was impossible for those from whom he had received such loyal and almost passionate devotion at one time not to feel as if he were unkind and untrue when he turned away.

Most of this bad press and adverse commentary on Moody had to do with his manner and personal style, and not with the substance of what he was preaching. And there was enough good press to assure Moody's success in England. One paper wrote: "He is a business man and he means business; every word he speaks is meant to lead to a definite business; if it does not do that, he regards it as thrown away." And as Moody prepared to leave England, one paper reported:

Let us frankly confess as we bid him good-by that we are heartily glad that he is what he is. We would not change him. Make him the best-read preacher in the world and he would instantly lose half his power. He is just right for his work as he is, original, dashing, careless . . . Mr. Moody reaches the masses more surely and widely because he is one of them himself, and because he has not been made eloquent and faultless by the trimming and restraining processes of a liberal education.

Back in Chicago, a newspaper wrote of the way Moody prepared for a meeting:

He gave orders like a general. There must be a good beginning. He said a good beginning meant half the battle. He urged the choir to sing as if it meant it. He did not want any lagging. The organist must make the organ thunder. He told the two hundred preachers who sat on the stage that they were there for work—not for dignity.

Theodore Cuyler compared Dwight Moody to Abraham Lincoln:

Lincoln and Moody possessed alike the gift of an infallible common sense. Neither of them ever committed a serious mistake. They were alike in being masters of the simple, strong Saxon speech, the language of the people and of Bunyan, the language that is equal to the loftiest forensic or pulpit eloquence.

And another observer, President Woodrow Wilson, tells the story of how he once saw Moody in a barber shop being attended to in the chair, and talking to the other barbers there. Wilson says there was nothing of cant, nothing didactic or sermonizing in Moody's talk, yet the impact was extraordinary:

I purposely lingered in the room after he left and noted the singular effect his visit had upon the barbers in that shop. They talked in mono-tones. They did not know his name, but they knew that something had elevated their thought. And I felt that I left that place as I should have left a place of worship.

Moody and Sankey continued with their Crusades in major American cities (1875 through 1877), and during this period Moody began to set down his practical advice to students: they should get a Bible and have it with them at all times; they should spend fifteen minutes a day in prayer and Bible study; they should believe the Bible is God's revelation to them, and act accordingly.

Moody also set down his advice to other Evangelists on how they should conduct powerful Revival Meetings:

1. Have a superfluity of energy and intention so your own ego does not get in the way. "Get so full of your subject that you forget yourself."
2. As for prayer, practice brevity. "If you can't pray short, don't pray at all. The men who make long prayers are generally the ones that pray least at home."
3. Choose particular persons to preach to. "I always selected a few people in the audience here and there, to whom I speak. If I can interest them and hold their attention, I have the entire audience. If any one of these goes to sleep or loses interest, I work to secure the attention of that one."
4. Don't turn the pulpit into a showcase for personal pyrotechnics. "Some men remind me of a windmill, with their practiced gestures. How would Moses have succeeded if he had gone down into Egypt and tried elocution on Pharaoh?"
5. Stay close to the subject and forget about oratory. "It is said of Cicero, the great Roman orator, that when he had spoken every one would go out of the building saying, 'What a magnificent address! What an orator!' But when Demosthenes, the Greek orator, had finished, the people would say, 'let us go and fight Philip!' He had fired them up with the cause; and what we want is to get the attention of the people away from ourselves and on to the subject."

Moody's basic attitude could be characterized as a radical pessimism about all worldly matters—as Henry Ward Beecher noted: "He thinks it is no use to attempt to work for this world. In his opinion it is blasted—a wreck bound to sink—and the only thing that is worth doing is to get as many of the crew off as you can, and let her go."

This explains why Moody did not have any interest in the Social Gospel, or even trying to ameliorate living conditions among the poor and dispossessed. In Moody's view, human nature was so riddled with original sin, it was a hopeless case:

> We are a bad lot, the whole of us, by nature. It is astonishing how the devil does blind us and makes us think we are so naturally good . . . the first man born of woman was a murderer. Sin leaped into the world full grown, and the whole race has been bad all the way down. Man is naturally bad.

This is as hard-line Fundamentalism as one can possibly get: there must be no liberal retying of shoestrings and pointing to any extenuating circumstances in one's life. Moody considered this the humbug of sentimental Christianity:

> I want to say very emphatically that I have no sympathy with the doctrine of universal brotherhood and universal fatherhood. I don't believe one word of it. If a man lives in the flesh he is a child of the devil. That is pretty strong language, but it is what Christ said. It brought down a hornet's nest on His head, and helped to hasten Him to the cross, but nevertheless it is true. Show me a man that will lie and steal and get drunk and ruin a woman—do you tell me he is my brother? Not a bit of it. He must be born into the household of faith before he becomes my brother in Christ. He is an alien, he is a stranger to the grace of God, he is an enemy to God, he is not a friend. Before a man can cry "Abba, Father," he must be born from above, born of the Spirit.

There is an echo here of the cave analogy from Book VII of Plato's *Republic*, in which prisoners are chained together and watch shadow plays on the wall, and only a few can ever hope to escape and glimpse the pure daylight on the outside of the cave. This world was as unreal to Moody as it was to Plato:

> We say this is the land of the living! It is not. It is the land of the dying. What is our life here but a vapor? . . . River of life for the healing of

the nations, and everlasting life. Think of it! Life! Life! Life without end!

But what separates Moody from Plato and the other pagan philosophers is not only Moody's belief in the Second Coming of Christ, but also his lively belief in hellfire and brimstone:

> If there is no hell, let us burn our Bibles. Why spend so much time studying the Bible? . . . If I believed there was no hell, you would not find me going from town to town, spending day and night preaching and proclaiming the Gospel and urging men to escape the damnation of hell. I would take things easy.

And as for the conversionary experience, Moody had no doubt whatsoever that it was completely efficacious:

> Salvation is instantaneous. I admit that a man may be converted so that he cannot tell when he crossed the line between death and life, but I also believe a man may be a thief one moment and a saint the next. I believe a man may be as vile as hell itself one moment, and be saved the next.

Finally, Moody believed in taking direct personal initiative at all times: "Don't wait for something to turn up; go and turn something up." He distrusted the modern mania of delegating responsibility through endless byways of bureacracy: "If there had been a committee appointed, Noah's ark would never have been built."

Moody's position, then, was extreme Fundamentalist, and this may also account for his overwhelming popularity in his Crusades. Like Jonathan Edwards before him and the Great Awakening, Moody held the spectre of hell in front of his congregations and he persuaded them that this would be their fate if they did not trust in the grace of God. It was, as we have seen, a message that modern Protestants were eager to hear. Dislocated and disoriented as they were by the increasing complexity of an industrial civilization, they responded to Moody's message of the inerrancy of the Bible and his promise of a personal salvation that would be immediate, trustworthy, and everlasting.

No wonder his great Crusades not only brought in hundreds of thousands of converts, they brought in hundreds of thousands of dollars as well—not only from industrial tycoons like Andrew Carnegie, John

Wanamaker, J. P. Morgan, and Cyrus McCormick, but from countless collections that were taken up from among the working classes.

Moody used this money for a variety of purposes. First, there was the actual financing of his Revival Meetings and Crusades, and Moody was careful to keep a scrupulous accounting of how much money was used for each major Evangelical undertaking: he was a model for later Evangelists in his concern not to give the appearance of wrongdoing in any financial matters.

Second, Moody helped to raise thousands of dollars for the support of the YMCA and other affiliated youth movements.

Third, he founded the Moody Bible Institute in Chicago in 1889 to perpetuate the teaching and study of the Bible, and over the next hundred years this organization would serve as one of the bastions of Fundamentalist doctrine and training.

Finally, Moody founded the Northfield Schools—the Mount Hermon School for Boys and the Northfield School for Girls—to provide religious training for secondary school students. Moody's objective was to give young men and women the opportunity of a solid college preparatory training which would, of course, have Bible study as the core. The emphasis was on enrolling gifted young people who would not otherwise have the opportunity of furthering their education because of economic hardship, and the academic work was supplemented with a work program that involved dairy farming, working in a steam laundry, and other activities that would not only help offset tuition costs but also teach practical skills that could be used in later life.

In 1878 Moody bought one hundred acres of choice farmland for the site of these Northfield Schools in Massachusetts, and ground was broken for the first dormitory in 1880. Moody chose as motto for the two schools a verse from Isaiah Chapter 27:

3 I the Lord do keep it; I will water it every moment: lest any hurt it, I will keep it night and day.

Under the stewardship of his son, William Revell Moody, the two schools put up more and more buildings over the next twenty years —Mount Hermon would have Crossley, Dwight's Home, Breckenridge, Overtoun, Dickerson, West Hall, and Memorial Chapel; Northfield would have Kenarden, Palmer, Russell Sage Chapel, Marquand, Stowe, Revell, Wilson, Weston, Merrill-Keep, Holton, and Gould Halls. In the years to come, Hermon would become known for its athletic program and its Sacred Concerts, and Northfield would host the Summer Religious Conferences.

Towards the end of his life, Dwight L. Moody retired back to the Pioneer Valley of the Connecticut River where he had been born, to spend his last days driving a simple horse and buggy along dirt roads around Bernardston, Gill, and Warwick. Here in the quiet beauty of the long lawns and distant foothills of the Green Mountains of Vermont, Moody died in 1899. He had already written this brief autobiography years earlier:

> Some day you will read in the papers that D. L. Moody of East Northfield, is dead. Don't you believe a word of it! At that moment I shall be more alive than I am now. I shall have gone up higher, that is all —out of this old clay tenement into a house that is immortal; a body that death cannot touch, that sin cannot taint, a body fashioned like unto His glorious body.
>
> I was born of the flesh in 1837. I was born of the Spirit in 1856. That which is born of the flesh may die. That which is born of the Spirit will live forever.

One of Moody's biographers, Gamaliel Bradford, summarizes Dwight Moody's life and work:

> It may be that in the future others will have different ways of overcoming man's separation from God, from those that appealed to Dwight L. Moody. But it will not be denied that in his day none worked more passionately, more lovingly, and more successfully to bring God to man and man to God.

1837   1899

The Autobiography of DWIGHT L. MOODY

SOME day you will read in the papers that D. L. Moody, of East Northfield, is dead. Don't you believe a word of it! At that moment I shall be more alive than I am now, I shall have gone up higher, that is all; out of this old clay tenement into a house that is immortal—a body that death cannot touch; that sin cannot taint; a body fashioned like unto His glorious body.

I was born of the flesh in 1837. I was born of the Spirit in 1856. That which is born of the flesh may die. That which is born of the Spirit will live forever.

AIMEE SEMPLE MACPHERSON. *United Press International Photo.*

BILLY SUNDAY. *Religious News Service Photo.*

MARTIN LUTHER KING, JR. *Religious News Service Photo.*

HERBERT ARMSTRONG shortly before his death. *Religious News Service Photo.*

JIM AND TAMMY BAKKER at home in Malibu. *Religious News Service Photo/Wide World.*

BILLY GRAHAM. *Courtesy Billy Graham Evangelistic Association.*

PAT ROBERTSON.
Religious News Service Photo/Wide World.

JIMMY SWAGGART.
Religious News Service Photo/Wide World.

ORAL ROBERTS.
Courtesy Beverly Hubbard Photo Library.

JERRY FALWELL. *Courtesy Old Time Gospel Hour.*

ROBERT SCHULLER in the Crystal Cathedral. *Religious News Service Photo.*

Chapter 7

TWENTIETH CENTURY EVANGELISTS

EVANGELISM HAS taken many forms in the twentieth century. The higher Bible criticism of Albert Schweitzer has coexisted with the Fundamentalism and showmanship of Billy Sunday and Aimee Semple McPherson. The twentieth century has also witnessed the growth of Evangelical organizations, from the Salvation Army and the Christian Science movement (both of which had their roots in the nineteenth century) to the Hare Krishna movement. Protestant, Catholic, Jewish, Eastern-inspired and secular voices have all been represented in twentieth century Evangelism.

Albert Schweitzer is one of the major Evangelical figures of our time, vastly misunderstood and underestimated for his role as one of the principal authors of the higher Bible criticism which has had such a disquieting effect on Fundamentalist doctrine and beliefs.

Of course there were earlier scholars who raised serious textual questions as to the authenticity and consistency of holy scripture. The first was Hermann Reimarus, Professor of Oriental Languages at Hamburg, Germany, who died in 1768 but left a posthumous volume entitled *Wolfenbüttel Fragments*, which claimed Jesus never intended for his teachings to be a part of any ongoing religion of Christianity but simply thought he was forecasting the end of the world. The controversy that was stirred up throughout Europe by this work accounts for why Napoleon Bonaparte in 1808 asked the famous German scholar Wieland point-blank if he believed in the historicity of Jesus.

The questioning went further: in 1835, Heinrich Paulus published

The Life of Jesus, in which he rejected outright all the supernatural miracles in the four gospels. In 1836, Ferdinand Christian Baur (1792–1860) challenged the Letters of Paul, claiming that only Galatians, Corinthians, and Romans could be authenticated. In 1840, Bruno Bauer began publishing a series of books that claimed Jesus never lived but was only an amalgam of the assorted sects and creeds of his time.

In 1863 the French author Ernest Renan introduced a major innovation for the higher Bible criticism when he published his book, The Life of Jesus. Renan's fluid writing style made his book seem to be conciliatory and orthodox: he asserted "The whole of history is incomprehensible without Jesus." Nonetheless, beneath the surface grace and charm of the book, Renan was raising so many doctrinal questions about the discrepancies to be found in Matthew, Mark, Luke, and John, that there was a clear implication that all four gospel writers could not possibly be reporting on the same historical personage. Renan's book had an enormous readership, even though no one could be quite sure whether this Life of Jesus did more to confirm or contradict the received view of the Bible.

By this time higher Bible criticism had become a major force in Europe, so much so that the Catholic Church was driven to excommunicate the Abbé Loisy for raising radical objections against the original Bible text. Loisy was declared a heretical "modernist" and his works were placed on the Index.

At this point we should pause and consider the underlying issue of this higher Bible criticism, which goes back to that question Napoleon asked Wieland: apart from the four gospels in the Bible, what real basis is there for belief in the historical existence of a man named Jesus? And why is this man's ministry not recorded in more detail by the Roman rulers who were occupying Jerusalem at that time, and why is there such a nagging absence of any objective commentator who may have been aware of the life and teachings of this man?

About the only reliable source we have that there was ever a real historical figure named Jesus is a brief passage that appears in The History of the Jews by Josephus, A.D. 83, which raises so many questions that we have to quote the passage in full:

At that time lived Jesus, a holy man, if man he may be called, for he performed wonderful works, and taught men, and joyfully received the truth. And he was followed by many Jews and many Greeks. He was the Messiah.

This passage seems agreeable enough on first reading, but the more one considers it, the more irritating it becomes. What exactly were the "wonderful works" this man is alleged to have performed, and why does Josephus pass over them so quickly? And what were the teachings that this man "taught men"? One would think if Josephus was writing a history of the Jews, he would be concerned enough to develop the doctrines that this Jesus was disseminating among his fellow Jews. Furthermore, if Josephus really believed what he said in that baffling third sentence, that "He was the Messiah," Josephus would devote more than these short cryptic sentences to the man and his works. And if Josephus asserts so emphatically that Jesus was the Messiah, then why does he seem to leave the question open in an earlier sentence when he implies that Jesus may or may not have been merely a man? And what, precisely, was that "truth" which this Jesus is said to have "joyfully received"? We are left with the impression that either Josephus did not care enough to explore any of these matters to his full satisfaction, which seems highly unlikely for a historian of his stature and integrity; or that Josephus realized it would probably be impolitic to come out and say what he really thought about Jesus for fear of offending the Jewish or Roman authorities, which seems much more likely in those perilous times. We are left, then, with no clear idea of what Josephus meant in this brief passage from *The History of the Jews*, and we are back where we started: without any firm verification of the life and teachings of Jesus, apart from what is given to us in the four gospels in the Bible.

The preceding is a fair example of the sort of questioning that goes on in higher Bible criticism: a text is quoted and then one considers whether it can be taken at face value or whether it raises more problems than it can explain on its own terms. The reader can judge for himself, based on this criticism we have just been giving the Josephus passage, how unnerving it can be to have a text destroyed in front of one's own eyes. And the reader should bear in mind that this passage under consideration is by a writer who is outside the mainstream tradition of Christianity, so our criticism does not touch on any vulnerable sensitivities that might be associated with the two thousand year tradition of Christian thought. We'll leave it to the reader to imagine what his feelings might be if we took a brief passage from one of the four gospels—say, the Sermon on the Mount—and subjected it to a similar textual criticism. Perhaps then the reader would have some idea of the maelstrom of controversy which has been stirred up by the higher Bible criticism.

As Europe was still reverberating with the impact of the French and German higher Bible criticism towards the end of the nineteenth century, suddenly a young man named Albert Schweitzer became the most conspicuous and outspoken of all scholars to raise serious questions as to the authenticity and consistency of holy scripture.

In his autobiography *Out of My Life and Thought*, Albert Schweitzer describes how he delivered the inaugural 1902 lecture before the Theological Faculty at Strasbourg, Germany. The lecture caused such a furor that there were protests against Schweitzer's appointment as university lecturer because of his methods of historical investigation into the life and teachings of Jesus, together with fears that Schweitzer would confuse or mislead theological students with his radical views.

As Schweitzer himself puts it, many people were shocked to learn that the historical Jesus had to be accepted as "capable of error" regarding the supernatural kingdom of heaven, the manifestation of which Jesus had proclaimed as imminent but which, of course, did not appear during the lifetime of Jesus. Schweitzer writes in *The Quest of the Historical Jesus*:

> Jesus did not share the simple, realistic expectation about the Messiah which was at that time widely spread among the Jewish people, and that it was by failures which He experienced after some initial success that He was brought to His resolution to face death.

This idea that Jesus did not believe in the literal coming of any Messiah, and that he experienced failures during his own lifetime, and that he actually changed his mind about the nature of his mission here on earth—these ideas present us with a Jesus who has never been taught in the annals of traditional Christianity. No wonder Schweitzer's lecture audience became so agitated, and no wonder his appointment as university lecturer was challenged.

In *The Quest of the Historical Jesus*, Schweitzer goes on to make even more revolutionary statements: "Jesus tries to divert the attention of believers from the supernatural Messianic Kingdom which they expected, by proclaiming to them a purely ethical kingdom of God which He Himself is attempting to found upon earth."

Schweitzer is claiming here that Jesus did not intend a spiritual kingdom of heaven, nor did he intend for there to be an apocalyptic Second Coming. Instead, Schweitzer claims Jesus was more concerned with creating a *"paradiso terrestre,"* an ethical heaven here on earth. Schweitzer describes the impact of this doctrine:

At first success attended His preaching. Later on, however, the multitude, influenced by the Pharisees and the ruler at Jerusalem, falls away from Him. In view of this fact He wrestles His way through to the conviction that, for the cause of the Kingdom of God and the preservation of His spiritual Messiahship, it is the will of God that He shall die.

Clearly this is not a Jesus to whom anyone can attribute divine infallibility: it is a Jesus who is unclear as to the precise character of his calling. Not even the most liberal Unitarians would dare to argue for such a reading of Jesus, yet Schweitzer is basing all of his claims on the strictest historical scholarship.

Schweitzer feels his conclusions open up an entirely new view of the Incarnation, and give us a new existential appreciation of what Jesus the man must have experienced in his lifetime:

The historical Jesus moves us deeply by His subordination to God. In this He stands out as greater than the Christ personality of dogma which, in compliance with the claims of Greek metaphysics, is conceived as omniscient and incapable of error.

Of course Albert Schweitzer's book was a bombshell—not only to those who insisted on the "inerrancy" of the Bible, but also to those who wanted to hold to the traditional view of the divinity of Jesus. As a result of the ensuing religious controversy, Schweitzer made a decision to turn his attention from theology to medicine and obtain his degree so he could devote the rest of his life to the healing profession of a doctor.

When Schweitzer finished his medical studies in Europe, he moved to Lambarene in the African Congo, where he set up a modest hospital for the natives there. He became, in effect, a medical missionary who was treating the African natives with the most modern scientific techniques, giving vaccines, delivering babies, and performing simple surgical techniques, and also teaching hygiene and basic sanitary practices to his patients. Word spread along the Congo that this white man in Lambarene was not like those earlier Christian missionaries who only wanted to convert natives to a weird new religion of some invisible trinity: the African natives knew that this white man was their friend who knew how to heal and care for them, and so gradually they began to come from great distances to the modest hospital outpost in Lambarene.

Albert Schweitzer lived out the rest of his life in Christlike devotion to the service of others, thereby exemplifying the ideal of that same religion he had done so much to unsettle with his earlier criticism. He even found time to continue with his organ playing, and was known worldwide as one of the leading exponents of the music of his countryman, Johann Sebastian Bach.

Even in Lambarene, however, Schweitzer still insisted on the accuracy of his earlier work of higher Bible criticism:

> I find it no light task to follow my vocation, to put pressure on the Christian faith to reconcile itself in all sincerity with historical truth. But I have devoted myself to it with joy, because I am certain that truthfulness in all things belongs to the spirit of Jesus.

Albert Schweitzer's life work is a fitting introduction to the problem of twentieth century Evangelism. One would think that Schweitzer's revolutionary undermining of the most cherished principles of traditional Christianity—the divinity of Jesus, the imminence of the Second Coming, and the inerrancy of the Bible—would make it a little bit more difficult for modern Evangelists to keep on insisting on the basic tenets of Fundamentalist thought.

However, Evangelism has never been deterred from pursuing its objectives by anything so ephemeral as scholarship, objectivity, or historical truth. All that a really determined Fundamentalist has to do is call for a reassertion of faith in the basic principles of Christianity —amply serving to dismiss contrary conclusions reached by Albert Schweitzer or other higher Biblical critics.

This may sound simplistic, but it's exactly what modern American Evangelists have been doing. The more the claims of higher Bible criticism have influenced liberal thinkers and theologians in America, the louder the Evangelists have shouted for a return to the claims of pure faith. And since Fundamentalism is by its very nature a massive reaction formation against any criticism of the Bible as the Word of God, it may be that Schweitzer and the other higher Bible scholars have only reinforced American Evangelists in their determination to cling to a literal interpretation of scripture. It's an ironic effect, that revolutionary truth-seeking would only fortify those conservative elements that are so hellbent on perpetuating the Official Party Line, but it's nothing new, as we saw the same reinforcement take place during the Counter-Reformation when the Catholic Church was actually strengthened by its resistance to the challenge of Martin Luther.

Of course one could say that modern American Evangelists are being unscrupulous and ahistorical, to go leapfrogging so blithely over the implications of higher Bible criticism. But whoever says that has simply misunderstood the nature of modern American Evangelism, and the best remedy for such a person is to read Sinclair Lewis' 1927 novel *Elmer Gantry*. This book is a classic portrait of the prototypical twentieth century American Evangelist: Elmer Gantry is a rough-and-tumble small town midwestern Evangelist with a knack for using the Bible to advance any point of view that seems appropriate to the moment. A cheating, lying, fast-talking hustler, Gantry is so adept at playing the shell game of conversionary religion that he manages to seduce every congregation he comes across. The book was made into a major motion picture in 1960 and won Academy Awards for Burt Lancaster and Shirley Jones, who played the leading characters.

Two of the real-life Evangelists of the early twentieth century come right out of this Elmer Gantry mold: Billy Sunday and Aimee Semple McPherson were both giant figures, flamboyant and theatrical, and their message was traditional Fundamentalist doctrine.

Billy Sunday's full name was William Ashley Sunday (1862–1935) and he had begun his career as right fielder for the Chicago White Stockings (1882–1890): his name is still listed in Major League record books as one of the fastest base runners of all time. In eight years of professional baseball play for three different National League teams (Chicago, Pittsburgh, and Philadelphia), Billy Sunday compiled a total of 2008 at bats, 498 hits, 55 doubles, 24 triples and 12 home runs. His lifetime batting average was a highly respectable .248 (compared with the all-time record batting average of .367 of Ty Cobb), and Billy Sunday's total stolen bases was a phenomenal 236, putting him well ahead of Rogers Hornsby (135) and Babe Ruth (123) although behind Honus Wagner (722) and record-holding Ty Cobb (892).

After Billy Sunday received his Call from the Lord in 1907, he hit the sawdust trail and began preaching against the Devil and Demon Rum. He was no mean businessman: with the dispatch of a Baseball Commissioner, Billy Sunday built up an Evangelistic organization that one commentator called "second in efficiency only to National Cash Register."

Once on the streets of New York in 1917, Billy Sunday preached to some 20,000 people on Broadway and 168th Street, where he stood and called New Yorkers "vile, iniquitous, low down, groveling, worthless, damnable, rotten, hellish, corrupt, miserable sinners." Billy Sunday attacked Harry Emerson Fosdick and his congregation as "a pack of pretentious, pliable, mental perverts (modernists), dedicated to the destruction of religion and one and all of them liars, so labeled by the authority of Almighty God." He also called for the expulsion of Nicholas Murray Butler as President of Columbia University for similar reasons.

With his freewheeling style of firecracking preaching, Billy Sunday railed against "hog-jowled, weasel-eyed, sponge-columned, mush-fisted, jelly-spined, four-flushing Christians." John D. Rockefeller thought this was dandy and he called Billy Sunday "a great power for good. I don't think it's any one thing he does or says that counts in particular. Mr. Sunday is a rallying center around whom all people interested in good things may gather."

Billy Sunday's preaching against Demon Rum did have an effect: together with lobbying efforts by the Women's Christian Temperance Union, Billy Sunday is largely responsible for passage of the Prohibition Amendment in 1919 as the law of the land.

The second prototypical twentieth century American Evangelist, Aimee Semple McPherson (birth date?–1944) was billed in her heyday as "the world's most pulchritudinous evangelist." At her Angelus Temple in Los Angeles, Aimee always wore a diaphanous gown and held a Bible in one hand and a bouquet of open roses in the other as she stood in a bright white spotlight and delivered her sermon. Her preaching was practical and punctuated with no-nonsense figures of speech such as "A church without the Holy Ghost is like an automobile without gasoline." Aimee was also no-nonsense about seeing to herself: she always kept one monthly collection from the Angelus Temple as her own remuneration.

What would have been an outstanding career by America's only significant female Evangelist was interrupted by a curious event. In 1926, Aimee Semple McPherson stepped into the waters of Ocean Park, California, and she disappeared from sight for thirty-six days. Rumors were rampant: she had been killed by a rival Evangelist, or she had been taken up bodily into heaven, roses and all. When she finally turned up, she told newspaper she had been kidnapped and escaped by walking twenty miles through the blistering Mexican desert. But then new rumors began: some said she had spent ten days hidden away in a cottage with Kenneth Ormiston, her radio announcer. H. L. Mencken had his own version of what really happened:

> Earlier in 1926 she had mysteriously disappeared, and there was a
> dreadful hullabaloo among her customers. When she returned just as

mysteriously she told an incredible tale of having been kidnapped. It was soon established that she had been on a love-trip with one of her employees, a bald-headed and one-legged electrician, and she was thereupon charged with perjury and put on trial. She escaped easily enough, but the scandal badly damaged her business, and she was soon supplanted as the ranking ecclesiastic of the United States by Bishop James Cannon, Jr. She died, almost forgotten, in 1944.

Obviously, a very managing woman, strongly recalling the madame of a fancy-house on a busy Saturday night. A fixed smile stuck to her from first to last.

One person who recalls attending one of Aimee's Revival Meetings when he was a young child is John D. Mitchell, President of the Institute for Advanced Studies in the Theatre Arts. The service took place in Rockford, Illinois, during the Great Depression. Dr. Mitchell comments:

At the meeting which I attended, Aimee timed her entrance. There was a buildup and she had a good sense of theatre. She entered all in white. She had striking blond, seemingly lacquered hair in marcel waves of the 1930s. (During this Evangelical session, she had something of a resemblance to a nightclub entertainer of the period, Texas Guinan.)

The meeting was like an old-style gospel tent circuit of Evangelist meetings, and her delivery and oratory was in that style. She had a loud, Ethel Merman type voice which really carried and her style was that of the converting-type speakers. During the break as the group was being stirred up and energized, there was (and as young as I may have been, it struck me with some amusement) a soloist singing a song which had been composed for her meetings, "I Have Struck Oil," and the accompaniment was a solo trumpet!

During the session, members of the audience were urged to come forth and be "born again" (perhaps this was not the term used then), to be converted and to openly present themselves before the audience having been moved by this Evangelistic meeting and by Aimee's preaching. Too, there was much urging and energy put into the collections and they were more than one as I recall, when the youthful entourage with which she traveled went about collecting from the audience. These young people were wearing a type of uniform undoubtedly designed for her Evangelistic travels.

. . . One never knew if the people who came forth had been plants or whether they were those who were genuinely moved and inspired to come forth and to embrace Christ and Aimee Semple's version of Christianity . . . She did seem, in spite of her divorces and things about her private life that came out from time to time in the Hearst newspapers, to succeed and she did seem to accumulate a great deal of money and many followers . . .

In addition to individual Evangelists, numerous Evangelical organizations also began to flourish in the early part of the century. Chief among these was the Salvation Army, originated in 1865 as "The Christian Mission" in Whitechapel, England, and later changed to "The Salvation Army" after an accidental military metaphor slipped out of William Booth's mouth when he was speaking about God's "Army of Salvation." The phrase stuck, and thereafter it was the Salvation Army.

General William Booth (1829–1912) had been an itinerant Methodist preacher who left Methodism over a disagreement of principle and became a nonaffiliated Evangelical. His Salvation Army adopted a quasi-military life-style and concerned itself with saving outcasts, drifters, the dispossessed, and street people who wandered into any of the Army's multiplying relief shelters. There the downtrodden could always count on a doughnut and a cup of coffee, although they would probably have to sing a few choruses of Arthur Sullivan's hymn "Onward, Christian Soldiers" and perhaps make a token confession of the sins of their past.

By the turn of the century, there were branches of the Salvation Army in America, Canada, India, Japan, and Australia. George Bernard Shaw, in the Preface to his 1905 play about the Salvation Army, *Major Barbara*, speaks of

the Salvationist, repudiating gaiety and courting effort and sacrifice, yet always in the wildest spirits, laughing, joking, singing, rejoicing, drumming, and tambourining: his life flying by in a flash of excitement, and his death arriving as a climax of triumph.

In the play itself, Shaw poses the dilemma of whether the Salvation Army should accept money from Undershaft, a distiller of alcohol and a cannon founder. Shaw's answer is that of course the Army should take the money, because it has to survive in the real world. The play is subtitled *Discussion in Three Acts* and is an analysis of the amorality of funding Evangelical causes. The twentieth century would see many other examples of the laundering of dirty money through donations to Evangelical causes.

Another Evangelical movement was the scientific methodology of faith healing, the Christian Science of Mary Baker Eddy. Mrs. Eddy's discovery of the principles of healing were set forth in her book, *Science and Health with a Key To the Scriptures* (1866), which showed ways in which the human mind could align itself with the Divine Intelligence which operates throughout the universe. Once this is done, extraordinary healing powers result.

The publication of *Science and Health* coincided with an accident Mrs. Eddy had in 1866 on an icy street, and her seemingly miraculous recovery from injuries after reading Matthew Chapter 9:

> 2 And, behold, they brought to him a man sick of the palsy, lying on a bed: and Jesus seeing their faith said unto the sick of the palsy; Son, be of good cheer; thy sins be forgiven thee.

From November 1878 through 1879, Mrs. Eddy delivered a series of thirty-nine lectures in Boston on the subject of faith healing, and in 1883 she filed suit in U. S. Circuit Court to determine that she was in fact the author of *Science and Health*. In 1893, there was a landmark case testing the validity of Christian Science, when Mrs. Eliza Ward was arrested and indicted for manslaughter because she did not give a patient under her care a life-saving operation but tried to use Christian Science principles. The patient died, and Mrs. Ward was held responsible for the death.

Faith in Mrs. Eddy's teaching became enormously popular in America, as is evidenced in this testimonial from *Historical and Biographical Papers: Sketches from the Life of Mary Baker Eddy and the History of Christian Science*:

> In many instances, Mrs. Eddy healed persons who did not come to her as patients. Their condition attracted her compassionate and loving thought. For instance, while she lived at Lynn and was passing along one of Lynn's streets, she saw a man sitting on the sidewalk who was so deformed that his knees touched his chin. Going to him and leaning over so that her face was close to his, she said, "God love you," and

went on without waiting. Almost immediately, the man arose and walked.

Another Evangelical movement in the early part of the century was the Jehovah's Witnesses, which took its witnessing name from Isaiah Chapter 43:

> 10   Ye are my witnesses, said the Lord, and my servant whom I have chosen: that ye may know and believe me, and understand that I am he: before me there was no God formed, neither shall there be after me.

Jehovah's Witnesses currently number around three million persons in over 206 lands, 25% of them in the United States. Originally an offshoot of the Mormons after the 1844 Millennium predicted by William Miller failed to take place, the Jehovah's Witnesses began in the 1870s as a Bible Study Class in Allegheny City, Pennsylvania, under the American religious leader Charles Taze Russell (1852–1916).

In July 1879, the first issue of *Zion's Watch Tower and Herald of Christ's Presence* appeared, and in 1881, Zion's Watch Tower Tract Society was formed. In 1909, the Society headquarters moved to its present location in Brooklyn, New York, where its printed sermons are syndicated in newspapers all over the United States, Canada, and Europe. The *Watch Tower* publishes over 11,630,000 copies of each issue, and it is translated into over one hundred languages including Swahili, Danish, Chinese, Afrikaans, Russian, Portuguese, Korean, and Dutch. Articles in the paper include attacks on higher Bible criticism and articles arguing against the theory of evolution.

Jehovah's Witnesses are mostly known in America for their door-to-door witnessing in local neighborhoods. In March 1986, the author of this book was working industriously on the rough draft manuscript of *Evangelism in America* when lo, there came a persistent knocking at the door of his 14th Street apartment in Manhattan, New York. As our author stopped work on his writing and got up to open the door, whom should he see there but an elderly couple who introduced themselves as Jehovah's Witnesses, and politely asked if they might have a few moments of our author's time.

Now, under any other circumstances, this sort of interruption of our author's work by complete strangers, interlopers as it were, would be most unwelcome. But at this particular time and under these highly unusual circumstances, our author warmly and hospitably invited the couple to enter his apartment, where he offered them comfortable seating and hot coffee and some fresh pieces of danish pastry. And before this couple could begin their witnessing to him about the Lord, our author turned the tables on them and explained the nature of the book he was working on, and he asked if they would be good enough to agree to be interviewed about their religious practice, if he promised them total anonymity in their answers. The couple gave their consent, and following is the exchange that took place:

Question:	You go from door to door, in particular areas of towns and cities, spreading the word about your religion. Do you run into very much hostility or resistance when you knock on doors?
Jehovah's Witness:	We are "pioneers" so we have to put in ninety hours a month in this witnessing. Sometimes if people don't want to be bothered, or if they have their own religion, we leave them alone. Sometimes people are just so disgusted with the way the world is going, they will just want to talk. Or maybe there has been a death in the family. Or they may just want to hear something from the Bible.
Question:	But your specific goal is not proselytizing?
Jehovah's Witness:	Our specific goal is to turn people to Jehovah God and the Bible. We show them what's what in the Bible, and that a person always has free will. Of course we believe we are the true religion, otherwise we wouldn't be Jehovah's Witnesses. We believe that very soon God is going to destroy the very evil, wicked, commercial, and political religious organization of this world, and usher in a new kingdom which Jesus Christ will rule over for a thousand years. Actually we believe that Christ's Second Coming is already here, that Christ's Kingdom was set up in 1914.
Question:	Even so, do you ever run into real hatred or anger? Do you ever get any doors slammed in your face?
Jehovah's Witness:	Well, they did it to Jesus.

Following the end of World War II, there was a proliferation of sects and cults in America, scattered and eclectic movements that sprang up in different parts of the country. Here is a partial listing of some of these Evangelical groups:

Gestalt Therapy	Synanon Growth Movement
Bioenergetics	Janov's Primal Institute
Jews for Jesus	Edgar Cayce Groups
Psychosynthesis	Arica
Carl Rogers' Non-Directive Therapy	Theosophy of H. P. Blavatsky
T Groups of Kurt Lewin	Gurdjieff Groups
Transcendental Meditation (TM)	Inner Peace Movement

We should also note the Evangelism of mind-altering chemicals such as LSD, a forerunner of the American underground drug culture. Timothy Leary, Allen Ginsberg, Aldous Huxley and other spokesmen advocated, each in his own language, that the country's youth "Turn on, tune in, drop out." Although this movement led some youths astray and caused a considerable number of premature deaths through overdosing and suicide, the use of LSD may have had some lasting religious significance, as Roy Wallis, writing in *The Dynamics of Change, Religious Movements: Genesis, Exodus and Numbers*, notes:

> LSD led many people in the 1960s in a more spiritual direction not because it failed to achieve what they sought, but because it manifestly succeeded in opening up to some of those who took it the possibility of another world, the experience of a realm beyond the mundane, which could then be explored by other—more explicitly spiritual—means.

Of course, there were fringe sects such as the UFO cult of 1975: Herff Applewhite and Bonnie Nettles, "Bo and Peep," who preached resurrection by being lifted up in an Unidentified Flying Object, to about two dozen followers in the Los Angeles area.

And there were fringe individuals such as former astronaut James Irwin, who attempted to discover the remains of Noah's Ark around Mount Ararat in eastern Turkey. Irwin had walked on the moon in 1971 and then became an ordained minister after he returned to civilian life. He spent several years in Turkey searching for the Ark before finally giving it up with the comment, "The Lord may have some other mission for me. I always want to be doing what the Lord wants me to do."

A more considerable movement was begun by L. Ron Hubbard, a

science fiction writer and son of a naval commander, who founded Scientology, which tried to link secular psychological therapy and growth with the dynamics of a religious cult. Hubbard had been committed to Oak Knoll Military Hospital in 1943 after reporting a sabotage which did not exist, but in 1950 a breathless Walter Winchell flashed to the nation the following news bulletin:

> There is something new coming up in April called Dianetics. A new science which works with the invariability of physical science in the field of the human mind. From all indications, it will prove to be as revolutionary for humanity as the first caveman's discovery and utilization of fire.

As Winchell predicted, in the next issue of *Astounding Science Fiction*, Hubbard announced Dianetics, a new form of scientific psychotherapy. The premise of this new therapy was that man is plagued with "engrams" or mental images resulting from painful experiences out of the past. These engrams can be cleared away through "auditing sessions," or carefully monitored counseling interviews during which electrical instruments are attached to the client's skin. The object was to monitor the client's responses to provide increased control over thought processes in that portion of the mind where emotional problems and psychosomatic illnesses were known to originate, and also to clear away the memory bin of those pesky engrams which were causing the discomfort. Clients paid Scientology counselors upwards of $300 an hour for these one-on-one auditing sessions.

In 1952, Ron Hubbard went on to announce Scientology as a new world religion, and by 1979 there were fifty-one churches worldwide, with twenty-three in America. By the time of his death in 1986, Hubbard was a multimillionaire: he had published over 589 works, with fiction sales numbering over twenty-two million copies and non-fiction works more than twenty-three million. Testimonials on the power of Scientology came from all fields, including the actor John Travolta and jazz pianist Chick Corea, who stated: "L. Ron Hubbard set a star-high goal for us. He documented it with pure science. He taught it with pure love. He's left nothing but pure inspiration."

Another self-help Evangelical organization was Werner Erhard's EST and its seminars. EST ("it is") teaches an exploration of reality through self-awareness techniques, and more effective communication with others through channels which had been previously blocked or unexplored. Over the past two decades EST claims it has influenced over 200,000 people in business and the arts, and helped them towards more vital career choices and personal self-expression.

During this period there was a sudden influx of Evangelical sects and cults which were strongly influenced by Eastern thought. In the 1940s and 1950s there was the phenomenal popularity of Kahlil Gibran's *The Prophet*, which offered a prophetic tradition that was completely outside the mainstream of Judeo-Christian religion. A Lebanese who wrote in Arabic, Gibran published his own ink drawings of mystical portraits and figures to accompany the text of *The Prophet*, so the whole book seemed vaguely spiritual and other-dimensional. Gibran's success in America was an augury of new interest in Eastern religion and life styles.

The various sects and cults that began to proliferate were all seeking a radically new concept of personal growth, and insisted on the central premise of a disciple's meek obedience to a guru or spiritual master —an idea derived from the second century B.C. holy book, the *Bhagavad Gita*:

> Try to learn the truth by approaching a spiritual master. Inquire of him submissively and do service to him. The soul that has realized itself can impart knowledge because it has seen the truth . . . [The disciple must] be a fool, a dog, a puppet before the master . . .

In many of these new Eastern sects there was a high incidence of membership turnover, recidivism, defections, apostasies, and dropouts. For many young American novitiates, it was too difficult to adapt to the stringent disciplines of meditation, endless litanies, and the perfection of intricate physical skills. Following are brief sketches of some of these Eastern physical disciplines:

1. Hatha Yoga—meditation, unity of mind, body, and spirit through practice of postures and self-massage, breathing exercises, leading to increased awareness and well-being.
2. T'ai Chi Ch'uan—Chinese art of moving for health and self-defense. Kicks, strikes, and evasive actions; teaches timing, grace, and coordination.
3. Tae Kwan Do—Korean martial art. Punches, lunges, kicks, knife hands. Introduced in 1988 Olympics as a competitive sport.

For many young Americans who may only have known Sunday School or an occasional genuflection as all the discipline that was required in one's spiritual life, these Eastern skills held an extraordinary fascination and challenge. Many loved the new concept of coordinating mind and body to achieve spiritual awareness, but some could not adapt themselves to such a rigorous life-style and abandoned it after a brief period.

As the various Eastern sects and cults were becoming ensconced in America as an authentic Evangelical movement, they received a significant endorsement and validation with the arrival in America of Bhagwan Shree Rajneesh, formerly Chadra Mohan, head of the so-called Rajneesh Movement. Rajneesh had experienced enlightenment at twenty-one in Poona, India, and in 1981 he immigrated to America, married the daughter of a Greek millionaire, and began teaching Emptiness, the Voice, and the Beyond to eager young Americans. Centered in Oregon, Rajneesh taught that the unknown anarchy of the psyche is suppressed by having gone through centuries of past births, and the true aim of the psyche is to attain egolessness and abandon "things." This was nothing new to readers who knew the doctrine of Karma and the Hindu teaching of the Great Chain of Being, but Rajneesh found a way of making it immediately relevant to dislocated Americans. After Rajneesh's turbulent eviction from the United States, his movement foundered, but its literature still attracts new members.

Hare Krishna is another Eastern Evangelical movement that found popularity in America. Founded in 1965 by A. C. Bhaktivedanta Swami Pabhopda, Hare Krishna appears to have Hindu origins but is essentially American in practice. Each person coming into Hare Krishna has a "godbrother" or friend to nurture and advise the person during entry.

We asked one Hare Krishna member, who has since left the movement, to tell us how she came to join the movement in the first place and what its experience meant for her life. She wrote:

If what happened was your father went to work everyday and came home and your mother made you dinner and that was your life; if you're twelve years old and it's 1972 and you just moved into a big new white colonial house with four bedrooms and aluminum suburban neighborhood where the schools were good—if you're twelve and the quiet and alone type and your oldest sister just went off to college and you weren't into socializing at school then you might just become close to your next oldest sister who is sixteen and again it's 1972 so she's reading *Siddhartha* and she's got a poster on her wall with a picture in water color blues of a peaceful boy playing a reed flute and underneath the picture is that different drummer quote from *Walden*, then should be in such desperate haste to succeed . . .

Describing the daily routine of Hare Krishna, she wrote:

I woke up at 3 A.M. most mornings and sometimes earlier, then I stumbled down the path to bathe on a dark quiet mountaintop field with some sleepers lying around me, the cold water felt good and I felt austere and I adorned my body in 12" shoots and with mud from the Ganges River in each spot a mantra, and creating with my finger the sign of Visnu . . .

Now my body was purified, a temple for the Lord within my heart, maybe he would accept my services and hear my prayers, I wrapped my sari around me and walked through the field to the cow path saying a Sanskrit prayer to my guru thanking him for opening my eyes with the touching of knowledge, and then I began to chant quietly the Holy names of god on my beads over and over again while pacing back and forth in the moonlight, I continued doing this until 4 A.M. and then I walked to the temple to begin preparing the tray with items for the worship in the form of deities in the temple . . .

Sitting on a lotus and contemplating the navel of Lord Visnu, Brahma sang these mantras to Lord Visnu, before creating the universe, with each breath out the entire material manifestation is created, and with each breath in it is destroyed—of course there are billions of years in between each breath . . .

This was at Hare Krishna commune in West Virginia, there was only the temple and tiny cabin with wood stairs and myself and my husband Tasmuna, and the priestess, lived there along with nine worshippable deities of Krisnu and his expansions . . .

We asked this Hare Krishna ex-member if she thought there was anything bizarre about a twelve year old girl living with her "husband" in a West Virginia commune practicing esoteric Eastern rituals at three in the morning, and she answered no. Then we told her we had heard reports of several murders which had taken place at that Hare Kirshna commune, and she answered:

As early as the 1970s, members of the New Vrindavana community farm that was Hare Krishna headquarters in West Virginia reported continued harassment by the local police, and in several incidents local people stormed the community and shot up the residences and caused injury to Hare Krishna members.

In 1983, there were reports of two children under ten who were killed by being locked in a refrigerator, and shortly thereafter their father also disappeared and his body was found far away from the farm. Although the West Virginia State Police investigated the incidents, no suspects were charged and no formal complaint was made. This family that was killed was outside the Hare Krishna movement, had given money to the community, and it may have been their mere association with the farm that triggered the killings.

This type of cult community living may strike us as an example of extreme alienation in young Americans, but it does have its vindication. Dr. Hardat Sukhdeo, a psychiatrist practicing in Newark, New Jersey, comments in Willa Appel's *Cults in America*:

> When I look around at our institutions—the family, the churches, the colleges—and the children tell me they're all fakes, they're right—they are. Our institutions are failing our young people, and so are our values. When we look at their parents, who have money but who are not happy, who are physically together but not emotionally together, they ask, "What do I want that for?" I think that if you really look at the questions that the people in cults ask, there's a lot to it.

The occasional police shoot-ups of Hare Krishna communes and reports of children being locked in refrigerators are nothing compared to what was about to break over news services in 1978, when another Evangelical cult community suddenly erupted in the mass suicide of almost a thousand members in the land of Guyana, South America. "Jonestown" was the pet Evangelical project of the Reverend Jim Jones, and he was the one who gave the signal for the appalling liquidation of all his followers in September 1978.

Jim Jones had grown up in Lynn, Indiana, where his father may have been a member of the local Ku Klux Klan (reports are ambiguous; Jones himself was never sure) and his mother may have dreamed that she would give birth to a son who would save the world. With this type of background it is no wonder that as soon as Jim Jones was old enough to realize that he had a calling, he traveled all the way to New York to meet with Father Divine in Harlem and discuss the techniques of Evangelism with him. Jim Jones then went to Brazil in 1962, and it was probably there that he got the idea of eventually founding an Evangelical settlement in nearby Guyana. When he returned to North America, Jones had an apocalyptic message that was as searing as it was imaginative—one can get some sense of his vision from the following excerpt predicting the end of the world, from *Six Years with God: Life Inside Reverend Jim Jones's People's Temple* (New York: A & W, 1979):

> I have seen, by divine revelation, the total annihilation of this country and other parts of the world. San Francisco will be flattened. The only survivors will be those people who are hidden in caves that I have been shown in a vision. Those who go into this cave with me will be saved from the poisonous radioactive fallout that will follow the nuclear bomb attack. This cave is what led our church to migrate to this little valley from Indianapolis, Indiana . . . We have gathered in Redwood Valley for protection, and after the war is over we will be the only survivors. It will be up to our group to begin life anew on this continent. Then we will begin a truly ideal society . . . People will care about one another. Elderly people will be made to feel needed and will be allowed to be productive . . . There will at last be peace on earth. I have seen this all by divine revelation . . .

This kind of apocalyptic oratory may strike some people as utterly flaky or wacko, but it is important to remember there was a certain borderline fringe of the populace that had been made perilously insecure by the perpetual threat of nuclear conflagration through the 1960s and 1970s. And after all, the vision that Jones is reporting to his congregation is nothing new in Judeo-Christian prophecy: his promise that he and his followers would be among the Elect survivors is an echo of Isaiah's promise to the Hidden Remnant in the Old Testament.

What matters is that Jim Jones had such a powerful effect on his listeners with all that subliminal imagery of mass slaughter and annihilation, together with his promise that they would be the ones to begin all over again. It is no wonder Jim Jones was able to gather together a group of ardent followers and relocate almost a thousand of them in 1977 to the Evangelical community of "Jonestown" in Guyana, just north of Brazil and south of Venezuela.

Of course Jim Jones was the central authority figure in Jonestown: he gave all the rules and received all the homage, and he even required his followers to describe the sexual fantasies they had about "Father Jones." It was, by all accounts, very likely the most bizarre and solipsistic theocracy that had ever been set up, from Savonarola's Florence and Calvin's Geneva, to Endicott's Salem and Brigham Young's Utah. Jonestown made all these other Church/State models look like so many Sunday School children at play.

And apparently that was the way a United States Congressional staff investigation group saw the whole thing also, when their members flew down to visit Jonestown in September of 1978. The Committee members toured the Jonestown grounds and they must have picked up some inkling of what hijinks were really going on there, because before they were done with their visit, Jim Jones made up his mind he had to prevent these people from flying back to the United States and giving a detailed report on Jonestown to Congress and the American people. And so, in a desperate and reckless move, Jones ordered his followers to fire on the Committee members before they could get back on their plane. There was a general massacre of the entire staff group, including Congressman Leo J. Ryan.

This was a gross miscalculation on Jones's part, and by this time he realized he was embarked on a homicidal course that was so brutal and stupid, there could be no turning back. It was like the middle of *Macbeth*, when the killer king realizes nothing matters anymore—Act III, scene iv:

> I am in blood
> Stepp'd in so far that, should I wade no more,
> Returning were as tedious as go o'er . . .

Jim Jones knew he had to wipe out all the evidence of what had been going on at Jonestown, and that meant wiping out everyone who had ever been a part of it. In a gruesome echo of that "total annihilation" sermon in which Jones claimed he saw the end of the world, Jim Jones now ordered the entire Jonestown community to line up and drink from a vat of kool-aid laced with cyanide. Nine hundred and twelve men, women, and children drank from the vile brew, and they all died agonizing deaths. It was one of the largest mass suicides in modern history.

What happened at Jonestown was an awful and appalling occurrence, the most bewildering atrocity associated with American Evangelism since the Salem Witch Trials killed twenty innocent men and women in the name of Puritanism. And like those Salem Witch Trials, the catastrophe at Jonestown raised certain basic questions about the nature of Evangelism itself: for example, how can a religion that purports to foster love and freedom of the spirit erupt in such vicious persecutions and atrocities as those of Salem and Jonestown?

One wonders how other Evangelists could continue in their self-appointed Calling, after so many and such furious eruptions of violence, anarchy, and error, without at least pausing long enough to consider what Oliver Cromwell said in 1650 to the General Assembly of the Church of Scotland: "I beseech ye, gentlemen, by the bowels of Christ, bethink ye that ye may be mistaken."

Yet the truly curious thing about Evangelism in America is the way it keeps on keeping on, in spite of whatever errors or scandals or outright catastrophes may cross its path. Like a many-headed Hydra, destroy one Evangelical enterprise and ten others will rise up immediately to take its place, so deep is the need for some vestige of conversionary experience in the American character. Of course the only way to kill a Hydra is to strike at the heart of it and burn out its core, which in the case of Evangelism would be the infantile regressive wish for some kind of utopia/peace on earth. But not many people are up to such a Herculean feat of self-confrontation, which is why Evangelism in America continues to be alive and well, in spite of the Salems and the Jonestowns in our recent past.

Even before the debacle of Jonestown, there were new Evangelists in America and they were initiating new fights and lobbying for special Evangelical causes, sometimes with an embarrassing single-mindedness. We would have to include Anita Bryant in her one-woman attack on homosexuality in all quarters, going so far as to advocate the death penalty for homosexuals and insisting that her Calling was clear: with the same conviction William Jennings Bryan had shown at the Scopes Trial, Anita Bryant characterized her cause as ". . . a battle of the agnostics, the atheists, and the ungodly on one side, and God's people on the other."

Another maverick Evangelist was Madalyn Murray O'Hair, whose militant atheism may have technically made her an anti-Evangelist, but nonetheless her zeal and determination were as fervent as the most Fundamentalist of American Evangelists. O'Hair proposed that because the First Amendment of the Constitution forbade Congress from

legislating any law affecting freedom of worship, that meant Congress
had no right to approve the use of God's name on public currency,
public buildings, or in public oaths. O'Hair insisted that God's name
should be removed from the Pledge of Allegiance, and the motto "In
God We Trust" be struck from all United States currency, together
with any reference to God that might be inscribed on the walls of any
federal or state or municipal buildings. It was an absolutely staggering
proposal in its scope and intent, and O'Hair went the route of civil
court suits and appeals, trying to press her case. After years of adversarial
court battles, O'Hair was not successful in changing any of the Deistic
expressions which our Founding Fathers thought fit to ornament on
our money, or the verbal affirmations on our public edifices.

During this period there were also innumerable secular Evangelical
movements. One example is a gnostic sect which advocated a world-
view using the principles of art to unify the opposites within the human
psyche: Aesthetic Realism was the philosophy of poet Eli Siegel, who
had written the important American poem "Hot Afternoons Have Been
in Montana," which won *The Nation* Poetry Prize in 1925. Aesthetic
Realism's key statement was: "In reality, opposites are one: art shows
this." Its most publicized conversionary experience was the change of
certain practicing homosexuals to a heterosexual life-style—David
Susskind devoted several of his television talk shows to interviewing
these "changed" individuals. On the surface, Aesthetic Realism looked
like not much more than a behavior modification technique; but Siegel's
world-view was much larger, being a curious mix of psychology and
literature, as illustrated in these lines from "Hot Afternoons Have Been
in Montana":

> Men work in factories on hot afternoons, now in Montana, and now
>   in New Hampshire; walk the streets of Boston on hot afternoons;
> Novels, stupid and forgot, have been written in afternoons;
> Matinées of witty comedies in London and New York are in
>   afternoons;
> Indians roamed here, in this green field, on quiet, hot afternoons,
>   in years now followed by hundreds of years.
> Hot afternoons are real; afternoons are; places, things, thoughts,
>   feelings are; poetry is;
> The world is waiting to be known; Earth, what it has in it!
>   The past is in it;
> All words, feelings, movements, words, bodies, clothes, girls,

trees, stones, things of beauty, books, desires are in it;
and all are waiting to be known;
Afternoons have to do with the whole world;
And the beauty of mind, feeling knowingly the world!
The world of girls' beautiful faces, bodies and clothes, quiet
afternoons,
    graceful birds, great words, tearful music, mind-joying poetry,
    beautiful livings, loved things, known things; a to-be-used and
    known and pleasure-to-be giving world.

Aesthetic Realism is an extension of the pluralism and unity of this poem, and its teaching is embodied in a major work entitled *Self and World*, published by Definition Press. One student of Aesthetic Realism, Barbara Singer Zalkan, describes the effect this movement had on her own life:

When I first heard of Aesthetic Realism through a friend at N.Y.U. in the fall of 1944, I had many things going for me, including a scholarship, but I was deeply sad. For one thing, I sometimes thought I didn't love my mother, and I thought I should. Also, I had a general feeling of loneliness and separation from people. I wanted to be popular, to be loved, but often I felt painfully different; I didn't fit in. I veered from feeling superior to people, to feeling inferior. I was trapped by something in myself which Mr. Siegel understood and helped me understand. It was the tendency to have unjust contempt: the "disposition in every person to think he will be for himself by making less of the outside world."

Studying this in myself and in others and learning about the coexisting but opposite desire to be fair and have good will, gradually changed my perceptions and reactions to things. The alienation I often felt is gone. Much anger, guilt, anxiety, and illness are gone. I feel friendly to people, however different they are from me. I fit in.

Among other non-Protestant Evangelisms, there were those who did not particularly want to encourage people to "fit in" but rather worked to unsettle them so they would have to face some unpleasant reality. One such unsettling Evangelical force is Elie Wiesel, who has been called "the conscience of the Holocaust."

Modern Protestantism has nothing to compare with the single-minded zeal of Jewish Zionism after World War II in its determination to set up a permanent Jewish homeland in the modern State of Israel. It is one of the most momentous and memorable Evangelisms in the history of man: led by Theodore Herzl, the creation of Israel represents the realization of a five thousand year dream of the Jewish people to cease their dispersal and wanderings over the face of the globe and return to a nation of their own. Minuscule in land mass and harassed by Arabs and Palestinians since its founding, Israel nonetheless exists and would seem to be the fulfillment of all Zionist aspirations.

But this was not to be so, because Elie Wiesel insisted there was still the ongoing task of making the world aware of what had happened during the Holocaust. Born in 1928 in Hungary, Wiesel is the embodiment of the promise Jews made to themselves following the liberation of Auschwitz, Dachau, Buchenwald, Treblinka, and Bergen-Belsen— "Never again!" Elie Wiesel has divided his time between writing, researching, and trying to unearth documents and locating survivors of the concentration camps who may be able to testify to the enormity of the crimes that took place there. Through his own Evangelical work, Wiesel is determined to keep the memory of the Holocaust alive for future generations.

During this period, the Catholic Church also witnessed Evangelical movements. In the early part of the century one maverick Evangelist, Father Coughlin of Royal Oak, Michigan, began broadcasting seemingly innocent children's programs in 1926, but more and more his political views began to spill over into his parochial school lessons: he would break away from a prepared text to denounce "the money changers and subversive socialists" who were ruining the country, and during the 1930s Father Coughlin campaigned vigorously on "Roosevelt or Ruin" programs. Coughlin was clearly becoming a national political force with a growing audience, until his Bishop silenced him in 1937 for making flagrantly anti-Semitic and pro-Nazi comments on his programs.

Within the Catholic Church itself there was a major Evangelical movement during the pontificate of John XXIII, when Ecumenical decrees began to give rise to the idea of a "Charismatic Church" which stressed the joy of service to God and a more liberal view of Christian life, seeming to set aside centuries of repression by "opening the windows" on the real world. John XXIII must have looked like a godsend of freedom to a century which had already endured the moral compromise of Pius XII, who might have helped save Jews from the Holocaust if he had not felt himself entrapped in a Vatican that was surrounded by the Fascism of Mussolini.

Pope John XXIII reversed the direction of Church morale and gave new dignity to the role of women, children, and lay persons who wanted more joy in the teachings of Jesus. After John XXIII, the Church lapsed back to conservativism with John Paul II, who issued edicts strictly opposing contraception and stressing clerical celibacy and insisting on an all-male priesthood.

One Catholic Evangelist during this period was Thomas Merton, whose autobiographical *Seven Storey Mountain* told of his conversion in the 1940s while a student at Columbia University working with Mark Van Doren. Merton joined the Trappist Order at Gethsemane, Kentucky, where he took a vow of silence and kept on writing books that earned him a vast readership. *Seeds of Contemplation* was a quasi-mystical exploration of soul force which could be focused on a hypnotic Jesus. Merton experienced tension with his superiors, who never seemed to be quite sure just what to make of his astonishing popularity.

At the same time as Merton's conversion, the American poet Robert Lax also converted from Judaism to Catholicism and wrote the allegorical book-poem *The Circus of the Sun*, which was a celebration of the acrobatics of spiritual life. For many years Lax helped edit the Catholic magazine *Jubilee* before he left America to live on the island of Patmos, Greece, where John had written the Book of Revelation.

An important Evangelical organization on the fringes of Catholicism was The Catholic Worker, founded by Dorothy Day. An ardent Communist before she met the French socialist Peter Maurin, Dorothy Day devoted her life to feeding the poor and subverting the bureaucracy of the State. In the 1930s, the *Catholic Worker* newspaper was founded and sold for one penny on streetcorners; it featured woodcuts by Fritz Eichenberg and other fine graphic artists; it ran articles on War Resistance and social service, and during the Second World War it advocated pacifism. The Catholic Worker practiced civil disobedience against air raid drills and harbored deserters and conscientious objectors being sought by the authorities, and since 1945 the Catholic Worker has steadfastly resisted civil defense efforts to guard against nuclear war, on the grounds that readiness would only hasten its arrival.

Dorothy Day's radical attitude towards Church/State relations is based on Matthew Chapter 22:

21   Render unto Caesar the things which are Caesar's; and unto God the things that are God's.

Dorothy Day tersely commented on this verse: "If we rendered unto God the things that are God's, there'd be very little left over for Caesar."

One Catholic Worker member, Jeannette Noel, writing in Vol. LIII, No. 7 of the *Catholic Worker*, Oct.–Nov. 1986, gives this portrait of Dorothy Day:

> Dorothy, a prophet of our time, dared to challenge the Church at a time when pacifism was not spoken of. She encouraged draft resistance and spoke out strongly on the subject. She knew from history that peace could not be achieved by war. She saw the horrible effects war had on the human race: God's creation destroyed, the shattered lives of men and women, the suffering of innocent children. She grieved, especially, at the sufferings of Nagasaki and Hiroshima. It was puzzling to her that ordinary people would not think of throwing another person into a raging fire, yet we, as a nation, so easily threw down fire on so many, and their children. War not only destroys human life, but brings about the dehumanization of the destroyers. How is it possible to follow Jesus, Who told us to love our enemy, while proceeding to kill that same so-called enemy? Yes, Dorothy believed in the revolutionary pacifism of Jesus.

The most dramatic act of Roman Catholic Evangelism took place early in the Vietnam War. The trial of the Catonsville Nine, including the two Berrigan brothers, Philip and Daniel, both Catholic clergymen, made national headlines and alerted America to a groundswell of protest that was beginning to register against this undeclared war that was turning into a bloodbath of atrocities and statistics.

On May 17, 1968, the nine defendants carried 600 individual draft files in two wire baskets from local board 33 in Catonsville, Maryland, and set fire to them with homemade napalm in a vacant parking lot. It was clearly an act of premeditated civil disobedience—deliberate, planned, and even announced in advance. The protest proceeded in a peaceful and orderly manner, intended to end in the arrest of all the participants so they could stand trial and call attention to what was happening in the Vietnamese war. As Daniel Berrigan commented, "We went into court as we had gone into the draft center—wide awake, neither insane nor amnesiac." The defendants were already notorious: six months before the burning of the draft board files, Daniel Berrigan had traveled to Hanoi on a peace mission to repatriate three American prisoners of war.

The trial was held in Baltimore federal court October 5–9, 1968. Trial evidence established that there were only 378 draft files, but the Catonsville Nine had indeed done exactly what they were alleged to have done. From the court transcript, one defendant, David Durst, tells why he did it:

> Well I suppose my thinking is part of an ethic found in the New Testament. You could say Jesus too was guilty of assault and battery when he cast the money changers out of the temple and wasted their property and wealth. He was saying It is wrong to do what you are doing. And this is our point: We came to realize draft files are death's own cry. We have not been able to let sacred life and total death live together quietly within us. We have cried out on behalf of life. The government has chosen to see our cry as anarchy and arrogance. Perhaps real anarchy lies in the acts of those who loose this plague of war upon a proud people in face of great and burning doubt. This doubt cried to heaven. Our cry too goes out in the name of life. Men around the world hear, and take heart. We are one among them. We believe that today we are at a joyful beginning. We are together and we are not afraid.

Daniel Berrigan, a Jesuit priest, also gave his reasons for acting as he did:

> I began to understand one could not indefinitely obey the law while social conditions deteriorated, structures of compassion breaking down, neighborhoods slowly rotting, the poor despairing, unrest forever present in the land, especially among the young people who are our only hope, our only resource. My brother's action helped me realize from the beginning of our republic good men had said no, acted outside the law, when conditions so demanded. And if a man did this, time might vindicate him, show his act to be lawful, a gift to society, a gift to history, and to the community. A few men must have a long view, must leave history to itself, to interpret their lives, their repute. Someday these defendants may be summoned to the Rose Garden and decorated, but not today.

Predictably, a verdict of guilty was returned for all nine defendants on each of three counts: destruction of U.S. property, destruction of Selective Service Records, and interference with the Selective Service Act of 1967. But the Berrigans and the other defendants had made their point, and after Catonsville the awful truth about Vietnam began to emerge and grieve the nation's conscience.

If the Roman Catholic Church produced the Berrigan brothers to protest the war in Vietnam during this era, Protestantism produced William Sloane Coffin, who was equally effective as radical gadfly to the Body Politic.

While Chaplain at Yale University, William Sloane Coffin was a key defendant, along with Dr. Benjamin Spock, in one of the most celebrated political trials of the period which called attention to what was rapidly becoming a national protest against the Vietnam war. What the Berrigan brothers began at Catonsville, Spock and Coffin brought to worldwide awareness, making Americans painfully conscious of what their country was doing in Southeast Asia with napalm and defoliation chemicals and daily body counts published in the *New York Times*. The nation was indeed embarked on a policy of dehumanization, and the Spock-Coffin trial underscored this.

Following the Vietnam trial, Coffin was appointed in 1977 as pastor of New York's prestigious Riverside Church. John D. Rockefeller had originally helped found the church as a haven for liberal Protestantism, and for many years it had been guided by Harry Emerson Fosdick in a strong tradition of political activism.

But the Riverside congregation may not have been prepared for the radical activism that William Sloane Coffin introduced there. During his tenure, Coffin made a 1979 visit to Tehran to conduct Christmas services for the American hostages, and Coffin also agitated against the Carter administration for America to acknowledge its own "past sins" in Iran, in order to find "a route of reciprocal justice" that might secure the release of the hostages. Coffin vigorously denounced Jimmy Carter's call for economic sanctions against Iran, comparing this policy to Lyndon Johnson's bombing of North Vietnam. "We scream about the hostages, but few Americans heard the screams of tortured Iranians."

Coffin made no bones about the fact that he believed America was the leading force for evil on the face of the earth. Invoking the prophet Amos in the Old Testament, William Sloane Coffin told the Cadet Corps at West Point in 1981 that "America was on a macho binge in foreign policy, heading for disaster." And at a memorial service for Sandy Pollack, an American Communist killed in a plane crash outside Havana, Coffin commented: "Sandy may not have believed in God, but God certainly believed in Sandy." Coffin made the same kind of reverse eulogy of Marxist Nicaraguan President Daniel Ortega at a reception at Riverside Church: "Daniel Ortega may not love God, but God loves Daniel Ortega."

In 1987, William Sloane Coffin resigned as senior minister of Riverside Church, allegedly leaving it in dire financial straits and with a legacy of pro-Marxist causes which Coffin had espoused during his tenure there. Coffin was moving on to take over the Presidency of Sane-Freeze, a nuclear disarmament lobby which he had worked with as part of his Riverside Church program.

During this twentieth century, modern American Evangelists have run the gamut from the vituperative anti-alcoholism of Billy Sunday to the bouquet of open roses that Aimee Semple McPherson always held; from the homicidal madness of Jim Jones to the vicious hatred of homosexuals by Anita Bryant; from the impassioned atheism of Madalyn Murray O'Hair to the moral courage of the Berrigan brothers and William Sloane Coffin. And behind this dizzying array of native American Evangelists, there is the integrity of the higher Bible criticism of Albert Schweitzer, who had to leave his German homeland to live out a life of service in Africa.

The spectacle of twentieth century Evangelism may strike us as bewildering to behold, but it is no more bewildering than the century itself, which witnessed such dire calamities as the Great Depression, the Holocaust, the dropping of the atomic bomb on civilian populations, and the dehumanizing Vietnam war.

If Evangelism in any era is a reaction against the strong social and political circumstances which give rise to it, then modern American Evangelism is a reflection of our times: a conduit for the basest and also the most noble instincts of our bewildered civilization.

Chapter 8

BLACK EVANGELISTS

FROM THE EARLIEST DAYS of the African Slave Trade to the American colonies, Black Evangelism attempted to realize some semblance of social justice for an entire people that had suffered the trauma of dislocation from their ancestral and cultural roots.

One of the most eloquent forebears of Black Evangelism in America was Harriet Tubman (1825–1915), who typified the Runaway Slave who was willing to endure any indignity in order to secure freedom. With almost hallucinatory religious fervor, Harriet Tubman told her biographer, Sarah Bradford, how she felt after her first escape from slavery in 1845: "When I had crossed that line, I looked at my hands to see if I was the same person. There was such a glory over everything."

During the American Civil War, and with a full awareness of its military significance, Abraham Lincoln issued the Emancipation Proclamation on January 1, 1863, which proclaimed that all slaves within any state then in rebellion against the United States "shall be then, thenceforward, and forever free." Lincoln fully intended to restore equity for all parties who had lost so much through the terrible and divisive Civil War. He said in his Second Inaugural Address:

> With malice toward none; with charity for all; with firmness in the right, as God gives us to see the right, let us strive to finish the work we are in; to bind up the nation's wounds; to care for him who shall have borne the battle; and for his widow, and his orphan; to do all which may achieve and cherish a just and lasting peace among ourselves, and with all nations.

Shortly after Lincoln's Second Inauguration, Grant accepted Lee's surrender at Appomattox Court House, but only a few days later, Lincoln himself was assassinated. The difficult era of Reconstruction was deprived of Lincoln's magnanimity, and the American Negro began a long and arduous struggle towards individual freedom and self-esteem: in the South, under the resentful eyes of the defeated Confederacy, and in the North, in the bewildering industrial cities.

By the beginning of the twentieth century, Black Evangelism had taken its separate road from mainstream Protestant Evangelism. Black Evangelists were concerned with one thing: how to interpret and portray what it was to be a Black in America, and how to counsel Blacks in the best way to adapt to a complex and often hostile environment.

Father Divine (1882–1965) may be one of the best known but least representative of modern Black Evangelists. Born as George Baker near the Savannah River, Father Divine traveled north to Baltimore and apprenticed himself to Samuel Morris, preacher at Baptist Church Colored. He went south again to Valdosta, Georgia, where he began to preach but was arrested and put on trial as a public nuisance and told to leave the state. He traveled north again, this time to Myrtle Avenue in Brooklyn, and here his preaching began to achieve notoriety. It was only a short trip over to Harlem, where Father Divine's church began to attract hundreds of followers.

Father Divine's preaching was flamboyant and theatrical: he would appear full blown in a huge puff of smoke that came billowing out of the pulpit of his Harlem church, and he would proclaim that he was God Himself who "repersonificates and repersonifitizes." Father Divine elaborated on this: "God is your father, your mother, your sister, and your brother, and you never had another."

Father Divine's attitude towards sex may have influenced Jim Jones in his practices at Jonestown in Guyana: Father Divine forbade members of his congregation to have sex with each other, even husbands and wives—although that did not preclude Father Divine from having sex with his own harem of chosen "Rosebuds," some of them the wives of congregation members. Father Divine also forbade congregation members to smoke or drink, and he ignored taboos against racial intermarriage and eventually married a white woman.

In 1919, Father Divine moved his congregation out to Sayville, Long Island, and in 1928 he counted 90 disciples in his church. During the Depression he set up soup kitchens for the unemployed, and was active in organizing the Peace Mission Movement ("Peace, it's wonderful!" was his way of putting it). In 1931 Father Divine was arrested in Sayville for creating a public nuisance and he was sentenced to serve six months in jail and to pay a $500 fine; four days later the sentencing judge suffered a heart attack and died, and Father Divine commented: "I sure hated to do that."

For all the off-beat humor of this account, one senses that Father Divine was a caricature, a white man's version of a stereotypical Black Preacher: shiftless, sex-mad, and delusional. It fits too neatly into the racist's prototype that Blacks are buffoons who confuse religion with voodoo and mass hysteria. But that's why Father Divine is interesting to us, because he is not the last Black Evangelist to be so pigeonholed into certain preconceived "Uncle Tom" images.

Frederick J. Eikenkroetter II, better known as "Reverend Ike," was founder of the United Church and preached that lack of money was the root of all evil. Such an innocent, simplistic message was sure to be popular, and Reverend Ike had a slick way of putting this easy theology into even easier words: "Why worship in some storefront church waiting to die so you can have that pie in the sky by and by? Get yours now, with ice cream on top!"

Congressman Adam Clayton Powell alternated duties in Washington, D.C., where he initiated important Civil Rights legislation, with a charismatic pastorate at the Abyssinian Baptist Church, where he preached African heritage and a gospel Christianity. Powell was such a formidable preacher and politican that his foes had to resort to scandal to undermine him: his first wife brought adultery charges against him which were trumpeted in the white press, and numerous rumors of Powell's flirtations with white women were fanned by the F.B.I.

K. C. Price, a more sophisticated Black pastor of a church in Los Angeles, conducts television sermons on Channel Eleven on Sunday mornings from 8:00–9:00 A.M. Price is urbane and has an instinctive sense of timing, preaching directly out of an open Bible that he holds in his hand. Yet for all his brilliance, he preaches a status quo Christianity that does not rock anyone's boat and so is deemed safe enough for network media coverage.

Behind all these stereotyped Black pastors, there was a more earnest and sober Black Evangelism working its way out in America, an Evangelism which had a deeper truth and a more revolutionary message than would gain acceptance on network television. The chief architect of this underground Black Liberation movement was a man named Marcus Aurelius Garvey (1887–1940) with his "Back to Africa" crusade of the 1920s.

Marcus Garvey was born in Jamaica and had come to America in

1916, when he began to urge the return of Negroes to their ancestral homeland in Africa. In a 1920 speech on "The Principles of the United Negro Improvement Association," Garvey spelled out what he was really after: "We are not engaged in domestic politics, in church building or in social uplift work, but we are engaged in nation building."

Garvey himself was attractive and articulate, and the "nation building" he had in mind was the founding of a modern Liberia. No wonder white America saw Marcus Garvey as a dangerous presence, and by all accounts Garvey was framed by the federal government because J. Edgar Hoover wanted him out of the way. Garvey was sent to prison, and when he got out there was a marked change in his views: he had become more conservative, he worked to support Calvin Coolidge, and he met with Ku Klux Klan members during the Bilbo era to try to keep racial issues from erupting into open violence.

But no one forgot that Marcus Garvey was an inflammatory personality, and his idea of establishing a modern African state for dispossessed American Negroes was disquieting to white Officialdom. Garvey was eventually deported to Jamaica in 1928, and most of his followers transferred their loyalties to Father Divine.

During this period one of the strongest voices in America was a great original talent of our theater and concert stage. Paul Robeson (1898–1976) had been named to the All-American football team from Rutgers University, graduated Phi Beta Kappa, and won a Rhodes Scholarship to Oxford University.

Returning to earn his law degree, Paul Robeson began one of the most phenomenal dramatic careers in American theatre. He starred in Eugene O'Neill's expressionist drama *The Emperor Jones* (1920), which explored through tom-toms and jungle foliage how power reverts back on itself. Robeson made the 1936 film version of Jerome Kern's 1927 stage classic *Show Boat*, singing with his magnificent baritone the masterpiece song which embodied the misery of all slaves everywhere, *"Ol' Man River."* And Robeson starred in Margaret Webster's 1943 Broadway version of Shakespeare's *Othello* with Uta Hagen as Desdemona and Jose Ferrer as Iago: the opening night of this production was so charged that one participant commented, "If a cat had walked across the footlights, it would have been electrocuted."

For all his stature as one of the great singers and actors of his time, Paul Robeson had been naive enough to think he could change the backlog of centuries of racist attitudes during his lifetime. The trouble began when Robeson accepted an invitation to travel and perform in the Soviet Union, where he was shown how Black people lived an idyllic life in a utopian Marxist state. The cruel truth was that while Paul Robeson was being given an idealized view of racial harmony, Josef Stalin was wiping out whole ethnic groups through genocide and mass starvation elsewhere in Russia. Nonetheless, Robeson was so transfixed by the status he saw accorded to Black people in Russia, he arranged for his son, Paul Robeson, Jr., to be educated in the Soviet Union between the ages of eight and twelve.

But when Robeson returned to America, he fell into a number of political entrapment situations, including a series of anti-Communist demonstrations in Peekskill, New York. Robeson was called to testify before the House Un-American Activities Committee, and when he indicated he was unwilling to sign an anti-Communist affidavit, the State Department revoked his passport. Robeson predicted at the HUAC hearings that the passport would have to be returned to him as a United States citizen, as indeed it was when the Supreme Court ruled against the State Department's action.

Even so, Robeson found himself seriously frustrated in his acting and concert career, and several of his documentaries and concert pieces including "The House I Live In" were cited as examples of his affiliation with the Stalinist left. Paul Robeson died in 1976 after a ten year illness during which time he lived with his sister in Philadelphia —a broken man whose career as artist and Evangelical spokesperson for Black people everywhere had been seriously curtailed by reactionary forces who tried to ostracize him for his views.

An even more potent force for Black Evangelism during this period was an obscure man named Elijah Muhammad, who was born Elijah Poole. He had no formal schooling past the fourth grade, and he arrived in Detroit at the age of twenty-five in 1923, where he came under the influence of W. D. Fard. Fard taught a strange blend of the Quran (Islamic Koran) and the Bible, and he had arrived at his own amalgam of Christianity and Islam. Fard taught that God's real name is Allah and that his true religion is Islam, and the appropriate name for followers of that religion is Muslims.

As an alternative religion for Blacks who felt they had been betrayed by the Judeo-Christian tradition, this new view of God as Allah had tremendous appeal, especially as it united them with one-fifth of the world's population who were already Muslim. In addition to changing God's name to Allah, Muslims taught that American Blacks should also change their own "slave" names to more appropriate Muslim names which would be given to them by their religious teachers.

In 1931 Fard founded the University of Islam in Detroit, and three years later he disappeared without a trace and was never heard from again. Elijah Muhammad took up Fard's work, but in 1942 Muhammad himself was arrested and charged with draft dodging and sentenced to five years in prison. He served three and a half years in the federal penitentiary in Milan, Michigan.

Thus at the outset of the Black Muslim Movement, Elijah Muhammad had already arrived at a fusion of Christianity with Islam, and he had also experienced what it was like to serve time in an American prison. Both these events would become crucially important for the future of the Black Muslim Movement. The next important step would be the meeting of Elijah Muhammad and Malcolm X.

Malcolm Little's father, the Reverend Earl Little, was a Baptist minister and organizer for Marcus Garvey, and Malcolm's earliest memory is how his father used to exhort his congregation to get ready to return to Africa, with phrases like "Adam driven out of the garden into the caves of Europe" and "Africa for Africans" and "Ethiopians Awake!" and "Up you mighty race, you can accomplish what you will!" But others on the outside heard these phrases also, and soon there were violent reprisals: the Reverend Earl Little was killed in Lansing, Michigan. His skull was crushed and he was laid across some tracks so a streetcar would run over him; his body was almost cut in half. As Malcolm writes in *The Autobiography of Malcolm X*: "Hence I have no mercy or compassion in me for a society that will crush people, and then penalize them for not being able to stand up under the weight."

It was not long before young Malcolm himself got into trouble, was arrested, and sentenced to ten years in February 1946—he was not quite twenty-one: "I had not even started shaving." While Malcolm was in Concord Prison, he began reading as many books as he could get his hands on, and he also began to formulate his own view of history:

> Human history's greatest crime was the traffic in black flesh when the devil white man went into Africa and murdered and kidnapped to bring to the West in chains, in slave ships, millions of black men, women, and children, who were worked and beaten and tortured as slaves . . .

> The devil white man cut these black people off from all knowledge of their own kind, and cut them off from any knowledge of their own language, religion, and past culture, until the black man in America

was the earth's only race of people who had absolutely no knowledge
of his true identity . . .

It's a crime, the lie that has been told to generations of black men and
white men both. Little innocent black children, born of parents who
believed that their race had no history. Little black children seeing,
before they could talk, that their parents considered themselves inferior.
Innocent black children growing up, living out their lives, dying of old
age—and all of their lives ashamed of being black. But the truth is
pouring out of the bag now.

The truth was indeed pouring out of the bag, but if Malcolm had
poured a little more he would have found things were not all that
clear-cut. One of the terrible ironies of this Black Muslim Movement
is that the original Muslims were probably the worst offenders in the
African slave trade, and slave trading in Arabia was still being carried
on right up to the twentieth century. And in the Middle East, Muslim
Fundamentalists make American Evangelists look innocuous enough.
Muslim Fundamentalism imposes a fanatical Puritanism on its people
that is as brutal as it is irrational: women are given public lashings for
wearing lipstick; men are stopped on public roads and given breath
tests to see if they have been drinking; children at school are encouraged
to tell incriminating things they overhear at home. In Ayatollah Khom-
eini's Muslim Theocracy, any Iranian can be shot on sight for no
reason at all. And unlike American Evangelists who have to beg their
TV audiences to send in free will gift offerings to keep them on the
tube, the Ayatollah has complete ownership and control of all radio
and television stations, and he also has an armed militia which is ready
to do his bidding and die at a moment's notice.

Malcolm X may not have known the historical facts about Muslim
Fundamentalism but he should have: Malcolm's single-minded blam-
ing of the "devil white man" and Christianity for all the crimes of the
world does not hold up under objective scrutiny. Malcolm X is correct
as far as he goes in his analysis of the African slave trade, but the fact
is that at this particular time in his life, he simply did not go far enough
in his thinking.

It was about this time, while Malcolm was still serving time in
prison and reading the history of the Slave Trade, that his brother
Philbert began writing to him that he had discovered "the natural
religion of the black man." Philbert belonged now, he said, to some-

thing called "the Nation of Islam" and he said Malcolm should "pray to Allah for deliverance." Others began urging Malcolm to "accept the teachings of The Honorable Elijah Muhammad," so Malcolm wrote to this religious leader in Chicago. Elijah Muhammad sent back an immediate reply, and he enclosed five dollars with his letter.

Malcolm was beginning to gain confidence in his new world-view. During a prison Bible class taught by a visiting Harvard Seminary student, Malcolm listened to the explication of Christian theology and finally he raised his hand and asked the teacher what color St. Paul was. Malcolm did not give the teacher a chance to reply, but went right on to answer his own question: "He had to be black . . . because he was a Hebrew . . . and the original Hebrews were black . . . weren't they?"

Malcolm reports the young Seminary student flushed bright red, but he had the courage to answer "yes." Malcolm went on to ask the teacher what color Jesus was. There was a pause, and the teacher made a compromise answer: "brown." After this interchange, Malcolm knew he was on the right track with his thinking.

When he was released from prison, Malcolm went to Detroit and lived with a Muslim family:

> I had never dreamed of anything like that atmosphere among black people who had learned to be proud they were black, who had learned to love other black people instead of being jealous and suspicious. I thrilled to how we Muslim men used both hands to grasp a black brother's both hands, voicing and smiling out happiness to meet him again. The Muslim sisters, both married and single, were given an honor and respect that I'd never seen black men give to their women, and it felt wonderful to me. The salutations which we all exchanged were warm, filled with mutual respect and dignity: "Brother" . . . "Sister" . . . "Ma'am" . . . "Sir." Even children speaking to other children used these terms. Beautiful!

It was at this time that Malcolm Little received his Muslim name of "Malcolm X"—the "X" standing for his true African name which he could never know. And at this time also, Malcolm X began to develop his own Black Evangelist position: it was the same basic distrust of the white man's Uncle Tom Christian religion which Reverend Ike had characterized as "pie in the sky by and by." But Malcolm X brought such lethal heat to the argument, the end result was fiercely anti-white and anti-Christian:

My brothers and sisters, our white slavemaster's Christian religion has taught us black people here in the wilderness of North America that we will sprout wings when we die and fly up into the sky where God will have for us a special place called heaven. This is white man's Christian religion used to *brainwash* us black people! We have *accepted* it! We have *embraced* it! We have *practiced* it! And while we are doing all of that, for himself, this blue-eyed devil has *twisted* his Christianity, to keep his *foot* in our backs . . . to keep our eyes fixed on the pie in the sky and heaven in the hereafter . . . while *he* enjoys *his* heaven right *here* . . . on *this* earth . . . in *this* life . . .

Christianity is the white man's religion. The Holy Bible in the white man's hands and his interpretations of it have been the greatest single ideological weapon for enslaving millions of non-white human beings. Every country the white man has conquered with his guns, he has always paved the way, and salved his conscience, by carrying the Bible and interpreting it to call the people "heathens" and "pagans"; then he sends his guns, then his missionaries behind the guns to mop up . . .

Like his father's espousal of the "Back to Africa" movement of Marcus Garvey, Malcolm X was developing a radical separatism which would set him apart from other Black leaders like Martin Luther King, Jr., who were working towards integration during this period. For Malcolm X, there could be no integration with the devil white man:

The Honorable Elijah Muhammad teaches us that since Western society is deteriorating, it has become overrun with immorality, and God is going to judge it, and destroy it. And the only way the black people caught up in this society can be saved is not to *integrate* into this corrupt society, but to *separate* from it, to a land of our *own*, where we can reform ourselves, lift up our moral standards, and try to be godly.

Events in the 1960s began to move rapidly and with bewildering violence in America: a high-powered rifle killed Medgar Evers, Field Secretary for the NAACP, in Mississippi; a bomb exploded in a Negro Christian Church in Birmingham, Alabama, killing four Black girls. At the same time, there was the awful corrosion of rumor and scandal: on July 3, a UPI dispatch reported that Elijah Muhammad, 67-year-old leader of the Black Muslim Movement, faced paternity suits brought by two former secretaries who charged that he had fathered their four children.

But that same year of 1963 saw one of the biggest publicity coups for the Black Muslim Movement, when World Heavyweight Boxing Champion Cassius Clay held a press conference and proclaimed he was a Black Muslim and changed his name: henceforward he would be referred to as Muhammad Ali. The effect was electrifying, and it was enough to make sportscaster Howard Cosell wince with incomprehension.

Over the next two years a mysterious thing began to happen: Malcolm X started to rethink his position of absolute separatism from the white man, and that led him to start questioning some of the teachings of Elijah Muhammad and the orthodox Black Muslim doctrine. This led to divisiveness within the movement, and a tension that was beginning to split Black Muslims between Elijah Muhammad and Malcolm X. There is no telling what would have happened if Malcolm X had been allowed to develop his new thought, and whether it would have made possible an alliance between Malcolm X and Martin Luther King, Jr., in the Civil Rights Movement that was to come.

But events would prove otherwise. In 1965, at the Audubon Ballroom in New York, between Broadway and St. Nicholas Avenue at West 166 Street, Malcolm X was giving a speech that raised serious questions about Black Muslim teaching. Suddenly there was a fracas in the rear of the auditorium. One eyewitness reports: "The commotion back there diverted me just for an instant, then I turned back to look at Malcolm X just in time to see at least three men in the front row stand and take aim and start firing simultaneously. It looked like a firing squad."

The hit men had used a sawed-off shotgun and two revolvers. Malcolm X was dead on arrival at the hospital. Police and Muslim leaders—particularly Louis Farrakhan, Muslim financial adviser— launched extensive investigations into the murder, and all indications point to internal dissension within the Muslim Movement which precipitated Malcolm X's assassination.

News of Malcolm X's death stunned the world. Dion Pincus, a teacher at New York University and a writer, comments:

> Malcolm was a true heroic force. It is always much easier to love King, and even though Malcolm was beginning to move away from Black racist-supremacy philosophy of separatism towards the end, and even though he began to lean more toward tolerant acknowledgement of King's integration approach, even so, Malcolm was like Thoreau in later days, demanding not so much the abolition of all standing order

but a better order, now. King was more Emersonian, but Malcolm seemed (to me at least) to emulate what Thoreau was about: correct and hard-nosed until his last years, when he began to mellow a little but lost not one whit of his ideals, merely gained hindsight and perspective.

Eldridge Cleaver learned of Malcolm X's murder while he was serving time at California's Folsom Prison, and as he wrote in *Soul On Ice*:

> If a man as valuable to us as Malcolm could go down, then as far as I was concerned so could any other man—myself included. Coming a week after the alleged exposé of the alleged plot to dynamite the Statue of Liberty, Washington Monument, and the Liberty Bell, a plot supposedly hatched by discontented blacks, the assassination of Malcolm X had put new ideas in the wind with implications for the future of black struggle in America.

Eldridge Cleaver went on to give the best summary of why Malcolm X spoke so powerfully to American Blacks who had suffered what he had been through in his own life:

> Malcolm X had a special meaning for black convicts. A former prisoner himself, he had risen from the lowest depths to great heights. For this reason he was a symbol of hope, a model for thousands of black convicts who found themselves trapped in the PPP cycle: prison/parole/prison.

When Eldridge Cleaver was released from prison, he became Minister of Information for the newly formed Black Panther Party, a more militant political movement. Cleaver went on to run as a candidate for President of the United States on the Peace and Freedom Party ticket, and while his candidacy was a predictable failure, it nonetheless gave Cleaver the opportunity to take his Evangelical message to the American people:

> The world capitalist system has come to a decisive fork in the road, and this is at the heart of our national crisis. The road to the left is the way of reconciliation with the exploited people of the world, the liberation of all peoples, the dismantling of all economic relations based upon the exploitation of man by man, universal disarmament, and the es-

tablishment of international rule of law with effective means of enforcement. The road to the right is refusal to submit to the universal demand for national liberation, economic justice, peace, and popular sovereignity. To walk this last path, the decision-makers must be prepared to unleash worldwide genocide, including the extermination of America's Negroes.

Cleaver was especially scathing on the subject of American Blacks being drafted to fight in the Vietnam war: "Black Americans are considered to be the world's biggest fools to go to another country to fight for something they don't have for themselves."

Black Evangelism was now deeply committed to political and social reform, but most particularly to raising Black consciousness about itself. Certain media spokesmen like Gil Noble of ABC television's *Like It Is* program were able to host a series of ongoing forums for Black leaders to speak their minds to a nationwide audience.

The Black Muslim Movement remained a very real force in America: H. Rap Brown worked with Stokeley Carmichael during the 1960s Civil Rights Movement but then went on to become a Black Muslim pastor. And continuing with the legacy of Martin Luther King, Jr., both Andrew Young and Jesse Jackson went their separate ways as spokesmen for the Black experience.

The American poet LeRoi Jones, author of the brilliant play *Dutchman* and numerous volumes of poetry including *Notes of a Dead Lecturer*, and one of the founders of the Congress of Afrikan People, explained his position in a 1979 Craft Interview with The *New York Quarterly* magazine:

> The first thing I tell them is, it's all political. I begin by letting them see how in art and writing, the first thing you look for is the stance. For example, what side is the person on? For instance, I couldn't see anyone being on the side of the majority of the people in this country, who could write poems in favor of capitalism or racism or women's oppression.

As for Leroi Jones's own name change to Amiri Baraka, the poet explains:

> I was given the name Ameer Baraka, which is an Arab name, by this Muslim Imam, who buried Malcolm X. I changed the name, swahilized it, when I became an Afrikan nationalist, to Amiri Baraka . . .

My own name change was meant to change my own self-perception, and the way others perceive me, Afrikan consciousness, Black consciousness, where we wanted to get rid of the American names, the slave names, and take on an identity which was in tune with African liberation. And while I certainly didn't feel that changing a name is going to bring revolution, I see no reason to drop it, as a lot of people might perceive that as trying to liquidate the whole revolutionary nationalist struggle that we went through in the 1960s.

Of course most of the Black Evangelist positions that are described in this chapter were evolving simultaneously with the Civil Rights Movement of the 1960s led by Martin Luther King, Jr., which will be dealt with in the following chapter. The sheer multiplicity of Black Evangelists during this period shows the tremendous depth and complexity of the Black Liberation movement that was taking place in the middle of twentieth century America.

Chapter 9

MARTIN LUTHER KING, JR.

MORE THAN ANY OTHER Evangelist in our time, Martin Luther King, Jr. had a solid grounding in theology and philosophical thought behind his quest for truth and social justice. This being so, it is important to document some of this crucial thought that went into shaping this modern American Evangelist, before we look at King's own life and work.

The first major influence on Martin Luther King, Jr. was a nineteenth century American and close associate of Ralph Waldo Emerson —Henry David Thoreau (1817–1872), whose "Civil Disobedience" (1849) states that man has a moral obligation to stand up against the State when there are any unjust laws. Thoreau thus set the stage for most of the important social protest movements of the twentieth century.

In fact, Thoreau's "Civil Disobedience" had a very curious history of its own, and its impact was felt all around the rest of the world before it had a significant effect here in America.

Leo Tolstoy read "Civil Disobedience" in Russia and knew that this essay validated his desire to free the peasants on his own land, and it also encouraged him to agitate for the freedom of other serfs who were eking out their wretched lives all across Czarist Russia.

Picking up on a reference to Thoreau in the works of Tolstoy, Mahatma Gandhi read "Civil Disobedience" in South Africa and commented: "It left a deep impression upon me," and he carried Thoreau's ideas back to India where he used them to confront the unjust laws of the British government there.

And finally, Martin Luther King, Jr. learned of the principle of Civil Disobedience by studying the life and work of Gandhi.

So King got it from Gandhi and Gandhi got it from Tolstoy and Tolstoy got it from Thoreau. And this brief essay "Civil Disobedience" had a worldwide effect that was almost as revolutionary as the full-length books of Darwin, Marx, Einstein, or Freud. The reason for the immediacy and relevance of this small work is that it was in the realm of moral thought, which gave it an authority and power that more complex works in other fields could not have achieved so easily.

In "Civil Disobedience," Thoreau states what should be obvious to everyone, that real government begins with the individual: "Let every man make known what kind of government would command his respect, and that will be one step toward obtaining it." He draws an important distinction between conscience and legislation: "I think that we should be men first, and subjects afterward. It is not desirable to cultivate a respect for the law, so much as for the right." He then looks at his own American government and he does not like what he sees:

> How does it become a man to behave toward this American government today? I answer, that he cannot without disgrace be associated with it. I cannot for an instant recognize that political organization as *my* government which is the *slave's* government also.

He goes on to define what he means by political virtue in a democracy: ". . . any man more right than his neighbors constitutes a majority of one already."

Thoreau is well aware of the consequences of this definition, and he warns the virtuous person that he must be willing to pay the price for his virtue. Thoreau himself paid the price: he sat in Concord jail rather than pay a poll tax to support a government that was abetting the Mexican War and slavery. Thoreau recommends such a course of action to others also: "Under a government which imprisons any unjustly, the true place for a just man is also a prison." But the alternative to this political virtue is too ghastly to contemplate: "Is there not a sort of blood shed when the conscience is wounded? Through this wound a man's real manhood and immortality flow out, and he bleeds to an everlasting death. I see this blood flowing now."

The thrust of Thoreau's argument, then, is a hardheaded assertion of moral principle: it is an appeal to the conscience and conviction of any individual who has the strength of his principles to stand firm and not yield to the forces of complacency and compromise.

Some thirty-five years later and halfway around the world, Leo Tolstoy was writing *My Confession*, a record of the great Russian author's religious conversion. After having written *War and Peace* and *Anna Karenina*, the fifty year old Tolstoy suddenly felt life was meaningless, and he was flooded with perplexity and questioning: Why? What next? In 1886, he turned these questions into book form: *What Then Must We Do?*

By this time Tolstoy had read Thoreau's "Civil Disobedience," and he freed the serfs on his inherited land and began urging reform of feudal practices in the rest of Russia. Tolstoy then went on to summarize the principles he wanted to live by: non-resistance to evil, abolition of State and Church, and renunciation of private property.

This was no purely ethical crusade that Tolstoy was embarked on: all of the radical social and political convictions that he felt called upon to advocate went hand in hand with his increasing belief in the reality of God.

Probably no Evangelical figure of modern times more completely embodies the power of moral passion than Mahatma Gandhi—a simple man who went naked except for a white dhoti tied around his loins, cheap wire frame spectacles, walking stick, and sandals made from the hide of a cow that had died a natural death.

In his autobiography *The Story of My Experiments with Truth*, Gandhi states that religion invariably has to be allied with some form of social action:

> To see the universal and all-pervading Spirit of Truth face to face one must be able to love the meanest of creation as oneself. And a man who aspires after that cannot afford to keep out of any field of life. That is why my devotion to Truth has drawn me into the field of politics; and I can say without the slightest hesitation, and yet in all humility, that those who say that religion has nothing to do with politics do not know what religion means.

Trained as a lawyer in England, Gandhi found a job in South Africa, and in 1893 he was traveling first class on a train to Pretoria in the Transvaal when a European passenger ordered him from the compartment and told him he must travel in a van reserved for colored at the rear of the train. Gandhi told a train official that he had a first class ticket and refused to move, so the official called a constable who removed Gandhi.

The next day Gandhi tried to take a second train, but had to change to a stage coach where the conductor ordered Gandhi to sit on the footboard. Gandhi refused, and another man began hitting Gandhi and the conductor cursed at him all the way to Pretoria. As soon as Gandhi arrived there, he called a meeting of all the Indians living in Pretoria to discuss their encounters with racial discrimination.

It was about this time that Gandhi read Thoreau's "Civil Disobedience" and Tolstoy's *The Kingdom of God Is Within You,* which stated that all government is based on war and violence and one could only counter these evils through non-violent resistance. Gandhi now organized more than two thousand followers on the grounds of Hamidia Mosque in Johannesburg where they burned their registration certificates as a public symbolic action. When Gandhi was sentenced to two months in jail, he decided to fill all the jails in the Union with Indians to dramatize the immorality of anti-Indian laws.

Finally Gandhi organized about six thousand men to march to Charlestown, across the Natal border. In June of 1914, Gandhi was able to meet with Jan Christian Smuts and to negotiate with him in March 1919, but the British retaliated by passing the Rowlatt Act which called for press censorship and summary justice for agitators. Gandhi responded by calling for a general strike and non-cooperation of all Indians in South Africa.

When Gandhi returned to his native India in 1921, he began a ten year tour of the country to advise workers and recruit followers to engage the entire country in massive civil disobedience against the Salt Tax in 1930. He also began the non-violent Salt March, walking each day about twelve miles, then doing one hour's spinning, then writing in his diary.

One can get some sense of the discipline Gandhi instilled in his followers from this May 5, 1930 news report:

> Suddenly at a word of command, scores of native policemen rushed upon the advancing marchers and rained blows on their heads with their steel-shod lathis. Not one of the marchers even raised an arm to fend off the blows. They went down like ten-pins. From where I stood I heard the sickening whack of the clubs on unprotected skulls. The waiting crowd of marchers groaned and sucked in their breath in sympathetic pain at every blow . . .

They marched steadily, with heads up, without the encouragement of music or cheering or any possibility that they might escape serious injury or death. The police rushed out and methodically and mechanically beat down the second column. There was no fight, no struggle; the marchers simply walked forward till struck down.

In 1937, the British finally yielded and offered a new constitution for India granting self-rule in stages, beginning with transfer of powers to the provincial governments. But in 1942, Gandhi launched another massive disobedience campaign and demanded that the British quit India right away.

Gandhi's moral conviction could be expressed in a single statement: for him, the Truth was God. As he said, "There is an indefinable mysterious power which pervades everything. I feel it, though I do not see it." For Gandhi, faith and action were inextricably linked: "What message can I send through the pen if I am not sending any through the life I am living?"

As with Tolstoy, Gandhi's social and political convictions went hand in hand with an ever-increasing belief in the reality of God: "God's voice has been increasingly audible as the years have rolled by." And Gandhi insisted that God's nature can be nothing other than love: "If love is not the law of our being, the whole of my argument falls to pieces."

Gandhi reiterated his conviction that the idea of social justice has to reflect the justice of God:

> I am a man of peace. I believe in peace. But I do not want peace at any price. I do not want the peace that you find in a stone. I do not want the peace that you find in the grave. But I do want that peace which you find embedded in the human breast, which is exposed to the whole world but which is protected from all harm by the power of almighty God.

Gandhi was successful in his efforts to win self-rule for India, but he did not live to see the fruits of his country's independence. Gandhi was assassinated in New Delhi on January 30, 1948.

The extraordinary success of Gandhi in achieving justice and freedom in South Africa and India were a harbinger for the life and work of Martin Luther King, Jr. However, King was not going to be facing adversaries who were foreign and Imperial colonizing powers, but his own white countrymen who paid lip service to the same Constitution and the same Christianity that King himself lived by and believed in. In this sense, King's challenge of integration in America may have been an even greater contest than Gandhi's, and his success would be an even greater victory.

Martin Luther King, Jr. was converted at the age of five in his father's Ebenezer Baptist Church, and in 1947 King himself was ordained and made assistant pastor at the same church. He graduated in 1948 from Morehouse and went on to Crozier Seminary in Pennsylvania.

While he was at these two schools, King studied the works of Thoreau, Tolstoy, and Gandhi. He also attended a lecture by Mordecai Johnson, President of Howard University, on the life and teaching of Gandhi and Tolstoy's idea of noncooperation with evil. He also attended a lecture on pacifism by A. J. Muste of the Fellowship of Reconciliation. And during this period, the work of Reinhold Niebuhr also influenced King with his insistence that Protestant liberals overestimated the role of reason and underplayed the need for faith: Niebuhr believed that evil was "stark, grim, and colossally real."

Thus at the outset of his Evangelical ministry, King had thoroughly assimilated the principles of Civil Disobedience and non-resistance to evil as they are embodied in the works of Thoreau and Tolstoy and Gandhi; he was also deeply impressed with the traditional Baptist practice of his own father; and he was influenced by the pacifism of Muste and Niebuhr's assertion of a faith-oriented theology.

Martin Luther King, Jr. was ready now to embark on his life mission, and circumstances were already conspiring to involve all America in its ordeal.

In 1954, the United States Supreme Court handed down their decision in *Brown v. Board of Education of Topeka*, outlawing segregation in schools across America, and almost immediately there was a massive outpouring of hatred on the part of Southern whites who may have sensed that the days of segregation were coming to an end. KKK crosses were burned on lawns and Klan terrorists made savage raids against Blacks. One youth, Emmett Till, a fourteen-year-old Black from Chicago, visiting relatives in Greenwood, Mississippi, was dragged from his house by three white men who threw him in the Tallahatchie River with a seventy-pound gin fan tied to his neck with barbed wire.

The political test came one year later, in 1955 in Montgomery,

Alabama, when a Black cleaning woman, Mrs. Rosa Parks, refused to stand on a bus when a white wanted her seat. She was arrested and charged with violating the city segregation code. Martin Luther King, Jr. went to Montgomery and helped organize the Blacks there in a boycott of the bus lines, and on Monday, December 5, the Blacks began walking to work and riding in car pools.

In a sermon at that time, King said: "We are here this evening to say to those who have mistreated us so long that we are tired—tired of being segregated and humiliated; tired of being kicked about by the brutal feet of oppression." But King insisted to the Blacks that their resistance would have to be non-violent, and he quoted Gandhi: "Rivers of blood may have to flow before we gain our freedom, but it must be our blood."

During this Montgomery bus boycott, King began to experience the entrenced apathy of American society, especially among his fellow clergy. He said, "Expecting the support of white ministers was the most pervasive mistake I have ever made."

At this time, King began receiving thirty to forty hate letters a day, and sometimes as many as twenty-five obscene phone calls a day. But he remained adamant in his insistence on non-violence: "If one day you find me sprawled out dead, I do not want you to retaliate with a single act of violence. I urge you to continue protesting with the same dignity and discipline you have shown so far."

King's personal situation reached a crisis one evening when he received a threatening phone call. He tells it in his own words:

> After a particularly strenuous day, I settled in bed at a late hour. My wife had already fallen asleep and I was about to doze off when the telephone rang. An angry voice said, "Listen, nigger. We've taken all we want from you. Before next week you'll be sorry you ever came to Montgomery." I hung up, but I could not sleep. It seemed that all of my fears had come down on me at once. I had reached the saturation point.
>
> I got out of bed and began to walk the floor. Finally I went to the kitchen and heated a pot of coffee. I was ready to give up. I tried to think of a way to move out of the picture without appearing to be a coward. In this state of exhaustion, when my courage was almost gone, I determined to take my problem to God. My head in my hands, I bowed over the kitchen table and prayed aloud. The words I spoke to God that midnight are still vivid in my memory. "I am here taking a

stand for what I believe is right. But now I'm afraid. The people are looking to me for leadership, and if I stand before them without strength and courage, they too will falter. I am at the end of my powers. I have nothing left. I've come to the point where I can't face it alone."

At that moment, I experienced the presence of the Divine as I had never before experienced Him. It seemed as though I could hear the assurance of an inner voice, saying, "stand up for righteousness, stand up for truth. God will be at your side forever." Almost at once, my fears began to pass from me. My uncertainty disappeared. I was ready to face anything. The outer situation remained the same, but God had given me inner calm.

Three nights later, our home was bombed. Strangely enough, I accepted the word of the bombing calmly. My experience with God had given me a new strength and trust. I know now that God is able to give us the interior resources to face the storms and problems of life.

On February 21, an all-white jury found the Blacks guilty of violating a state anti-labor law prohibiting boycotts, and eighty-nine leaders of the movement, including twenty-four ministers and the drivers in the car pool, were found guilty. On March 19, King was fined $500 plus court costs. Later, a federal panel ruled the Alabama bus laws unconstitutional, and when news of this ruling became public there was havoc in Montgomery: armed whites opened fire on buses, a pregnant woman was shot in the legs, a teenaged Black girl was beaten, and Ralph Abernathy's home and church were bombed. On February 18, 1957, *Time* magazine ran a cover story on Martin Luther King, Jr., and he was quoted as saying:

Our use of passive resistance in Montgomery is not based on resistance to get rights for ourselves, but to achieve friendship with the men who are denying us our rights, and change them through friendship and a bond of Christian understanding before God.

In September 1957, in Little Rock, Arkansas, the Central High School was ordered to admit nine Black students, but Arkansas Governor Orval Faubus deployed the Arkansas National Guard around the school with orders to keep the Black students out. President Eisenhower responded to this situation by federalizing the Arkansas National Guard, and he also dispatched a thousand regular United States

Army Paratroopers to Little Rock to patrol the streets and keep order. The small Southern city had become an armed camp, and at this time King addressed his followers with an extraordinarily ironic appeal for pragmatic measures. As he said:

> Let's do as Gandhi did in South Africa. Let's consider what the whites say against us and consider whether they have any good arguments . . . They say that we smell. Well the fact is some of us do smell. I know most Negroes do not have money to fly to Paris and buy enticing perfumes, but no one is so poor that he can't buy a five cent bar of soap.

Meanwhile J. Edgar Hoover had dispatched FBI men to Albany, Georgia, convinced that King and the entire Civil Rights Movement were under the influence of an international Communist conspiracy. Shortly thereafter, King, sentenced to jail for his activities, used the occasion to write a letter from Birmingham jail that is comparable in moral passion to any letters Paul wrote to the early Christians. King's letter begins:

> My dear fellow clergymen:

> While confined here in Birmingham jail, I came across your recent statement calling my present activities "unwise and untimely" . . .
> Perhaps it is easy for those who have never felt the stinging darts of segregation to say, "Wait." But when you have seen vicious mobs lynch your sisters and brothers at whim; when you have seen hate-filled policemen curse, kick and even kill your black brothers and sisters; when you see the vast majority of your twenty million Negro brothers smothering in an airtight cage of poverty in the midst of an affluent society; when you suddenly find your tongue twisted and your speech stammering as you seek to explain to your six-year-old daughter why she can't go to the public amusement park that has just been advertised on television . . . when you are harried by day and haunted by night by the fact that you are a Negro, living constantly at tiptoe stance, never quite knowing what to expect next, and are plagued with inner fears and outer resentments; when you are forever fighting a degenerating sense of "nobodiness"—then you will understand why we find it difficult to wait . . .

Again and again, King repeated his commitment to non-violence and Christian love in the face of the most savage hatred, as in this sermon:

Do to us what you will. Threaten our children and we will still love you . . . Say that we're too low, that we're too degraded, yet we will still love you. Bomb our homes and go by our churches early in the morning and bomb them if you please, and we will still love you. We will wear you down by our capacity to suffer. In winning the victory, we will not only win our freedom. We will so appeal to your heart and your conscience that we will win you in the process.

Finally in 1963, during the mass demonstration March on Washington which took place on August 28 with celebrities like Harry Belafonte, Sidney Poitier, Marlon Brando, Joan Baez, Mahalia Jackson, and Charlton Heston appearing before the 250,000 people assembled outside the Lincoln Memorial, and after Roy Wilkins and A. Philip Randolph had spoken to the huge gathering, Martin Luther King, Jr. came forward to deliver his Evangelical message:

I say to you today, my friends, that in spite of the difficulties and frustrations of the moment I still have a dream. It is a dream deeply rooted in the American dream. I have a dream that one day this nation will rise up and live out the true meaning of the creed: "We hold these truths to be self-evident, that all men are created equal." I have a dream that one day on the red hills of Georgia the sons of former slaves and the sons of former slave owners will be able to sit down together at the table of brotherhood. I have a dream that my four little children will one day live in a nation where they will not be judged by the color of their skin but by the content of their character.

I have a dream today.

I have a dream that one day the state of Alabama, whose governor's lips are presently dripping with the words of interposition and nullification, will be transformed into a situation where little black boys and black girls will be able to join hands with little white boys and white girls and walk together as sisters and brothers.

I have a dream today.

. . . This will be the day when all of God's children will be able to sing with new meaning "My country 'tis of thee, sweet land of liberty, of thee I sing. Land where my fathers died, land of the pilgrim's pride, from every mountainside, let freedom ring." And if America is to be a great nation this must become true. So let freedom ring from the prodigious hilltops of New Hampshire. Let freedom ring from the mighty mountains of New York. Let freedom ring from the heightening Alleghenies of Pennsylvania . . . But not only that; let freedom ring from Stone Mountain of Georgia. Let freedom ring from Lookout Mountain of Tennessee. Let freedom ring from every hill and mole hill of Mississippi. From every mountainside, let freedom ring.

When we let freedom ring, when we let it ring from every village and hamlet, from every state and every city, we will be able to speed up that day when all of God's children, black men and white men, Jews and Gentiles, Protestants and Catholics, will be able to join hands and sing in the words of the old Negro spiritual, "Free at last! Free at last! Thank God Almighty, we are free at last!"

J. Edgar Hoover's response to King's stirring Evangelical message was to release the Willard Hotel tape, with its alleged evidence of King's philandering with white women. Shortly thereafter, the FBI formally requested permission to tap King's telephones. And when President Kennedy was assassinated in Dallas, Texas, on November 22, 1963, Martin Luther King's comment was, "This is what is going to happen to me also. I keep telling you, this is a sick nation. And I don't think I can survive either."

Yet for all the harassment of Officialdom, King's personal faith in the reality of God only increased. In that same year, 1963, a collection of his sermons, *Strength to Love*, was published and it contained this statement:

The God Whom we worship is not a weak and incompetent God. He is able to beat back gigantic waves of opposition and to bring low prodigious mountains of evil. The ringing testimony of the Christian faith is that God is able . . .

On July 2, 1964, President Lyndon Johnson signed the Civil Rights Act into law, and in that same year Martin Luther King, Jr. received the Nobel Peace Prize. J. Edgar Hoover's response to King's international recognition was to have an FBI man mail an anonymous package with a tape containing all the recordings of King's alleged dalliances to Coretta King with the following note: "KING, THERE

IS ONLY ONE THING LEFT FOR YOU TO DO. YOU KNOW WHAT THAT IS."

One astute observer commented on this bizarre and perfidious chain of events:

> Hard to estimate what effect King's extramarital affairs had on his own conscience. Hoover had no conscience, and it's surprising that King left himself wide open for Hoover's base assault, which must have been a blow to Coretta King.

As the Vietnam war escalated in 1967, King pointed out that there were twice as many Blacks as whites fighting in combat for "the greatest purveyor of violence in the world today—my own government."

By this time King was beginning to sense he would not live to see the fruits of his labors. More and more he spoke of his own death, as in the following sermon in which he expressed his concern for what would be said at his own funeral:

> Tell them not to mention that I have a Nobel Peace Prize. That isn't important. Tell them not to mention that I have three or four hundred other awards. That's not important . . . If you want to say that I was a drum major, say that I was a drum major for justice. Say that I was a drum major for peace. That I was a drum major for righteousness. And all of the other shallow things will not matter. I won't have any money to leave behind. I won't have the fine and luxurious things of life to leave behind. But I just want to leave a committed life behind. And that's all I want to say . . .

In 1968, with riots in downtown Memphis, Tennessee, King spoke out even more plainly about the sense of his own impending end:

> It really doesn't matter with me now. Because I've been to the mountaintop. Like anybody I would like to live a long life. Longevity has its place. But I'm not concerned with that now. I just want to do God's will. And He's allowed me to go up to the mountain. And I've looked over. And I've seen the Promised Land. And I may not get there with you. But I want you to know tonight that we as a people will get to the Promised Land. So I'm happy tonight. I'm not worried about anything. I'm not fearing any man. Mine eyes have seen the glory of the coming of the Lord. I have a dream this afternoon that the brotherhood of man

will become a reality. With this faith, I will go out and carve a tunnel of hope from a mountain of despair . . .

On April 4, 1968, Martin Luther King, Jr., was standing on the balcony of the Lorraine Motel in Memphis, Tennessee, when he was hit by a high powered rifle, .30-06, and the bullet ripped through the right side of his face and tore away the lower jaw and neck. King fell in a pool of his own blood on the floor of the balcony.

When news of King's death reached the rest of the country, some Blacks were unable to contain their rage and riots broke out in 110 cities and thirty-nine people were killed over several days of arson and anarchy in the streets. The man who had had a dream was slain, and his followers were heartsick at the waste.

But King had achieved his vision. On his crypt, in marble, in South View Cemetery in Atlanta, Georgia, were the words from that old Negro spiritual that King had made come true: "FREE AT LAST, FREE AT LAST, THANK GOD ALMIGHTY I AM FREE AT LAST."

Martin Luther King, Jr. was unique among modern Evangelists in his power to mobilize faith into action. As he himself once said of Gandhi, King was "able to lift the love ethic of Jesus above mere interaction between individuals to a powerful effective social force on a large scale."

Chapter 10

BILLY GRAHAM

ONE OF THE MAINSTAYS of modern American Evangelism, a man who may have been seen and heard by more human beings than any other single figure since the beginning of time, Billy Graham represents the most visible expression of Fundamentalism and therefore is probably the most influential Bible preacher of all time.

Born in 1918, Billy Graham was a farm boy from North Carolina who had the stage presence of a stork-like archangel, "an Elijah-like authority" whom John Connally once characterized as "the conscience of America," an Evangelist whom *Newsweek* magazine described as "fervent banality . . . the ultimate perplexity of a religious leader with oatmeal for brains."

His biographer, Marshall Frady in *Billy Graham: A Parable of American Righteousness*, calls Billy Graham "the megastar of his age: his rangy wheat-haired form has been personally beheld, the reverberant bay of his voice immediately heard, by more people over the face of the earth than any other single human being in the history of the race."

Billy Graham's childhood consisted of doing farm chores: he was up at 3:30 A.M., worked all day, and then his mother scrubbed him clean each evening as she recited scripture to him. She comments:

> To me he lives almost a divine life. My doctor said he seems like there's a natural glow about him—which I thought was really something to come from a doctor. But you know, after he was born, I prayed that God would take him and use him. When he went off to school, I prayed

that every day for seven years up there in that bedroom. I don't think
it could be said that my prayer was not answered.

His mother comments on the kind of Christianity that Billy Graham
was surrounded by in his early childhood: "We were never among the
more emotional of the Christian people. We were just never that type.
There were so many cults, you know, that are—well, emotional. That
was not us." Nor was it Billy, as he himself comments on his own
conversion experience at the hands of Mordecai Ham, a Kentucky
Evangelist:

> I can't say that I felt anything spectacular. I felt very little emotion. I
> shed no tears. In fact, when I saw that others had tears in their eyes, I
> felt like a hypocrite, and this disturbed me a little.

Billy went on to become a Fuller Brush salesman, with awesome
success. Grady Wilson comments: "The area sales manager didn't quite
see how just one single human being could possibly sell that many
brushes in that space of time." Billy attributes his success in selling
on a simple quality he had in superabundance:

> I believed in the product. Selling those little brushes became a cause
> to me. I felt that every family ought to have a Fuller brush as a matter
> of principle . . . Sincerity is the biggest part of selling anything.

He went on to complete his education at Bob Jones University,
Wheaton, Illinois, at Florida Bible Institute and Seminary at Davidson.
Then began a curious phase of Billy Graham's Evangelical career:
suddenly the spontaneous oratory began to spill over inside of him,
and he began to preach to anyone who would stand still and listen to
him. He preached outside Belk's Department Store, where everyone
ignored him; he preached at the Hillsboro River to a cypress tree, with
frogs and alligators looking on. As one colleague commented: "He'd
preach to a stump if there was nothing else, anything that'd just stand
still for a minute."

Gradually, Billy Graham acquired the team that was to stay with
him during his Evangelical career: George Beverly Shea, who was
singing on a gospel radio program; Cliff Barrows, who was conducting
a Youth for Christ service near Asheville; and Grady Wilson, whose
job was to keep Billy in touch with the earth. In 1949, Billy Graham

got a major boost when William Randolph Hearst, looking for any social force that was fiercely anti-Communist, sent out a two word memo: "Puff Graham"—thereafter, Henry Luce's *Time* and *Life*, and competing *Newsweek* photographers and reporters began to accompany Graham and his team on their various Revival Tours.

One former colleague, Charles Templeton, describes Billy Graham's chief asset:

> It was the transparency of his spirit, I think. Here was a guy with absolutely no guile, no pretenses or defenses at all. Just this tremendous endearing sincerity and goodwill, and his simple yearning for lost souls . . . Even today the actual thinking in his preaching is simply dreadful —but somehow, when it came to the altar call, nobody could touch him. Billy would invariably have more people come forward than anybody else would . . .

Another colleague comments:

> An Evangelist can't be complicated. They are great persuaders, not explainers. And all Billy ever really had was passion. All the great Evangelists have that—extraordinary passion—which is why most of them are so virile in their preaching. They give themselves, not with intellect, but just with tremendous passion to their message.

Billy Graham began to go on Crusades around the world, together with his team of Associate Evangelists and the cheapest suits available —Stephen Olford commented on Billy's visit to a small Welsh mining town, "I really believe it was the first time in my life I ever saw anybody in a pink suit."

Charles Templeton reports on how Billy's preaching style began to develop at this time:

> I began to notice after a while that Billy seemed to be taking on, more and more, a largeness and authority in the pulpit, to be going now for a certain magnificence of effect. It became fascinating, really impressive, to watch him.

Charles Templeton had a falling out with Billy Graham at this time, over the specific content of Graham's Evangelical message. Templeton

challenged Billy on how he could turn aside from the theory of evolution so easily, and Billy answered him: "Wiser men than you and I
will ever be, they have already encountered and examined all those
arguments, and they have concluded that the Biblical record can be
completely trusted, and these are men far wiser than we are." That
did not sit well with Templeton because it seemed like a lame excuse for not thinking. So Templeton made his ultimate challenge to
Graham:

> Billy, what is the Great Commandment? . . . to love the Lord thy God
> not only with all thy heart and all thy soul but also with all thy mind.
> Not to think, Billy, is a sin against the Great Commandment . . .
> You've committed intellectual suicide!

At those words Billy began to feel a pain at the base of his skull,
and as they were driving across the Salt Lake Desert, he experienced
his greatest spiritual crisis. Graham stopped the car, got out, peeled
off his shirt, and kneeling there in the hot sand under a blazing sun,
Billy Graham prayed: "Lord, help me. I don't have the knowledge.
I'm placing myself completely, heart and mind, without intellectual
reservations, in your hands."

From that moment on, Billy Graham claims he felt "The Word of
God is enough." And it was about this time, or shortly thereafter, that
Billy Graham began to rail against so-called "intellectuals": Nietzsche
and Freud and John Dewey, men who had corrupted our modern
world by thinking too much. Frady quotes Charles Templeton: "What
drove Billy on in his ministry and gave him his power was precisely
what drove me out of the ministry. I was unable to accept that you
can refuse to think."

America was beginning to enter into a complex period: there was
the struggle of the Civil Rights Movement at home, and the Vietnam
war abroad. One observer claims this is partly what helped Billy Graham's popularity: "He preaches the life of certitude. There are no
doubts, no real choices to be made, no expanses of experience where
right and wrong, the nourishing and the corrupting, the healing and
the killing, cannot be easily distinguished."

By this time Billy Graham was broadcasting his "Hour of Decision"
weekly program over thousands of radio and television stations nationwide, and it had the largest audience of any religious program,
with over fifteen million in 1954. The Billy Graham Evangelistic

Association was sending out over 100 million pieces of literature each year, and receiving over 2.5 million letters a year. As Marshall Frady characterizes the organization: "Graham's ministry is administered from Minneapolis, in a manner that has become a mix of IBM, McCann-Erickson, Sears Roebuck, Blue Cross, and the morning devotionals at Vacation Bible School."

Billy Graham also pioneered a spanking clean image of his finances and those of his Evangelistic Association. It was a matter of public record that the only money Graham ever saw was his own straight salary of $59,000 plus housing and expenses. In addition, Billy Graham was a member in good standing of the Evangelical Council for Financial Accountability.

A dedicated family man and faithful husband to his wife Ruth, Billy Graham has also been scrupulously careful to avoid the slightest hint of scandal with women, going so far as not to allow himself to be left alone in a room with only one woman nor to ride on elevators with unescorted women.

As the most conspicuous crown of his Evangelical ministry, Billy Graham began to be a sort of *ex officio* minister to almost all the incumbent Presidents of the United States. Harry Truman would have none of him, but Dwight Eisenhower actually shared his deathbed prayers with Billy; John F. Kennedy played golf with him; Lyndon Johnson asked Billy's advice on running mates, and once even inquired of Billy which Vietnamese towns and villages he thought ought to be bombed; Richard Nixon tried to use Billy's considerable moral prestige as a fallout shelter during the Watergate scandal.

Billy's rationale for these indiscriminate Oval Office associations was ingenuous: "I feel that my role is of a preacher, a spiritual influence on whatever President is there."

In 1957, Billy Graham began a ninety-seven day Crusade in New York City, using an Executive Committee made up of Norman Vincent Peale, William Randolph Hearst, Jr., Eddie Rickenbacker, Henry Luce, and Ogden Reid. Graham trained volunteers to work at Madison Square Garden by making them take twelve hours of classes, which included the importance of using deodorants and mint breath lozenges. The Hotel New Yorker provided Graham with a free suite, along with free rooms for all his close associates.

On the opening day of the Crusade, May 15, 1957, such celebrities as Walter Winchell, Dorothy Kilgallen, Pearl Bailey, Gene Tierney, Ed Sullivan, Dale Evans, and Sonja Heine graced the stage as Billy

Graham began to preach. His message was strident, simplistic, and ersatz doomsday:

> Modern art is nothing but a splotch—man is scarcely recognizable. He is portrayed not as we know him, as a creature bearing the image of God, but as a blur, an irregular splotch, something abstract, something uncertain, indistinct . . . We have explored the mysteries of the universe, but have not solved the riddle of our souls . . . All the scientists, the greatest intellects on this earth—they haven't been able to solve the problem of sorrow . . . I am a Western Union boy! I have a death message! I must tell you plainly—you are going to Hell! You listen! Don't you trifle with God! Don't you think you can barter! You are a sinner! You have come short of God's requirements! Your punishment is sure!

At the end of his message, Billy Graham began his call for the congregation to stand and come forward to make their commitment to Christ. Charles Templeton was right—when it came to the altar call, nobody could touch Billy Graham. As Cliff Barrows conducted the choir to sing through several choruses of "Just As I Am," Billy Graham turned his eagle-eyed attention on every part of that vast Madison Square Garden as he announced:

> I'm going to ask you now that there be no walking around, no moving of any kind, no talking . . . I'm going to ask you now to come. Up here, down here, you way up there in those last rows . . . You may be a church member, you may not be, but you've never had that living encounter with God, something's missing in your life. Father, mother, young person, you need to come. If you don't come tonight, you may never come, you could go home tonight and have your life taken away from you before the sun rises tomorrow . . . Father, mother with gray hairs and bifocals and bunions and bulges, have you given yourself to Christ? He loves you, he wants to save you, he died for you . . . If you have friends, they will wait on you. I want you to come. You come now . . .

The subliminal effect of all these subtle death threats and cosmetic slurs and hypnotic repetition of that one word come/come/come/come/come had its effect: slowly, with ushers and individual choir members leading the way, from all over the great auditorium, people began to rise and make their way down to the large space in front of the pulpit. Billy Graham stood there motionless, head thrust forward in clenched fist, waiting for more to come.

Slowly, more did come. Then Billy Graham spoke a few words with the hundreds of people gathered together in front of him. He told them Christ had received them, and he asked them to bow their heads in a brief prayer. Then he sent them off to counseling rooms under the platform where trained advisers were waiting to talk with each person and give them special literature on how to follow through in their new commitment to Christ. Sixty-four percent of those who came forward were already members of some church so they were simply told to return to their congregations and give themselves to its ongoing activities with renewed vigor. The remaining 36% of unaffiliated Christians were given advice as to how they could seek out appropriate church membership in their vicinity.

Following Madison Square Garden, there were Crusades at Yankee Stadium where 100,000 persons turned out, and there was a giant rally at Times Square where 120,000 persons gathered to hear Billy Graham damn the sins of 42nd Street, just as Billy Sunday had done 40 years earlier to a crowd of 20,000 at Broadway and 168th Street.

Then Billy Graham was off on a world tour—first there was a twelve-week stand in England, where newspapers made wry comments: "Whatever wrestling Billy Graham has done with Satan, there are no claw marks."

Billy Graham met with the aging Winston Churchill, who told Graham he had no hope left for the world. Then he moved on to Scotland, where Graham was labeled as "pietistic kool-aid." He did a four-day whirlwind Crusade in France, then through Germany, and finally, against the advice of the American State Department, he took his Crusade to Moscow. Then he went to Australia where over half the country's population turned out to hear him. Then he went on to Africa, and to India.

During these worldwide Crusades there were criticisms of Billy Graham's message, although Marshall Frady insists that people still couldn't help liking the man:

One of the curious ironies that has abided through the course of Graham's career is that, personally he always strikes one as immeasurably more refreshing and large-spirited than his message . . . Out of his simple huge goodwill and sheer compulsive affection for people—he has always been stricken with an authentic desperation for salvaging what he deems lost and unhappy souls . . .

Still the criticisms were there, and occasionally they could be caustic: one observer noted Billy Graham's Crusade produced "popcorn conversions—from tight hard kernels, suddenly pop!—puff into instant papery Christian popcorn."

The eminent Protestant theologian Reinhold Niebuhr had a more substantial criticism to make of Billy Graham's message—he felt it was too pat and facile for the complexities of our anguishing age: "Ambiguity of all human values, the serious perplexities of guilt and responsibility, and particularly of guilt associated with responsibility, which each true Christian must continually face."

Perhaps the most catastrophic criticism of Billy Graham was what Graham himself said about Martin Luther King, Jr., when King made his 1963 speech in Washington. Martin Luther King, Jr. had said he had a dream that someday he would see little black boys and black girls walking hand in hand with little white boys and white girls. Billy Graham rejected King's vision outright. Frady relates that Graham insisted that only when Christ returns to the earth will little black children be able to walk with little white children. Billy Graham believed that all of King's efforts towards integration and social reform were foredoomed to failure until the Second Coming of Jesus. This was the old dichotomy of Fundamentalist versus Social Gospel— Dwight L. Moody believed the world was damned and not worth trying to patch up on social or political levels, whereas Dorothea Dix, Susan B. Anthony, and Dorothy Day believed a committed life could make a very real difference in the real world.

The success of Martin Luther King, Jr. in his Civil Rights Movement stands as a monument to Billy Graham's indecision and inability to join the crucial issues of his day. As Evangelist, Billy Graham waffled on almost all the major social and political issues of America: he remained silent during the Watts riots, and he was curiously unsure about America's role in Vietnam. When Martin Luther King, Jr. said that expecting the support of white ministers was the most pervasive mistake he had ever made, Billy Graham was one of those white ministers who had disappointed King: King had come to Graham to enlist his support in protesting the Vietnam war, and Graham had declined to take a public stand on the matter.

To be sure, Billy Graham had made an enormous gesture of concern

during that war, by joining Bob Hope in a touring U.S.O. company
which played at service camps on the Vietnam mainland. And that
gesture may go a long way towards fixing Billy Graham's Evangelical
role in our age: he is the Bob Hope of the gospel, a consummate stand-
up showman who has no more authentic persona than maintaining
his momentum and getting the right lines out at the right time.

As the Vietnam war continued to accelerate in intensity and senselessness, Billy Graham continued to vacillate. When Richard Nixon
began the 1972 Christmas saturation bombing of North Vietnam,
religious leaders from all over America pleaded with Billy Graham to
use his moral influence with Nixon and try to make him reconsider.
But Graham would not consider doing such a thing: he told his col-
leagues he considered himself more a New Testament Evangelist than
an Old Testament Prophet: "I don't want to get involved on either
side" was his way of putting it.

But Billy Graham was involved, whether he wanted to be or not.
He had listened to Lyndon Johnson go on and on about what he was
hoping to achieve through the bombing of Vietnam, and now he was
listening to General Westmoreland, General Abrams, and Richard
Nixon. He later admitted the whole thing puzzled him no end: "I
didn't know what was really going on." Strange words from a man
who claimed he had never experienced any doubt, and who said during
a 1960 visit to the Holy Land: "I've never known a moment of despair."

But Billy Graham's greatest crisis of confidence came during the
long ordeal of Watergate. Graham was genuinely fond of Richard
Nixon and he had the highest regard for Nixon's intellectual honesty.
As Graham commented,

> I just could never conceive of him breaking the law deliberately. And
> all those people around him, Haldeman, Erlichmann, Dwight Chapin
> —they seemed to be people who were so clean. They were even Chris-
> tian Scientists, you know—family men, clean-living, with an active
> interest in their church. All of them seemed so upstanding.

Billy had come up against the old appearance/reality riddle, and
apparently his Christian faith has not been much help in enabling
him to deal with it. One gasps at such naiveté in someone who has
supposedly traveled in the real world and claims to be familiar with
the Bible.

But the real gasping came when Billy sat down and listened to the

Watergate tapes and read through the transcripts where Richard Nixon's cynical mind and liberal use of four-letter words were right out there in black and white. In fact it was Richard Nixon's use of blasphemies and obscenities that seemed to trouble Billy much more than the actual crimes of Watergate: "I just didn't know that he used this type of language in talking to others . . . I rarely have ever heard Mr. Nixon use even words like 'damn' or 'hell,' and even when he did, he would look over at me and say, 'Excuse me, Billy.' "

Billy finally blamed the whole thing on Nixon's use of too many sleeping pills, and let it go at that. But clearly, there had been damage done to Billy Graham's view of himself and the world. And the public was also beginning to realize that Billy Graham's spanking clean Boy Scout image was really nothing but a sort of moral myopia.

More and more, Billy Graham began to withdraw into a wistful twilight zone of the soul that was filled with unknown terrors:

> I've been frightened all these years—just terrified. People have expected me, for instance, to be more of an authority on everything than I've really been able to be. And I'm still scared. I'm sure terrible traps are being set for me all the time. I probably will fall before it's over with.

When Billy Graham peeled off his shirt and knelt down to pray in the middle of the Salt Lake Desert in the early part of his Evangelical career, he told the Lord he was placing himself completely, heart and mind, without intellectual reservations, in the hands of the living God. It looks as if Graham got what he had asked for: an Evangelism that was totally without individual heart or mind and utterly without intellectual reservations. All that he has had, all that he really asked for in that Salt Lake Desert, was the passion to keep on with his faith— and now, towards the end of his Evangelical career, his greatest dread is "for the passion to be gone—like it happens with others in their old age in the Bible. For the fire to go, to die . . ."

But that only happened to those Old Testament Prophets who had lived lives of unthinking passion; it did not happen to Prophets like Abraham and Job, who made a point of keeping their wits about them and having the mental acumen to see through false counselors and downright lies.

Newsweek magazine, in reviewing Marshall Frady's biography of Billy Graham, summed up the emptiness of the Evangelist's life with accurate irony:

. . . an aging spellbinder whose simplistic certitudes have hardened into "an almost Plexiglas imperviousness to criticism," living in a mountaintop retreat patrolled by lethal guard dogs, asphyxiating in fame. This is, in short, a success story.

Chapter 11

RADIO AND TELEVISION EVANGELISTS

TWENTIETH CENTURY EVANGELISM embarked on an entirely new era of proselytizing when it discovered the most pervasive preaching medium of all time: radio and television.

Just as Martin Luther was mightily assisted in the dissemination of his Reformation message all over Europe by the use of the new Gutenberg printing press, so contemporary Evangelists are enormously amplified in their impact through the use of the new electronic media to reach mass audiences all over America.

To understand the growth and development of televangelists in our time, we should go back to examine the first radio and TV Evangelists, and how they use this new preaching technique.

In 1920, the first radio station began broadcasting programs of music across the country, and by 1960 there were over 200 million radio and television sets in America. Now, for the first time in history, people could stay in the comfort of their own homes and tune in their favorite Evangelists for a daily message. These same people could even phone in their freewill gift offerings through the use of toll-free numbers that flashed across their TV screens.

In fact the phenomenon became so specialized that entire radio and television networks were created to carry family gospel programming, complete with phone-in talk shows and sacred concerts and scripted radio dramas such as *Unshackled* to complement the usual staple of Revival sermons and conversionary Crusades.

But at the very beginnings of this electronic Evangelism, there was a note of vague foreboding. We've already noted how Father Coughlin's 1926 children's radio program grew in notoriety until Coughlin himself had become such an inflammatory political force that he had to be silenced by his Bishop. It would be an important augury for things to come in this new pervasive medium.

One of the pioneer radio Evangelists was Charles E. Fuller, who conducted *The Old Fashioned Revival Hour* from his headquarters in Long Beach, California. There was a kind of mindless joy to this weekly radio program as its theme song chanted out:

Heavenly sunshine, heavenly sunshine,
Flooding my soul with glory divine;
Heavenly sunshine, heavenly sunshine,
Hallelujah, Jesus is mine!

Charles E. Fuller was enormously important for the future of electronic Evangelism because the format of his radio show included the basic ingredients that would characterize almost all the later radio and television Revival programs: there was a choir singing gospel hymns, occasional guest celebrities who came by to be interviewed about their experiences in the faith, and then there was the message which Fuller himself directed to the nationwide radio audience. And there were, indeed, significant people out there listening to Fuller's message: young men like Billy Graham and Jerry Falwell, both of whom credit Fuller's *Old Fashioned Revival Hour* as having a lasting influence on their own later Evangelical work. Falwell even went on to title his own weekly TV program *The Old Time Gospel Hour.*

Another radio Evangelist who was astonishingly influential in America was Norman Vincent Peale, whose book *The Power of Positive Thinking* converted millions to a new way of thinking. Peale presented the essence of his message on both weekly radio and television programs, using a simple conversational approach to show people how they could solve their life problems through mental adjustments of attitude. The first and certainly the most successful of all self-help Evangelists, Peale turned American Protestantism into a kind of how-to-do-it gym class where one could learn how to leapfrog over any life obstacle provided one really set one's mind to it.

This "positive thinking" of Norman Vincent Peale was cut from the same cloth as Dale Carnegie's best-selling book *How to Win Friends and Influence People.* Theologically, both Carnegie and Peale were throwbacks to early Pelagianism, which denied original sin and taught that man was capable of achieving good without the assistance of divine grace. As St. Augustine was the first to point out, this Pelagianism is one of the most subtle and pernicious heresies for Christianity to identify and come to terms with.

There has always been a Pelagian tinge to almost all Christian reform movements, with the implied promise that you can achieve anything you set your mind to: all you have to do is think positively and then wait for it all to come true. This is irrational and infantile wish fantasy, and there is indeed a sort of Walt Disney mentality behind both Dale Carnegie and Norman Vincent Peale. In their Good Humor world there is no real doubt, no radical evil, no mental or emotional illness, only a kind of nonstop complacent optimism.

Of course both Dale Carnegie and Norman Vincent Peale became immensely popular in America because their message fit so neatly into the mythos of Horatio Alger's making good in the Land of Opportunity. And of course both Carnegie and Peale also had the strong thrust of free enterprise capitalism going for them.

On first sight, both Carnegie and Peale may seem bland and innocent enough until one remembers some of the realities of our twentieth century: think of Auschwitz or Dachau or Buchenwald, and suddenly the whole notion of Winning Friends and Influencing People becomes trivial and irreligious. Or think of our dropping atomic bombs on Hiroshima and Nagasaki, and the Power of Positive Thinking becomes a despicable blemish on whatever culture spawned these myopic self-help Evangelisms. The concept of overcoming all obstacles by sheer will and self-help techniques complacently ignores the more complicated issues of our time.

Nevertheless, as we said, it would be a great mistake to underestimate the influence of Dale Carnegie and Norman Vincent Peale on contemporary American Protestant thought. If one wants to locate a theology underlying certain conversionary Evangelists, one would have to trace it back to Carnegie and Peale: their two best-selling books provide the basic tenets of self-help and positive thinking that come back again and again in the preaching of such Evangelists as Robert Schuller, Pat Robertson, Jim Bakker, Oral Roberts, and Jimmy Swaggart. It is a thinly disguised Pelagianism of self-help, self-healing, self-saving, and self-delusion.

One of the most persistent American Evangelists began with a weekly radio program, *The World Tomorrow*, and later transferred it to television. Herbert W. Amstrong, a multimillionaire preacher whose program ratings outranked those of Billy Graham and Oral Roberts combined for income and listenership, taught a strict Fundamentalism and always referred to an open Bible to verify every one of his assertions.

One assertion was that Herbert W. Armstrong himself was the only true "chosen apostle of Christ" since the first century, and he published articles in his *Plain Truth* magazine to back up this claim. He also created courses at his Ambassador College in Pasadena, California, to confirm it. It was all a part of Herbert W. Armstrong's worldwide "Church of God," which reached gargantuan proportions during his lifetime.

But then a quirky thing happened. When it came time for Armstrong to retire from his television ministry, he turned *The World Tomorrow* program over to his son, Garner Ted Armstrong, who was young, good-looking, and extremely photogenic—a sort of Tyrone Power of the gospel. Garner Ted conducted *The World Tomorrow* in a much more free-wheeling and liberal manner than his father had, until finally it was perceived that he had departed from Fundamentalist teaching altogether and was presenting the scripture as more figurative than literal. In addition, there were rumors about Garner Ted's cavalier womanizing, and charges he was using *The World Tomorrow* television program as a personal dating bureau.

When Herbert W. Armstrong got wind of what Garner Ted was up to in 1978, he hit the ceiling and ousted his son from the ministry on charges of heresy and immorality. Herbert W. Armstrong then came out of retirement, took back *The World Tomorrow* program and restored it to strict Fundamentalist doctrine. Since the death of Herbert W. Armstrong, *The World Tomorrow* program continues along these orthodox lines with alternate moderators, David Albert and Richard Ames.

Eric Butterworth is another radio Evangelist whose weekly scripted programs present a leisurely approach to life's problems which is sane and amiable. Butterworth presents half-hour messages that are a kind of gnostic scientism, exhorting his listeners to use the resources of their own minds.

Harold Camping, President of WFME Family Radio, conducts Evangelical call-in talk shows in which he gives scriptural answers to personal questions. Always sober and unflamboyant, Camping is one of the most knowledgeable of all Fundamentalist Evangelists and whether one agrees with his interpretation or not, one has to be awed at Camping's chapter-and-verse scholarship of the Bible. He is one of the few Evangelists one can always learn from.

Roy Masters, speaking on behalf of his Foundation for Human

Understanding, presents his Evangelical broadcasts over WMCA and WOR radio. Masters teaches people to solve their problems by controlling their emotions. An ex-hypnotist, Roy Masters insists pride is the biggest problem in human affairs and he can be a bloodhound in scenting out hidden pride in anyone's hard luck story. Masters learned from the practice of hypnotism that people should not allow themselves to be unduly influenced by stressful circumstances in their environment, but should stay calm and not resentful so they can trust to their own gut hunches about a situation. This is a fairly insightful approach, and Roy Masters has written several books illustrating the method, of which *How to Survive Your Parents* is probably the most incisive.

From radio to television is an inevitable step in our time, and some Evangelists have been able to do it with such extraordinary success that they have become staple figures on the tube, as much as Johnny Carson, Lucille Ball, or Jackie Gleason.

It has been estimated that all the TV gospel shows reach a total of sixty-one million Americans each year. Jeffrey Hadden, a sociologist at the University of Virginia, predicted correctly that because of all this TV exposure, the Christian Right "is destined to become the major social movement in America" during the latter half of the twentieth century. Hadden's 1981 book, *Prime Time Preachers*, is a useful discussion of some of the leading televangelists of our time.

What is the chief attraction of the televangelists?

Personality, for one thing. Anyone who has worked in television knows the camera falls in love with certain people and makes them look uncommonly good, while it makes others look muddy and indistinguishable. Whatever one may think of the Evangelical message of Jim Bakker or Jimmy Swaggart, one can't deny that these two preachers pick up awfully well on the TV tube. Tammy Bakker, on the other hand, always looks top-heavy and over-made-up, in a state of perpetual distress. It's not her fault; it's just the way the TV camera picks up on her. Television is a fickle industry, and if someone has the right photogenic personality, that goes a long way towards establishing him or her as an attractive figure.

Then there's the glamor of the televangelist's presentation: Jimmy Swaggart may move around onstage with an open collar and his necktie all askew, but his back-up choir is neatly fitted in colorful robes and every curl is kept carefully in place. It's a dramatic contrast and is one of the subliminal messages that makes Swaggart's ministry so attractive.

Music also plays a large part in any good televangelist show: whether it's a trained choir such as Billy Graham uses under Cliff Barrow's direction, or whether the entire congregation joins in the singing as in Robert Schuller's Crystal Cathedral, the effect can be stirring and emotional and it helps set the stage for the televangelist's message.

Finally, as to this televangelist's message: the one thing you can always say about televangelism is that whatever the Biblical persuasion, be it Fundamentalist or Pentecostal or Charismatic, in one way or another every televangelist will manage to program his message so it builds to an authentic sense of frenzy. Billy Graham, Jerry Falwell, Ernest Angley, Rex Humbard, Jimmy Swaggart, Robert Schuller—in their separate ways and using their radically different individual approaches, each of these televangelists will invariably orchestrate his preaching so it reaches a fever pitch of frenzy before he is done.

Sometimes this frenzy may assume the low-key soft-spoken sincerity of a Pat Robertson, as he makes glistening eye contact with the camera and pleads for his TV viewers to send in one more freewill gift offering. Sometimes the frenzy may take an opposite tack and assume the statuesque posturing of a Robert Schuller, standing with his arms outstretched as he gives a still life imitation of Christ of the Andes. Sometimes the frenzy will spill over into an actual speaking in tongues, as Jimmy Swaggart often does on camera as he approaches the spasmodic peak of his preaching.

But whatever form it takes, frenzy is frenzy. It is libidinal high wire voltage and it's the closest you can come to simulating explicit sexuality on camera. And it's the heart and soul of televangelism.

Why is frenzy such an inextricable part of televangelism in America? To answer this question, we have to look around us. If we grant there is an awful void underlying our materialist culture, and if we also grant many Americans are so preoccupied with the details of daily life that they are only half aware of some dreadful emptiness inside their own lives, and if we also grant these same people would give anything to break free briefly and abate their gnawing hunger for genuine values and a meaningful spiritual experience—if we grant all these things, then we can see why this thinly veiled sexual frenzy is such an integral part of televangelism.

Because the more a televangelist can simulate an inspired possession by the Holy Ghost which sends him into paroxysms of rapture, the more his television viewers at home may experience a strong wish for the same Dionysian frenzy they see being enacted on the TV screen in front of them.

We can see this phenomenon of frenzy at work in other types of mass audience appeal. Following are three examples:

1. A hundred years ago, every touring carnival had a sideshow attraction known as the "geek," who was usually a homeless drifter, down on his luck. To keep himself in cheap wine, this geek would hire himself out to the sideshow where he would perform one of the most degrading acts imaginable: he would bite the heads off live chickens. Local folk would pay a dollar to go inside the canvas tent and watch as the geek picked up a chicken, poked its head in his mouth, and chomped down on its neck until he had decapitated it with his teeth. The chicken's headless body would be released to the sawdust floor where it would flutter around in a feathered frenzy, madly flapping as the blood spurted out in rhythmic gushes. It was a primitive exercise in frenzy and the yokels loved it.

2. At the massive Nuremberg Party Rallies, Adolf Hitler would always begin his speeches in a very calm and quiet voice, seeming to be the height of reasonableness and sanity. As the speech went on, Hitler would gradually build in intensity and pitch until he had reached a shrieking hysteria which would whip his listeners into a state of frenzy where they would agree with anything he wanted them to believe. It was a pretty delirious exhibition of programmed frenzy.

3. Leonard Bernstein is generally acknowledged to be one of the great conductors of all time, but he was not always so admired for his gesticulations and gyrations on the podium. In a scathing 1946 review in the *New York Herald-Tribune*, Virgil Thomson wrote:

> With every season his personal performance becomes more ostentatious, his musical one less convincing. There was a time when he used to forget occasionally and let the music speak. Nowadays he keeps it always like the towering Italian bandmasters of forty years ago, a vehicle for the waving about of hair, for the twisting of shoulders and torso, for the miming of facial expression of uncontrolled emotional states . . .

What else is Virgil Thomson describing here but a modern Evangelist, someone who is inexplicably phallic and Dionysian in his sexual frenzy? As if one needed further confirmation, Bernstein himself is quoted by Joan Peyser in her biography *Bernstein* as saying his only criterion for the performance of any new work is: "Will it give me an orgasm?"

This common characteristic of frenzy, then, will function with any type of mass audience appeal, from geek, to maniacal dictator, to symphony orchestra conductor. And it will also be an inextricable part of any successful televangelist. In fact one could probably argue that a televangelist's genius for bringing in freewill gift offerings and for scoring well on Arbitron ratings is in direct relation to his ability to simulate an authentic sense of frenzy on camera.

It should go without saying, however, that any televangelist who can go into screaming hysteria on camera does not necessarily enhance our respect for the sanity or the sincerity of the message he is trying to put over. Some televangelists may have an inborn talent for weeping on camera or being able to tap into hysteria. But that doesn't mean they are to be taken seriously as purveyors of legitimate religious experience.

Even so, as far as TV is concerned, if a televangelist is good at projecting an authentic sense of frenzy, that's usually enough to fill the bill. The camera will pick it up and convey it faithfully to the nationwide television audience out there.

And who is this audience that is tuning in on these televangelists and responding to their authentic sense of frenzy? Here is a firsthand account of that audience—the American playwright Stuart Sheffer recounts some early memories of his grandparents in Tennessee who watched televangelists regularly and always responded to the appeals for freewill gift offerings:

From what I gather, while my grandparents retained a fanatical religious faith, at some point they stopped going to church except for special occasions such as Christmas or Easter. Despite being in generally good health until their final illness, they preferred to get their religion by watching TV ministers such as Oral Roberts, Billy Graham, and Rex Humbard.

I have no idea why they did this. Religion was one of many topics my parents forbade us from discussing with our grandparents. All I remember was their house was filled with newsletters, requests for money, and gifts for donating money to these evangelists. I can still see on top of their television next to one of their many Bibles, a tiny gold replica of Oral Roberts' prayer tower.

The worst part of their love for these evangelists was every time we visited them we had to watch whatever evangelist was on. Unlike the revival, there was no emotion allowed on our part. We had to sit there in total silence watching the show. Whispering or even obviously not paying attention was swiftly punished by my grandfather. The only time we were allowed to do anything beyond watch the set, was when it came time to pray and we were allowed to bow our heads.

How did all this televangelism get started in this country?

It is ironic that both radio and television Evangelism, which have grown to be such bastions of American Protestantism, should each have been pioneered by a Roman Catholic. Just as Father Coughlin inaugurated the first radio Evangelism in 1926, so the first legitimate televangelism was begun by Bishop Fulton J. Sheen on Easter Sunday, 1940.

Bishop Sheen did a series of religious talks in that 1940 adventure, and he returned in 1952 to an astonishing audience response. Thereafter his *Life Is Worth Living* television talk show was aired regularly from the Adelphi Theatre in New York in front of a live audience.

Sheen's message was essentially Catholic but it was designed for all faiths. Wearing a black cassock with a wide red sash, a red skullcap and a flowing red cape, Bishop Sheen was always sedate and had an uncanny sense of timing and an impeccable instinct for positioning himself in portrait poses as he told spritely anecdotes that brought a twinkle to his Irish eyes. Sheen's wit was infallible: when he received an Emmy Award for his series, he commented to the television audience, "I'd like to thank my writers—Matthew, Mark, Luke, and John."

It's also ironic that both Catholic pioneers of radio and television should have been terminated by their superiors: Father Coughlin was silenced by his Bishop, and Bishop Sheen had a running feud with New York's Cardinal Spellman which made him leave his television program in 1957. Sheen accepted an appointment as Archbishop of Rochester, New York, in 1966, for the last three years of his ministry.

But Bishop Fulton Sheen's *Life Is Worth Living* program showed that televangelism was a natural medium for preachers, and he thus paved the way for the major Protestant Evangelists of the 1960s and 1970s. And of all these later televangelists, none was more adept at handling the new medium to achieve spectacular success, and none fell to such depths of nationwide disgrace and scandal, than Jim Bakker.

Jim Bakker was born James Orson Bakker in 1940 in Muskegon, Michigan. As a young man, Bakker experienced a terrible accident:

while driving his father's Cadillac on a date, he ran over a young boy who suffered a broken collarbone and several cracked ribs and a ruptured lung. The boy miraculously survived the accident, and as Jim Bakker writes in his 1976 autobiography *Move That Mountain!*, it made an irrevocable change in his thinking: "At that moment Jesus became the only thing in my life."

Bakker went to North Central Bible College in Minneapolis where he was known as "Holy Joe" because of the intensity of his prayer vigils. He married Tammy Faye La Valley and they both left school to begin Evangelical work together. Bakker was ordained in 1964 by the Assemblies of God as a Pentecostal preacher, and he and Tammy became itinerant Evangelists traveling around the small towns of North Carolina.

In 1965, Bakker and his wife joined televangelist Pat Robertson and served as guest hosts on the *700 Club*; Jim and Tammy also inaugurated a children's puppet show on television. It was here that Jim Bakker accidentally discovered his gift for making TV appeals for freewill gift offerings, when he stood onstage and let tears stream down his face as he pleaded with viewers to send in contributions to save the Christian Broadcasting Network.

Jim and Tammy left Pat Robertson and went with Paul Crouch to launch their own Trinity Broadcasting Systems; subsequently, the Bakkers moved on to create their own PTL Network ("Praise the Lord" or "People That Love," whichever designation Bakker gives it on a particular day). PTL announcer "Uncle" Henry Harrison describes the phenomenal success of Jim and Tammy: "They were just a cute little couple that people felt good about watching."

Jim Bakker threw himself into TV programming at PTL. He once commented, "My specific calling from God is to be a television talk show host." The PTL Network grew to 24 hour broadcasting and reached over thirteen million households in America, grossing upwards of $51 million a year. Wife Tammy Bakker kept on recording gospel song records, several of which became best sellers.

Jim Bakker also developed a 2,300-acre theme park, Heritage U.S.A., and in 1986 the park had 6.5 million visitors, ranking it third behind Disneyland and Disney World.

Marjoe Gortner in his documentary *American Gospel* assesses Bakker's talent: "Bakker can turn it on. He gets a little crazy and he starts preaching, and he has those phones lighting up. He's a very good preacher and a smart businessman."

There were rumors of untoward behavior: in 1979, the *Charlotte*

Observer charged that money raised for Bakker's overseas work had been diverted to expenses at home. The FCC held hearings, where PTL executives testified the Bakkers had indeed used donations to buy sports cars, a houseboat, a mink coat, and other luxuries. But Jim Bakker produced documents to refute the specific accusations and all charges were dismissed.

But the rumors persisted: one PTL ex-Vice President described how Bakker seemed to be indifferent to the human aspect of programming: ". . . little old women wanted just to touch his hand, people who had given him their life savings. But he wouldn't give them the time of day . . ." There were also rumors about Tammy: gossip had it that she had a crush on country music singer Gary Paxton, and it was making Jim Bakker terribly jealous.

But in spite of all the rumors, allegations, and gossip, Jim and Tammy Bakker kept on with their highly successful PTL Network show, and they seemed to be destined for ever higher horizons in their Evangelical work.

Then suddenly in March 1987, Jim Bakker shocked the country by announcing his resignation as head of the 500,000 member PTL ministry. On March 19, Bakker formally relinquished control of PTL to Moral Majority leader Jerry Falwell. No one knew what to make of it.

Then, gradually, the scandal began to surface. The immediate and proximate reason for Bakker's resignation of PTL in 1987 was a 1980 tryst he had had with Jessica Hahn, a former Church secretary from Long Island, New York, in a Florida hotel. There were also insinuations that a second PTL executive had joined in the goings-on at the hotel with Jessica Hahn. And there were allegations that over the next seven years, Bakker had paid out over $265,000 in hush money to keep the lid closed on what had happened.

The plot continued to thicken: Bakker began hinting that another televangelist (presumably Jimmy Swaggart) was trying to use this sordid information to effect a hostile takeover of the PTL Network. In desperation, Bakker had turned to Jerry Falwell to prevent that from happening. Whatever the truth of that specific allegation, it is fairly certain Jimmy Swaggart was responsible for Jim Bakker's being defrocked of his ministry by the Assemblies of God.

As soon as these scandals surfaced, other rumors began: Reverend John Ankerberg went on Larry King's Cable News Network and accused Jim Bakker of having had homosexual experiences in addition to that adulterous one-night stand.

At this point, Jerry Falwell suddenly waxed indignant. Having assumed temporary guardianship of PTL to keep the organization from foundering, Falwell now announced he was assuming permanent custody of the enterprise.

Jim Bakker, in turn, accused Jerry Falwell of having engineered the whole takeover of PTL from the outset. Falwell rejoined: "That's like accusing someone of stealing the *Titanic* just after it hit the iceberg."

But the scandals did not end here. Jim Bakker's mismanagement of PTL had left the organization close to bankruptcy, and facts began to come out about some of Bakker's exorbitant spending on himself and Tammy from PTL monies: Bakker had six homes, including a $449,000 house in Palm Desert, California; a $300,000 condominium in Highland Beach, Florida; and he had spent $300,000 in renovations on his Gatlinburg, Tennessee home in the Great Smoky Mountains. Bakker had also purchased a $100,000 Rolls Royce vintage 1953, as well as a 1983 Mercedes Benz, and had spent $60,000 more on a Rolls Royce which was to be used as a decoration on the roof of a hotel. There were minor items that also galled onlookers: Bakker had spent $800 for a Gucci briefcase, and he had engaged private tutors for his two children. In addition, Tammy Faye had spent $5,000 for an air conditioned doghouse, and she had undergone cosmetic surgery.

The really interesting question is how Jim Bakker had been able to get away with so much reckless spending under the aegis of the PTL management. For one thing, he had as many as forty-seven bank accounts and seventeen Vice Presidents for the organization, so Jim Bakker was the only one who ever knew how much money there was in PTL treasuries. He had also paid PTL Board members for their services in perks and gratuities so they would turn a blind eye to what was going on: one Texas minister received $100,000 for the landscaping of his church, and others received free vacation trips.

The total income for PTL in 1986 was $129 million, and the PTL assets were formidable: the cable television services were worth between $20 and $50 million, and the theme park Heritage U.S.A. was worth another $178 million.

It is a fair estimate to say that the projected assets of PTL were close to half a billion dollars, and perhaps because of this prodigious wealth, Jim Bakker seemed to have been operating on a kind of psychological Calvinism: as founder and chief executive of PTL, he felt he deserved the various emoluments he paid himself as proof of his spiritual prowess. At the time of the Great Eruption, Bakker was even planning a convention center for his theme park to be called "The Crystal Palace."

But once the scandals broke, desperate PTL employees began holding auctions of some of the household items, which the Bakkers had accumulated, to raise short-term cash: they sold off gold-plated toilet fixtures, most of the cars, the mink coats, even the Gucci briefcase. But revenue from these auctions could not cover the overdue bills which were accumulating at a breakneck pace: PTL television programs were marketed to some 160 stations nationwide, and already eighteen stations had dropped the PTL Club program for nonpayment of bills. Forty other stations were beginning to make noises about doing likewise.

About this time, federal investigators began to take notice of the situation. Representatives of the Justice Department, the Postal Service, and the Internal Revenue Service began to descend on PTL headquarters in Gort Mill, South Carolina, to examine the organization's books and documents. There was talk of indictment for criminal fraud, wire fraud, and mail fraud. At the same time, the House Ways and Means Oversight Subcommittee began investigations into the tax-exempt status of PTL and ten other Evangelical organizations.

In July 1987, there were public bankruptcy hearings in Columbia, South Carolina, to confront the $68 million debt that had accumulated. And there was a tricky legal question: whether the 120,000 "lifetime members" of PTL, each of whom had contributed over $1,000, should be considered creditors of the organization—in which case they would be entitled to refunds of their contributions, and could even lay claim for damages.

Jim Bakker engaged noted trial lawyer Melvin Belli to try to reinstate him as head of PTL, but by this time the real damage was so widespread it wasn't simply a matter of letting Bakker back. The entire Evangelical community had been shaken to the core, and televangelism had experienced a crisis from which it might never fully recover.

David Hubbard, President of Fuller Theological Seminary in Pasadena, California, commented: "Skeptics have fuel for their fires. They may see this as reflecting on the excesses of the whole Evangelical movement." Martin Marty, Professor of Modern Christianity at the University of Chicago, said "I don't think there's ever been a nationally perceived scandal like this. It's like the cocaine issue in professional sports. Every league, every franchise is affected by the image of a problem." And Jeffrey Hadden, Professor at the University of Virginia, commented:

They've all had to fight the Elmer Gantry image, the image of all the television Evangelists as a bunch of no-good shysters. And that's the key, I think, to why Jerry Falwell jumped into PTL in the first place. He knew that if it got out of control, there was a lot for everyone to lose.

There were also internecine hostilities that began to erupt among the Evangelists themselves: in Bakker's own PTL organization, some executives could not wait to attack him, with one officer commenting: "I wonder if Jim even has a conscience anymore." Evangelist Pat Robertson seemed almost exultant at what was taking place: "I think the Lord is housecleaning a little bit. I'm glad to see it happen."

There were deeper implications to this so-called "Holy War" that was taking place. To be sure, sex scandals were nothing new to the field: sex had been used to undermine Evangelists ever since Salome pleaded with Herod for John the Baptist's head. Aimee Semple McPherson, Father Divine, Garner Ted Armstrong, Adam Clayton Powell, Jim Jones, and Martin Luther King, Jr. were all beleaguered with rumors of sexual adventures, as if their charisma would be tainted by the imputation that they were super-libidinal.

And to be sure, the exposure of any single Evangelist as a typical Elmer Gantry type of huckster and hustler might be enough to tarnish the entire field of Evangelists.

But in this particular instance, there was more than sex and huck-sterism at stake: there was a very specific doctrinal issue that was causing the conflict. Jim Bakker, who had built up the PTL Club organization, was a Pentecostal Charismatic Fundamentalist whose followers knew that he practiced healing, speaking in tongues and the eccentric be-havior characteristic of Baptist Charismatics. Jerry Falwell, the alleged usurper of the PTL Club, was a conservative Fundamentalist who did not practice faith healing, speaking in tongues, or any of the other unusual Pentecostal or Charismatic practices. And Jimmy Swaggart, the alleged interloper who was threatening a hostile takeover of PTL, was a Pentecostal Fundamentalist but not a Charismatic.

So behind the sex and money scandals, the "Holy Wars" were really a doctrinal conflict between the three major movements of the South-ern Baptist Church: the question was whether Evangelical Christianity should remain strictly Fundamentalist, or whether it should be allowed to develop along more liberal Charismatic or Pentecostal lines.

And no matter how this Falwell-Bakker-Swaggart dispute would resolve itself, the underlying question about the future of American Protestantism would take some time to sort out its final answer.

Meanwhile the 2 billion dollar televangelist industry hung in the balance. There were some 221 stations committed to broadcasting various Evangelical programs across America, and some 60 syndicated nationwide programs were still being produced. All these Evangelical programs in one way or another reflected the basic Falwell-Bakker-Swaggart conflict: some programs adhered strictly to Fundamentalist conservativism, while others practiced the more liberal Pentecostal or Charismatic approaches.

One of the most influential televangelists over the years has been Rex Humbard of Little Rock, Arkansas. Conducting his syndicated radio and television programs over 650 stations in 18 countries, Rex Humbard performs out of his Cathedral of Tomorrow with 5,000 seats, and he also has access to the Gospel Big Top which holds 6,000.

Rex Humbard's Pentecostal message is "You Are Loved," and he disseminates this on his regular program To Tell the World. Marjoe Gortner assesses Rex Humbard's preaching style: "The worst. He's the worst on the air. He has no charisma. He is flat; he has a terrible haircut; his wardrobe—he should get a new tailor. It's always an amazement to me how he can be so successful."

Rex Humbard was one of the first to react strongly to the 1987 Jim Bakker scandals. Humbard felt the disclosure of Bakker's sexual and financial misdeeds could be potentially ruinous to the entire Evangelical community: "The credibility of the televised Evangelists is probably the lowest I can ever remember."

Another televangelist who has been enormously influential over the years is Ernest Angley, broadcasting out of Akron, Ohio. Angley's Revivalism takes the form of the crudest type of faith healing: repeatedly shouting out "IN THE NAME OF JESUS," Angley claps hands on the lame, the blind, the deaf, the retarded, as he commands the devil to leave the bodies of the afflicted. Angley's own body goes through contortions as he simulates the exorcism that is taking place with heaves, bellowings and grunts, all to the chorus of the repeated chant "IN THE NAME OF JESUS." Marjoe Gortner comments on Ernest Angley: "He's still doing the same thing he was doing when I was four years old. 'Hey! Hallelujah!' He's a relief. People are filled with tension all day and, hallelujah! It's great. It's like seeing a cheap, sleazy movie."

George Vandeman conducts a half hour TV lecture series entitled It Is Written, which presents solid Bible study combined with timely social and historical allusions. Probably the blandest of televangelists, Vandeman is laid-back and leisurely and appeals to those who prefer the illusion of common sense to the *sturm und drang* of more histrionic Evangelists.

One may wonder at this point why there are so many male televangelists and so few female Evangelists. Since Aimee Semple McPherson, there have been very few women who have succeeded in the field and this may have something to do with the peculiar nature of Dionysian frenzy we were discussing earlier: the curious frenzy which is associated with this phallic aspect of Evangelism seems to have been arrogated by male Evangelism. To be sure, there have been regional female Evangelists who present a modest form of conversionary preaching: Mother Angelica, a Catholic nun of the Franciscan Order, broadcasts out of Birmingham, Alabama, and was promoted by Pat Robertson on a TV program.

Perhaps the most successful of all female Evangelists since Aimee Semple McPherson was Katharine Kuhlman, who preached a Charismatic message of divine love and used a 700-voice choir to back up her message. Kuhlman had a strident voice that delivered a no-nonsense forthright sermon which confronted the viewer with the point-blank choice of accepting God's love or not. At the time of Kuhlman's death in 1976, she was the leading female Evangelist in America, with over three-quarters of a million regular viewers.

In addition to the major televangelists who continue to broadcast nationally, almost every section of America has its own indigenous Evangelists who preach to regional areas. We can take a random sampling of some of these local televangelists from four major parts of the United States: the Midwest, California, Texas, and Florida:

1. In the Midwest, broadcasting out of Grand Rapids, Michigan, Richard and Martin De Haan and Paul Van Gordner conduct their popular *Day of Discovery* program for the surrounding states of Ohio, Indiana, Illinois, and Wisconsin. Even so, the nationwide audience for this *Day of Discovery* program is so immense that in 1980 it ranked fifth in Arbitron ratings, ahead of both Jim Bakker and Jerry Falwell.

2. In California, aside from the many network TV programs like *The World Tomorrow* which originate out of the Los Angeles area for nationwide audiences, there are local televangelists who serve the regional area. Lloyd Ogilvie in Hollywood and Gene Scott in Los Angeles are two of the most representative.

3. In Texas, Robert Tilton conducts a self-help Evangelist program

called *Success-N-Life* out of Dallas, Texas, and Kenneth Copland broadcasts a Revival program from his Eagle Mountain Chapel in Fort Worth. Copland is so successful that he is able to make his TV congregation pledge to tithe their entire incomes as freewill gift offerings to his ministry.

4. In Florida, accommodating a mix of Southern Baptist Fundamentalists, tourists from out of state, and retired Senior Citizens, James Kennedy broadcasts a regular Revival program from his 7,000-member Church in Fort Lauderdale.

With the advent of this new electronic Evangelism, both radio and television, there were several simultaneous reactions against the phenomenon: a fierce anti-Evangelism began working to counteract what was perceived to be the chicanery and fraud that was going on in the business.

Anti-Evangelism is nothing new—in the early part of the century, H. L. Mencken let loose at a vocation that he despised:

If I hate any class of men in this world, it is Evangelical Christians, with their bellicose stupidity, their childish belief in devils, their barbarous hoofing of all beauty, dignity, and decency. But even Evangelical Christians I do not hate when I see their wives.

Perhaps the most effective critic of contemporary Evangelism is a man we have been quoting throughout this chapter on radio and television Evangelists—Marjoe Gortner. A film actor today, Marjoe Gortner made a film based on his own life experience entitled *Marjoe*, in which he documents the cynical exploitation that takes place when a parent sets out to program an offspring into performing as a Child Evangelist. The movie shows six-year-old Marjoe Gortner standing on a studio platform, cartwheeling his arms in midair as he denounces sin with a grown-up frown on his face, urging his congregation to repentance through the saving love of JE-sus. The film is an excellent exposé of the hustle and corruption that goes on behind the scenes of most Revival circuits across the country, and the sight of this earnest child dancing around and trying to con his gullible audience would be downright laughable if the whole thing weren't so base and degraded. Marjoe Gortner has been at work on another film, *American Gospel*, using his assessments of today's leading television Evangelists.

Another critic of contemporary American Evangelism is the Amazing Randi—Canadian-born James Randi—a magician by trade. On the April 22, 1986 *Tonight* show on NBC, Randi showed how the faith-healing Evangelist Peter Popoff of Upland, California, used fraudulent methods to perform miraculous cures onstage. Randi demonstrated how Popoff's wife was busy working the audience, secretly identifying persons with different ailments which Popoff would then call out and seem to heal miraculously. Popoff went even further and told the audience to toss all their pills and medications onstage, and the assorted vials and bottles that came sailing through the air included insulin, nitroglycerin, digitalis, and other life-saving drugs. Randi claimed the whole routine was a scam and an example of how dangerous Evangelism could be when it tried to usurp the role of appropriate medical care. In response to Randi's charges, the Peter Popoff Evangelistic Association of Upland accused Randi of trying to publicize a book he was writing exposing Evangelists. *Free Inquiry* Editor Paul Kurtz commented that, fraudulent or not, the kind of Evangelism the Popoffs were practicing could be extremely deleterious because "many people will be misled into thinking they have been healed when they are not, and that, in some cases, they may give up needed medicine."

An anti-Evangelist organization called Fundamentalists Anonymous was founded in New York in April 1985 by Richard Yao, a graduate of Yale Divinity School and a former Fundamentalist himself. Patterned after Alcoholics Anonymous, Yao's organization holds weekly discussion groups, puts out newsletters, and has a help line (212-696-0420) for persons who have become "hooked" on Fundamentalism and want to get off but are incapable of kicking the addiction "cold turkey." Richard Yao comments: "If Fundamentalism works for you, that's great. We just work with those who come to us and say, 'Help me get out.' The fact that 13,000 people have come to us so far proves there is a need for what we do."

Whatever we may think of televangelism, the hard fact is that—scandals notwithstanding—these so-called "God Shows" are here to stay. In fact they have become so much an organic part of legitimate TV fare that they are rated along with straight entertainment programming.

In 1980, Arbitron ratings for the top ten religious shows ranked the leading Evangelists as follows:

1. ORAL ROBERTS   2.7 million viewers
2. REX HUMBARD   2.4 million viewers

3. ROBERT SCHULLER   2 million viewers
4. JIMMY SWAGGART   1.9 million viewers
5. DAY OF DISCOVERY   1.5 million viewers
6. JERRY FALWELL   1.4 million viewers
7. JIM BAKKER   .6 million viewers

Arbiton estimates of these national TV audiences, about 75% were female, 30% were in the 18–39 age group, and most of the viewers canvassed were white.

Since those 1980 Arbitron ratings, there were considerable fluctuations of audience viewing, and a more recent Gallup Poll for Spring 1987 shows a considerable downward spiral in audience approval ratings for the major televangelists:

ORAL ROBERTS   from 66% in 1980 to 28% in 1987
JIMMY SWAGGART   from 76% in 1980 to 44% in 1987
PAT ROBERTSON   from 65% in 1980 to 50% in 1987
ROBERT SCHULLER   from 78% in 1980 to 61% in 1987

As we said earlier, it's a fickle industry and televangelists have to take their lumps along with prime time soap operas, sitcoms, and quiz shows. Television is a fiercely competitive business, and all the prayers in the world won't pay the bills when the Arbitron ratings begin to slip.

Chapter 12

FOUR CONTEMPORARY EVANGELISTS

WE COME NOW to four contemporary American Evangelists—Oral Roberts, Pat Robertson, Robert Schuller, and Jimmy Swaggart—who have all had a significant impact on Revivalism in our time.

Oral Roberts was born near Ada, Oklahoma, in 1918. Both his parents were part-Indian, and were Pentecostal.

Oral Roberts grew up in almost total poverty in Oklahoma, and in his youth he knew what it was to struggle against massive physical impediments: he stuttered incessantly, and he suffered from a severe case of tuberculosis. Once while he was lying in bed enduring the "final stages" of tuberculosis, Oral Roberts saw his father's face miraculously change to become the face of Jesus, and thereafter Oral was healed of his tuberculosis.

Apparently Oral Roberts' experiences in overcoming these early obstacles adumbrated his later phenomenal career as a Charismatic Evangelist, especially as he received no formal theological training. During the course of his ministry, Oral Roberts has preached to over 5 million television viewers each year, received over 6 million letters annually, and in 1986 his organization reported a gross revenue of over $140 million.

In the early 1960s, Oral Roberts professed to receive the command of the Lord to build Oral Roberts University, a $150 million campus complex in Tulsa, Oklahoma, that enrolls over 4,600 students and is a perennial national basketball contender. As soon as this University was completed, Oral Roberts received another command from the Lord to build the City of Faith Hospital, a multi-millon-dollar healing center. To raise money for this project, Oral Roberts reported a vision he received:

> I felt an overwhelming holy presence all around me. When I opened my eyes, there He stood . . . some 900 feet tall, looking at me . . . He stood a full 300 feet taller than the 600-foot-tall City of Faith. There I was face to face with Jesus Christ, the Son of the Living God. I have only seen Jesus once before, but here I was face to face with the King of Kings. He stared at me without saying a word; Oh! I will never forget those eyes! And then, He reached down, put his Hands under the City of Faith, lifted it, and said to me, "See how easy it is for Me to lift it!"

Needless to say, the response to this vision was overwhelming, and Oral Roberts received the $5 million he needed to complete the City of Faith Hospital.

At other times when Oral Roberts needs money, he resorts to marketing assorted religious novelties such as animated film strips of Bible stories, prayer cloths with a print of Oral Roberts' magic right hand, tiny bags of cement which will eventually end up in one of Roberts' building projects, and miniature sacks of cornmeal.

Marjoe Gortner praised Oral Roberts for his forthright Evangelical techniques and his savvy in using the electronic media:

> He's one of the best preachers ever. Powerful. He pulls you right in with passion, power, and strength. And a con man from the word go, but a good ole boy, a very good businessman and a strong, charismatic person. He once told me, "Marjoe, when you talk to a camera, just pretend it's a person sitting in a chair alone." When Oral Roberts talks to a camera, he has them place the lens within 12 to 15 inches of his face for a close-up. And he talks to that lens like it was a person. You get the feeling that he really is talking to you personally.

Oral Roberts describes his principle of faith healing, which is the central part of his ministry:

> The first step towards being healed and made whole in spirit, mind, and body begins with a prayer of confession that "I am sick." That is to say, "There's something out of harmony within me."
>
> Sickness in its broad sense means a lack of total harmony in one's being. Disharmony could take the form of sickness in the body, a

spiritual depression, backsliding, or unconfessed sin. Or it could be a mental depression, a down spirit.

If you are like I am, you experience down moments in your life and sometimes you feel you just can't get up. Finances get you down and you just can't see a way for your bills to be paid. You don't feel that things are going right in your marriage or on the job and you feel like giving up. When these things happen, you're sick. You feel defeated in a sense, you go blind, because in that attitude of defeatism you cannot see any more than a person who is physically blind. You're sick and in need of God's healing.

Of course the only meaningful test of such an approach is whether it works or not. And Oral Roberts has accumulated countless testimonials and case histories of healing based on his Evangelism. Here is one by "A.Z." of Pennsylvania:

I had been suffering from rheumatoid arthritis in my neck for ten years when I decided to attend your one-day service in Philadelphia last year. I didn't go to the meeting to pray for my own healing. I went to pray for my family and friends. But my Seed-Faith prayers were returned to me in the form of my own need, and my neck was healed that very same day!

Two years of wearing a neck support collar and taking medication for pain was finally over.

Brother Roberts, the healing presence of the Lord was powerful in your service that afternoon. When you told the people in the audience who had pain in the area of the neck to move their necks around, I did. And as soon as I did, the pain stopped and has never returned! Praise God!

Here is another testimonial by "A.C." of Arizona:

When I began watching your Sunday TV program, I was a complete doubter. I had been a truck driver for the last ten years, but as a result of a serious trucking accident in which I fractured my back, I was unemployed. At that point in my life I was broken in body, spirit, and finances.

Your TV program was the only thing that gave me any hope. Since you seemed to care about me and my needs, I wrote for your books and told you my many problems. You sent me books and I started corresponding with you. Actually, your letters kept me going. I watched your program every Sunday. What you said began to make sense to me, and when you announced the City of Faith, I wanted to be a part . . .

One day I had gotten to the end of my rope. I had a pistol in my hand ready to end it all when the mailman came by. There was a letter from you, inviting me to a laymen's seminar. You saved my life that day, Brother Roberts, and I knew right then I had to go to Tulsa.

During the 30-hour bus ride to the seminar I suffered excruciating pain in my back. I thought, "I'm going to have to get off and go back home. There's no way I can take 30 hours of this."

But I stayed on. I'm so glad I did because something wonderful and completely unexpected happened several hours later. Before I reached Tulsa, it suddenly occurred to me that for the first time in over a year and a half I was in no pain!

At first I could hardly believe it. But I have been free of the back pain ever since.

Of course such testimonials and case histories may strike us as contrived or hallucinatory, mere exercises in dream logic or infantile wish fulfillment which could not stand up under rigorous scientific analysis.

But it is not so easy to dismiss faith healing as a mere chimera. For one thing, we should remember healing was a large part of Christ's ministry on earth: making the lame walk, giving sight to the blind, even raising Lazarus from the dead (John Chapter 11). And one cannot say this was an exclusive power of Christ himself, as the power to heal by faith was specifically given by Jesus to each of the original disciples in the three versions of the Apostolic Charge when Jesus ordered them to go forth and preach his gospel and heal in his name (Matthew Chapters 10 and 28, Mark Chapter 16).

One can try to translate the experience of faith healing into accurate psychoanalytic terms. Sometimes an ailment or condition will persist over a given period of time until it becomes ready for remission, and this "readiness" may take the form of a predisposition that may coincide with a so-called "faith healing." If this happens and the subject experiences a remission of the ailment or condition, whether organic or psychosomatic, the event itself will seem to be miraculous.

One remembers Freud himself began his early practice by using hypnosis on his patients, as Breuer had done before him, and it was only when Freud discovered the cathartic method of free association that he was able to dispense with the mediation of hypnosis and encourage his patients to deal with their unconscious material directly out of their own stream of consciousness. A simple account of this technique is given in the opening pages of Freud's *Interpretation of Dreams*.

But whether one approaches the problem from the point of view of hypnosis or the cathartic method of free association, one cannot help but be impressed with the remarkable power of suggestion which functions strongly in either technique. And it is this same power of suggestion that dominates the work of faith healers like Oral Roberts, who risk their reputations on the fairly valid assumption that enough people out there will be suffering from psychosomatic illnesses which are reaching the point of remission, and given the right time and the right place, a strong suggestion can transform a predisposed subject from illness to health.

Oral Roberts did not rest content with having built a phenomenal career on his talent for faith healing. Pressed by a tightening economy and a backlog of unpaid bills, in 1987 Oral Roberts announced to the world that he would be "called home" if he was not able to raise $8 million by the end of March 1987. As the deadline—in this case, quite literally a deadline—drew nearer, Oral Roberts stayed isolated in his Prayer Tower on the campus of Oral Roberts University to keep vigil as he waited for the contributions to come in. It was a kind of cosmic blackmail, with Oral Roberts using his own life as the stakes.

The fund-raising gimmick worked: on March 23, 1987, Jerry Collins, the owner of pari-mutuel dog racing tracks in Sarasota and Orlando, Florida, flew to Tulsa, Oklahoma, and handed Oral Roberts a check for 1.5 million dollars, which completed the $8 million goal. Oral Roberts had saved his life for another year.

Two months later in June 1987, Oral Roberts turned his attention to resurrecting others. He announced he had raised the dead, and would give further demonstration and documentation in due time. One wag commented if it was so easy for Oral Roberts to raise the dead, how come it was so hard for him to raise cash? And in the August 3, 1987 issue of *Time* magazine devoted to the cover story "God & Money," there were two Letters to the Editor which summarize the reaction of a cross-section of America to these claims of Oral Roberts. The letters are worth quoting in full:

Oral Roberts' extraordinary claim of being able to raise the dead (Religion, July 13) brings to mind this question: If Roberts is so sure of his resurrection, why was he so worried about the possibility of his death back in March?

Anne E. McKee
Bloomington, Indiana

Oral Roberts can raise the dead! Good. He should resurrect Thomas Jefferson, James Madison, and George Mason so these gentlemen can explain exactly what they meant by separation of church and state, the right to bear arms, and other sticky points of our Constitution and Bill of Rights.

Anita Wilburn Dorsett
Houston, Texas

And Martin Gardner, in an insightful article in the August 13, 1987 *New York Review of Books*, quotes one of his friends in Tulsa, Oklahoma, who likes to say, "Oral may be a charlatan, but he's *our* charlatan."

Pat Robertson, the American Evangelist who is best known for testing the political waters of the 1988 Presidential elections, is himself descended from two United States Presidents, William Henry Harrison and Benjamin Harrison, and he is the son of a United States Senator, A. Willis Robertson.

Pat Robertson, Phi Beta Kappa graduate of Washington and Lee University, may well be the most educated of all contemporary Evangelists: a graduate of Yale Law School, he failed to pass the New York State bar exam and so turned to a business career before becoming a full-time Evangelist.

One item in Pat Robertson's biography which touched off controversy concerns his service in the Marines during the Korean conflict: in 1986 Robertson filed libel suits against former Rep. Pete McCloskey and Rep. Andrew Jacobs over their claim that Robertson tried to use his father's influence to avoid combat duty in Korea. Robertson's suit charged that both McCloskey and Jacobs "made wanton and reckless statements denigrating my role with the U. S. Marine Corps while serving in the Korean conflict."

Marjoe Gortner assesses Pat Robertson's appeal as an Evangelist:

He's a graduate of Yale and a very intelligent man. If you look at his business structure, it reflects it—he's a real businessman. Robertson sticks to the format of *The Tonight Show* on the *700 Club* (his Christian talk show), which appeals to the guy who owns a Western Auto store. He's preaching the same message as the others, but to me it's not as interesting, because it's just so corny. They sit there talking about business. Here's a man and his business was down and now it's up. Oh! Isn't that wonderful! It's just so sick.

Pat Robertson conducts his *700 Club* television show with black co-host Ben Kinchlow serving as a sidekick who is ready to pick up the ball whenever Robertson falters. The *700 Club* has had guest celebrities such as F. Lee Bailey, Anwar Sadat, Ronald Reagan, Jimmy Carter, and Gerald Ford, all of them aware of the tremendous exposure Robertson gives them on his Christian Broadcasting Network.

Pat Robertson occasionally indulges in a bit of long distance faith healing on the program:

My *700 Club* co-host, Ben Kinchlow, and I had been praying on the air, and each of us was given a word of knowledge by the Holy Spirit, "Someone has a heart that is enlarged, and God is causing that heart to resume its normal size in your chest cavity—and it's just miraculous what is happening."

In his books, Pat Robertson seems to give extraordinarily intelligent and scientific explanations for the practice of faith healing, such as the following passage:

Perhaps the reason so few people see miracles in their lives is their ignorance of the way power is activated in the universe. God's power underlies all reality. The material world as we see it consists of atoms and subatomic particles, which we further learn are composed of energy in the form of electrons and neutrons. In other words, matter is merely a form of energy. The great paradox is that what we perceive as real and tangible is actually an illusion. The reality is energy, and behind energy is the spiritual power of God.

This certainly seems to be intelligent and scientific at first reading, until we stop and think about it. Is Robertson equating God with energy in the form of electrons and neutrons? Or is he equating God with some mysterious spiritual power that is directing the flow of these electrons and neutrons? Whichever it is, how does Robertson propose keeping this God from the mechanistic trap which has been the curse of all materialist philosophies since the sixteenth century work of Hobbes? And does Robertson really care about the silliness of his statement, or is he simply showing off his sophomoric expertise in nuclear physics in order to impress his *700 Club* viewers?

One is inclined to understand why Pat Robertson keeps Ben Kinchlow at his side on the *700 Club*: to keep him from going off on such expeditions. But if the underlying theology gets muddled, Robertson can always fall back on accounts of his faith healing:

> During the years I have served Jesus, it has been my privilege to see a number of instantaneous miracles. I prayed for a woman in Calgary, Alberta, Canada, who had been deaf in one ear for fifty years. Her deaf ear opened instantly and she could hear perfectly . . .

This woman was not present at the *700 Club* broadcast so we have to take Pat Robertson's word for the miraculous cure. And that seems to be the way Robertson prefers it:

> Each year through my *700 Club* television program, I see or hear about some fifty thousand people who have received miraculous answers to prayer—most of them instantaneous. Tumors and cysts disappear, cancer is healed, disfiguring scars vanish, twisted limbs straighten, retarded children develop mental acuity, diseased organs become normal, marriages are restored, miracles of finance take place . . .

The indiscriminate scramble of all these good works is breathtaking: organic healing is mixed up with cosmetic cleansing and working the stock market and getting higher IQ scores and rehabilitating a bad marriage. Robertson is not above using phrases such as "God's marvelous system of money management," which he defines as "how to get more wealth if you really need it, and also, more importantly, how to manage your money and use it in line with God's overall plan for your life." This kind of entrepreneurship makes God sound like a Mutual of Omaha representative.

Pat Robertson is, in fact, the most adroit entrepreneur on the Evangelical scene today: he is President and Chief Executive Officer of the Christian Broadcasting Network; he oversees an annual income of some $233 million; he owns four television stations and five radio stations;

he employs a staff of over 800 people; his network is the world's largest supplier of cable TV programming; and he publishes a periodical newsletter, *Perspective*. Robertson's *700 Club* receives over 4 million prayer calls a year, has 4,500 volunteers, 60 counseling centers, and is the heaviest user of WATS phone lines (800 calls).

Pat Robertson's theology can be summed up in the predictable Fundamentalist positions: he is against abortion ("We are offering up 1.5 million babies a year upon the altar of sensuality and selfishness"); he is against homosexuality; he is against the ERA ("The husband is the high priest of the family"); and he is pro-Creationism.

Pat Robertson made his commitment to Christ in 1956, in the Neo-Pentecostal or Charismatic movement, which believes in baptism in the Holy Spirit, laying on of hands, and speaking in tongues. In 1963, in a spontaneous ploy to keep his television talk-show on the air, Robertson asked 700 people to pledge $10 a month for a total of $84,000 a year. It worked, and ever since the talk show has been called the *700 Club*.

In his 1972 autobiography *Shout It From the Housetops*, Pat Robertson tells of his marriage to his wife Dede and how she went off on a trip and he sold all their worldly possessions while she was away. He said he would continue to do this until she proved "her willingness to submit herself to my spiritual leadership."

The February 17, 1986 cover story of *Time* magazine ran a photo of Pat Robertson and an article on "Religion, Politics and Money" which quoted Robertson on a number of his positions. As to his possible Presidential candidacy: "The only thing for me is, where would God have me serve?"[1]

Robertson may present this public image of ingenuous waiting on the Lord, but nonetheless goes on with deliberate and calculated organization of his political machinery. As to his views on the legislative and judicial branches of government: "I believe that the courts have usurped the legislative function to an alarming extent . . . It is the churches that could take the lead. It is not something Government can get involved in . . ."

This boggles the mind of anyone who has taken a high school course in Civics and understands the basic principle of Church/State separation. As to his thoughts about social reform:

The prophet Isaiah says we are supposed to lift the yoke of oppression. And I think whether it is economic oppression, civil rights oppression of minorities, oppression against women or oppression against billions

of people under Communist domination, there is a positive duty to at
least assist people in their struggle for freedom . . . I think that if we
have the opportunity to assist these wars of liberation, as in Afghanistan
or Nicaragua or Angola, we should do that . . .

This proclamation of support for all wars of liberation against the
forces of oppression may sound bizarre coming from a man who is an
avowed foe of the Equal Rights Amendment for women and who
opposes equal rights for homosexuals. As to his thoughts about the
future:

I think that freedom is breaking forth in the world. All the U.S. has to
do is to stay strong and to stay the course. That is assuming we don't
fall from within with moral decay. If we have a spiritual renewal, which
is urgently needed, there is no question that the long-term outlook for
the U.S. is very, very bright. We religious broadcasters are a symbol
that a profound spiritual renewal is taking place in our country.

It is interesting that Pat Robertson sees televangelists as the brightest
hope in the free world, especially in light of the many recent scandals.
But then elevator operators would probably claim that elevator operators were the brightest hope in the free world, and paperback book
publishers would probably claim paperback book publishers were the
brightest hope. It all depends on whom you're talking to.

Behind the self-puffery, Pat Robertson may seem to be espousing a
platform of conservative politics, but underneath it is something quite
different. It offers us a demonstration of how dangerous the Evangelical
viewpoint can be when it enters into the realm of politics where debate
is vital to the democratic process. For example, there is this statement
Robertson made about the Republican takeover of the Senate in 1980:
"It was the direct act of God . . . that Strom Thurmond (R.-S.C.)
became head of the Judiciary Committee rather than Teddy Kennedy."

Awesome as such a comment is, Pat Robertson carries the same
kind of Theocratic head into the realm of finances in his book *The
Secret Kingdom*: "I was praying one day in 1969, and the Lord spoke
plainly to my inner man: 'The stock market is going to crash.' "

Robertson claims the Lord told him to put all his money into
government securities. It's nice to know the Lord is up on the Dow-
Jones averages but one trembles to contemplate what this kind of
thinking could do if it were installed in the Oval Office. One also

wonders how Pat Robertson's inner man could ever reconcile itself with something as unsanctified as majority rule, especially if this inner man had just been spoken to by the Lord.

It may seem a relief to leave Evangelists who are enamored of American politics, and see Robert Schuller standing in full cassock with his arms extended and a broad smile on his face as he proclaims: "This is the day the Lord has made! Let us rejoice and be glad in it!"

So begins each *Hour of Power* message from Robert Schuller's Crystal Cathedral in Garden Grove, California. This Crystal Cathedral, designed by architects Philip Johnson and John Burgee, was built in 1980 for $25 million and seats 10,000 people. It is in the shape of a four-pointed star which spans 415 feet and has 10,611 panes of glass on all sides. Inside the great glass edifice are fresh flowers, caged canaries, the world's largest pipe organ, and giant closed-circuit TV screens for those people in the congregation who are seated too far away from the pulpit to see Robert Schuller's broad smile. The Crystal Cathedral is one of the spectacular showcases of modern American Evangelism.

And Schuller's *Hour of Power* is one of the amazing media events in modern broadcasting. The 1980 Arbitron ratings already cited rank Schuller's *Hour of Power* in third place nationally with over two million viewers, slightly behind Oral Roberts and Rex Humbard, and well ahead of Jimmy Swaggart, Jerry Falwell, and Jim Bakker's *PTL Club*. In 1986, the Crystal Cathedral reported $35 million in gross revenues with $31 million in expenses.

Robert Schuller's message is something he calls "Possibility Thinking," which is a Pelagian form of self-help deriving from the Positive Thinking of Norman Vincent Peale. "Possibility Thinking" aims at boosting one's self-esteem through dynamic suggestion, and Schuller has published a slew of books that develop this approach: *Reach Out for a New Life; You Can Become the Person You Want to Be; Positive Prayers for Power-Filled Living; Peace of Mind through Possibility Thinking; The Peak to Peek Principle;* and *Be Happy You Are Loved.* Schuller explains:

In each of our *Hour of Power* messages, both printed and spoken, we have maintained that anyone can succeed if he or she makes a commitment to possibility thinking. By success we mean the achieving of a predetermined objective that makes manifest a person's chosen value system. By possibility thinking we mean that mental attitude which assumes that any objective that is noble, admirable, or beautiful can be realized even if it appears to be impossible.

In helping others to realize their full potential, Robert Schuller speaks of the Jonah complex: we fear an encounter with God because we fear the best much more than we fear the worst. Here Schuller may have hit on an important insight into human nature, for surely it is our own aspirations towards excellence that render us most timid and impotent in our own eyes. Yet the problem with this Possibility Thinking is that Schuller has an absolute mania for doggerel catch-phrases and homilies, flip mnemonic maxims and axioms that are as easy to keep in mind as they are offensively simplistic. A prime example is his coinage of the "Be-Happy Attitudes," a mongrelization of the sublime Beatitudes in the Sermon on the Mount. Following are some other examples of pat platitudes Schuller tosses out from his pulpit in the Crystal Cathedral:

> Turn scars into stars.
> It takes guts to leave the ruts.
> Inch by inch, everything's a cinch.
> The dream precedes the scheme.
> the attitude of gratitude
> fountains on the mountains
> nest on the crest
> Speak from the peak.
> Never believe in never.
> The cross is a minus turned into a plus.

That last one could appear sacrilegious if it weren't so ridiculous. And indeed, all these clichés are so tepid they are ultimately innocuous —the only real blasphemy is imagining 10,000 people seated there in that Crystal Cathedral drinking in trite insights as if they were pearls of wisdom.

Marjoe Gortner is more bothered by the manner than the matter of Schuller's Evangelism:

> I don't like Schuller. He talks s-o-o-o slowly and that's b-o-o-oring. He was never a traveling evangelist like the others. He's got that middle class approach. He comes off as an intellectual. His cleric robe is sort of a first for a full Gospel preacher. He's elevated high above the

congregation, more like a priest in a Catholic parish. He's taken the traditional Church and just put the full Gospel message in it. That's his gimmick.

In one of his self-help homilies, Robert Schuller describes how we tend to become what we expect other people to expect us to be:

Ultimately I am not what I think I am.
I am not what you think I am.
I am what I think you think I am.

The trouble with this sort of makeshift psychology is that it ignores the profound damage that can be done to the human psyche by such image projections. For example, how could one apply Schuller's formula to an outright psychopath like Iago in Shakespeare's *Othello*, who boldly announces to the audience "I am not what I am"? Or what about someone suffering from a split self-image that a schizophrenic parent imposed on him? Sometimes such pathological image projections may become so virulent as to become life-threatening, and in such cases it seems dastardly to preach a simplistic formula "I am what you think I am." Sometimes one can only come to terms with fractured egos and radically scattered self-images through extensive work in classical psychoanalysis.

Indeed, Robert Schuller's self-help theology of Possibility Thinking does presume a healthy and ordinary psyche, which is apparently the constituency of Schuller's pastorate. However, the sad irony is that such a cross-section of blandly "normal" plain folks are not the ones who usually go for any of the Herculean labors and soaring visions that Schuller keeps talking about in his sermons. These are Readers Digest types who are what Nietzsche had in mind when he condemned the "human, all too human" mediocrities who inhabit our modern world. All these blandly normal plain folks would much rather sit and listen to Herculean feats of achievement, than actually go out and practice them.

One good thing needs to be said about Robert Schuller, and that is that he is relatively harmless. Unlike some other contemporary Evangelists, Schuller has the good sense not to tamper in areas that are beyond his ken, like politics, abortion, divorce, homosexuality, or prayer in public schools. He is content to preach the insipid homilies of his Possibility Thinking within his $25 million Crystal Cathedral complete with tweeting caged canaries, fresh flowers, and the world's largest pipe organ—and his 10,000 member congregation loves him for it.

And so, like the Cheshire cat, Robert Schuller's broad smile gets broader and broader as the years go by.

Jimmy Swaggart is a Louisiana moonshiner's son, a high school dropout, and has been speaking in tongues since the age of nine. He is the cousin of rock star Jerry Lee Lewis, a Pentecostal preacher and gospel singer in his own right, with several gold albums which have sold well over thirteen million copies.

The Jimmy Swaggart Evangelistic Association in Baton Rouge, Louisiana, owns a 4,300-member local church, eight radio stations, with daily and weekly television programs syndicated over 222 TV stations across the country with a gross of $142 million in 1986.

The Jimmy Swaggart Bible College opened in 1984 with 18,000 annual applications for 400 openings. The printing plant produces 24 million items a year. Jimmy Swaggart has mission offices in fifty-three countries, and his weekly hour broadcasts originate from the Family Worship Center in Baton Rouge, with 7,000 seats.

During a typical service, Jimmy Swaggart begins by playing the piano or electric organ and singing with his backup choir. During his singing and playing, his left leg keeps conspicuous time to the strong Nashville rhythm of the gospel hymn. Then for his message, Jimmy Swaggart takes center stage and begins prowling the platform back and forth, slowly and deliberately, whipping the wire of his microphone behind him as if it were an evolutionary tail he is trying to get rid of. Gradually, Swaggart's pace begins to accelerate as his preaching heats up, and he pulls his necktie askew so he is open-throated as he begins shouting out loud and stamping his foot on the floor and dancing in paroxysms of exclamatory rapture. As he reaches the climax of his message, he begins speaking in tongues, babbling out indecipherable phrases and incomprehensible locutions with all the earnestness of someone speaking perfectly appropriate and syntactical English. His congregation explodes with applause and gives him a standing ovation. It's a good show.

Marjoe Gortner reports:

> I like his preaching style, that type of real entertainment. He's just like an old-time preacher. His message makes me sick. He's still talking about the most ridiculous things: God made woman to be in the home.

> The whole thing is very sexual. When Jimmy Swaggart sits down to play, the way he spreads those long legs and starts singing to the old ladies—the same ones who love Mike Douglas. He's got that pure thing in his voice . . .

Besides how God made woman to be in the home, what else does Jimmy Swaggart preach? Like most other Fundamentalists, he attacks Communism, secular humanism, pornography, AIDS, the ERA, and he says "The Supreme Court is an institution damned by God Almighty" for allowing abortions.

In 1986 in *Spin* magazine, Jimmy Swaggart began lashing out at Rock and Roll for encouraging "mass suicides, premarital sex, homosexuality, bestiality, and necrophilia." In retaliation, Bob Guccione, the publisher of *Spin*, began distributing posters of Jimmy Swaggart dressed in drag from *The Rocky Horror Show*. Guccione explains: "He raises $150 million a year and attacks Rock and Roll. He's the one who got teen and rock magazines banned from Walmart stores."

In 1987 during the "Holy Wars," Jim Bakker claimed it was Jimmy Swaggart who got Bakker ousted from the ministry and then precipitated the takeover of Bakker's *PTL Club*, forcing Bakker to turn PTL leadership over to Jerry Falwell. Bakker claimed Swaggart wanted to amalgamate PTL with Jimmy Swaggart Ministries to create the largest gospel congregation in the world.

Swaggart was smart enough to stay out of the ensuing public conflict between Bakker and Falwell and continue on with his own ministry. Which is just as well because when he is on, Jimmy Swaggart is an inspired performer who simulates the grace of God in his preaching and singing. And that's about all one can ask of any televangelist.

On February 21, 1988, Jimmy Swaggart stood in front of his congregation in Baton Rouge, Louisiana, and confessed he had sinned and would cease preaching indefinitely.

ABC News reported that Marvin Gorman, a television Evangelist from New Orleans, had provided church officials with photographs of Swaggart entering and leaving a motel room with a known prostitute. In 1986, Swaggart had accused Gorman of similar adulterous affairs and Gorman had filed a $90 million lawsuit against Swaggart which was later dismissed.

In 1987, many believe it was Jimmy Swaggart who informed the leadership of the Assemblies of God denomination about Jim Bakker's adulterous liason with Jessica Hahn, which brought about the scandal that almost wrecked the PTL Club. At that time, Swaggart said from his nationwide TV pulpit:

> When a preacher has been found out and it is fact—not hearsay— that he has performed an act of adultery, a hearing is convened and he then has to step down.

The Associated Press reported that Swaggart went even further privately, saying that Jim Bakker and his PTL ministry was "a cancer that needed to be excised from the body of Christ." And in March 1987, while on a California Crusade, Jimmy Swaggart made the following public reference to Bakker:

> God deliver us from these pompadour boys—hair done, nails done, fresh from the beauty shop, preaching the Gospel.

Now in February 1988, Jimmy Swaggart was standing in front of his own congregation, confessing publicly that he himself had committed the same sin. Swaggart said,

> I do not plan in any way to whitewash my sin or call it a mistake. I call it a sin.

Swaggart apologized to his congregation; to his wife, Frances, who sat behind him; and to Almighty God. He then announced he was giving up his pulpit for an undetermined period of time. "We will leave that in the hands of the Lord," Swaggart said.

Swaggart did not have long to wait for a decision. On Monday, February 22, the Assemblies of God church announced it had removed Jimmy Swaggart from his pulpit for three months. The church elders had accepted the preacher's "true humility and repentance" and announced that he had been offered two years of "rehabilitation." Louisiana District supervisor Cecil Janway reported:

> We accept his confession of specific incidents of a moral failure. Based on his detailed confession and the evidence we observed of true humility and repentance, we have offered him rehabilitation, in accordance with the bylaws of the general council and Louisiana District of the Assemblies of God.

Glen Cole, pastor of the Capital Christian Center in Sacramento, California, and one of the thirteen church officials who examined Swaggart, commented:

> He tried and tried and tried through prayer and fasting and everything he could do to lick it and it beat him.

On Wednesday, February 24, 1988, Debra Murphree, a 27-year-old, tattooed prostitute, went on WVUE-TV in New Orleans and identified herself as the "known prostitute" in question, and told how she had performed pornographic acts for Jimmy Swaggart for about a year, in various places in New Orleans:

> I seen him drive down the street every week, you know, and maybe sometimes he wouldn't stop unless he knew I was there—maybe once or twice a month.

At about the same time, an avalanche of phone calls began coming into the Assemblies of God headquarters in Springfield, Missouri, protesting the "inadequate" punishment that Swaggart had been given by the church hierarchy.

To compound the televangelist scandals that had already surfaced thus far, on February 25, 1988, Jimmy Breslin broke a story in the *New York Daily News* of a hooker named "Precious" who had been flown down to South Carolina to meet with Jim Bakker several times. "Precious" claimed she was later approached by three men in New York who said they were from Baton Rouge, Louisiana, and that these men paid her $100 to swear a deposition against Bakker. One of these men, she claimed, had "a $60 haircut" and forced her to have sex with him in the car afterwards, and then refused to pay her extra for her sexual favors. "Precious" identified the man who had sex with her as Jimmy Swaggart when she later saw him on one of his television Crusades. To get revenge, "Precious" began phoning in to all the different television Evangelism programs that displayed their special 800 telephone numbers on the TV screen, and when someone would answer she would ask, "Do you know what Jimmy Swaggart does with girls?" "Precious" would then tell her story to whomever would listen.

Breslin implies in his story that with this sort of thing going on, the truth was bound to surface sooner or later. But Pat Robertson, who was actively engaged as a Presidential candidate during this period, didn't see it the same way. On Tuesday, February 23, 1988, former television Evangelist Robertson charged that all these revelations about Jimmy Swaggart's sexual misconduct were deliberately timed and orchestrated for nationwide exposure by Vice President George Bush, who was also running for President, just prior to the Republican primaries in South Dakota and Minnesota.

According to the *Daily News* Washington Bureau, Robertson claimed the Swaggart disclosure was part of a "dirty tricks campaign" originating from the Bush organization with the goal of embarrassing Robertson before the March 5 vote:

> For a bit of information to lie dormant since last October and to surface in the headlines of the papers two weeks before the primary—to think that that's accidental stretches the credulity of almost everyone.

For his part, George Bush said Robertson was "making bizarrre statements in order to make news."

To place all these television Evangelism scandals in the context of Judeo-Christian religion, one would have to go back to the Genesis story of creation where Adam and Eve are expelled from Eden because of sexual disobedience. Further on in the Old Testament, there is the extraordinarily dramatic scandal that is told in II Samuel Chapter 12, where Nathan the prophet accuses David of taking Bathsheba after he killed her husband Uriah the Hittite. Nathan tells a parable about a man who took a lamb from a poor shepherd,

5 And David's anger was greatly kindled against the man; and he said to Nathan, As the LORD liveth, the man that hath done this thing shall surely die:

6 And he shall restore the lamb fourfold, because he did this thing, and because he had no pity.

7 And Nathan said to David, Thou art the man. Thus saith the LORD God of Israel, I annointed thee king over Israel, and I delivered thee out of the hand of Saul;

8 And I gave thee thy master's house, and thy master's wives into thy bosom, and gave thee the house of Israel and of Judah; and if that had been too little, I would moreover have given unto thee such and such things.

9 Wherefore hast thou despised the commandment of the LORD, to do evil in his sight? thou hast killed Uriah the Hittite with the sword,

and hast taken his wife to be thy wife, and hast slain him with the sword of the children of Ammon.

David admits his guilt, and he records in the fifty-first Psalm his enormous outpouring of remorse and contrition:

1 Have mercy upon me, O God, according to thy lovingkindness: according unto the multitude of thy tender mercies blot out my transgressions.

2 Wash me throughly from mine iniquity, and cleanse me from my sin.

3 For I acknowlege my transgressions: and my sin is ever before me.

4 Against thee, thee only, have I sinned, and done this evil in thy sight: that thou mightest be justified when thou speakest, and be clear when thou judgest.

5 Behold, I was shapen in iniquity, and in sin did my mother conceive me.

6 Behold, thou desireth truth in the inward parts: and in the hidden part thou shalt make me to know wisdom.

7 Purge me with hyssop, and I shall be clean; wash me, and I shall be whiter than snow. . . .

Both sexual transgression and unconscious homicidal wishes seem to be central to Judeo-Christian cosmology, but the story of David and Bathsheba would not be complete without adding its most extraordinary outcome. Further on in II Samuel chapter 12 it is reported,

24 And David comforted Bathsheba his wife, and went in unto her, and lay with her: and she bore a son, and he called his name Solomon: and the LORD loved him.

Thus a new king of Israel was born out of the scandal—Solomon, who was to reign for forty years and become known to all ages for his wisdom and uprightness. It would seem to be important to keep in mind that beyond scandal and judgmental punishment, God works in mysterious ways.

¹In November 1987 Robertson declared his candidacy for the Republican nomination for President. Although he came in a surprising second in the January 1988 Iowa caucuses, his campaign disintegrated as he made unsubstantiated claims about missiles in Cuba and hostages in the Middle East. He won no primaries or caucuses, and as of the New York primary trailed Vice President Bush in the race for the nomination, 800 delegates to 17.

Chapter 13

JERRY FALWELL

JERRY FALWELL, the genial self-appointed spokesman for the New Christian Right in America, began his ministry in 1956 at the age of twenty-two in an abandoned Donald Duck bottling plant.

Pastor of the Thomas Road Baptist Church in Lynchburg, Virginia, Jerry Falwell had grown up listening to Charles E. Fuller's *Old Fashioned Revival Hour*, so it was only natural that when it came time for Falwell to choose a name for his own radio and television program, he should call it *The Old Time Gospel Hour*. It has the same format as Fuller's earlier radio show, with gospel choir, informal sermon, and perhaps a few guest testimonials. Falwell's program is carried over 681 radio and television stations across America, and it reaches some 21 million listeners and viewers.

When Jerry Falwell was a child, his father killed one of Falwell's uncles in a family feud, and later Falwell's father died an agonizing death from alcoholism. This may go far in explaining Jerry Falwell's predisposition to getting himself embroiled in so many internecine conflicts such as Republican Party pressure groups and the more recent "Holy Wars" that broke out following Falwell's takeover of Jim Bakker's *PTL Club*. It may also explain Jerry Falwell's obsession with morality and strict Fundamentalist doctrine, as well as his mania for a slick veneer of righteousness and respectability: the man seems to be addicted to three-piece polyester suits, so much so that he has been characterized as "a sophisticated snake oil salesman."

Marjoe Gortner sums up Jerry Falwell:

He's kind of country, and down home. He appeals to that little guy out there who wants to speak up and say something—just doesn't know what he wants to say. He hears this good ole boy who talks in his language, and I think that could be very harmful. While some preach God's message, Falwell preaches Falwell's message, which is more like that of the old John Birchers or the Ku Klux Klan.

Jerry Falwell himself estimates there are over 110,000 local churches in the United States that are Fundamentalist in conviction and, by forming a loose coalition of these churches, Falwell's ambition was to form a "Moral Majority" that could do real political damage: for example, knock out liberal United States Senators like Frank Church, George McGovern, and Birch Bayh.

Jerry Falwell asserts his basic faith as follows:

I believe that God's role for America is as a catalyst, that he wants to set the spiritual time bomb off right here. If that is the case, America must stay free. And for America to stay free we must come back to the only principles that God can honor: the dignity of life, the traditional family, decency, morality, and so on.

The time bomb image in the above statement may be more revealing of Falwell's mind-set than he realizes: it makes God into a cosmic terrorist whose saving grace is like an act of arson in guerrilla warfare rather than any sublime beatitude.

But it's that phrase "and so on" which is the real tip-off on how open-ended and potentially dangerous Falwell's basic approach is: whatever values Jerry Falwell chooses to say are "principles that God can honor" may be added on to the above listing, but whatever values Falwell says God cannot honor have to be kept off the list. It's this kind of arbitrary thought process that allowed Falwell to feel real compassion and forgiveness toward Jim Bakker's confessed one-night stand of adultery with Jessica Hahn, but which slammed the door shut on any hope of forgiveness for Bakker's alleged history of homosexual episodes.

Jerry Falwell is not one to split hairs about such things, and his momentum is so powerful he keeps right on going. Occasionally he tosses out a few lines of metaphoric imagery to show he means business: "We have stretched the rubber band of morality too far already. A few more stretches and it will undoubtedly snap forever."

In 1971 Jerry Falwell founded Lynchburg Baptist College, then changed its name to Liberty Baptist College to avoid any association with the word "lynch." Then he changed its name to Liberty University. As Chancellor of this school, Falwell has poured over $40 million into its construction program and administration, and he plans to bring the current enrollment of 7,000 up to 50,000 by the year 2000. One may note in passing that those Fundamentalist Evangelists who preach the imminent Second Coming of Jesus most earnestly are usually the ones who make the most careful business projections of how things will fare on earth by the turn of the century, in case the Second Coming does not take place after all.

Liberty University has a 4,400-acre campus, and enforces a strict student dress and conduct code: ties and dresses are to be worn at all times by the appropriate sexes, and there is to be no listening to "rock, disco, country and western, Christian rock, or any other music that is associated closely with these types." No profanity, no smoking, no drinking of alcoholic beverages, no dancing, no going to movies—it is, in effect, a monument to Fundamentalist doctrine. And speaking of monuments, Liberty University has one of the most curious and bizarre shrines that has ever been conceived by the mind of man. In the center of the campus there is a tombstone-shaped shrine that is dedicated to all the fetuses that have ever been aborted since the 1973 Roe v. Wade Supreme Court decision legalizing abortions in America.

Jerry Falwell takes enormous pride in Liberty University and sees it as the vanguard school of Fundamentalism; he once commented, "Liberty University is to Evangelical Christianity what Brigham Young is to Mormons and Notre Dame is to Catholics."

Falwell has had his brush with the federal government in the management and disbursement of funds that go to make up the budget of Liberty University. In 1973 the Securities and Exchange Commission sued the Thomas Road Baptist Church for issuing allegedly fraudulent bonds; Falwell promised he would be more responsible in the future, all the while insisting on the Calvinist principle that "material wealth is God's way of blessing people who put him first."

"The Moral Majority" phrase that has been the label for the New Christian Right was first coined in 1979 through a chance remark Falwell made: "Out there is a moral majority waiting to be tapped." Like William Booth's inadvertent reference to the Salvation Army, the phrase stuck and became synonymous with Jerry Falwell's Fundamentalist movement. The idea that there may be a majority of Fundamentalists out there in America is reminiscent of a comment H. L. Mencken once made: "Heave an egg out of a Pullman window and you will hit a Fundamentalist almost anywhere in the United States today."

Falwell's Moral Majority has its own cable television service to promulgate its views: the Liberty Broadcasting network reaches over a million American homes with conservative Fundamentalist views that are approved by Falwell and his Liberty University Board. These strict views include the condemnation of every manifestation of moral decay, homosexuality, sexual promiscuity, perversion, pornography, abortion, and the undermining of traditional family values; as Falwell puts it succinctly: "They must be made to see that moral Americans are a powerful group who will no longer permit them to destroy our country with their godless, liberal philosophies."

For fund-raising purposes, Jerry Falwell's Moral Majority has been known to cloak itself under the titles of several front organizations such as The Conservative Caucus; The Roundtable; Committee For the Survival of a Free Congress; Christian Voice; American Conservative Union; Young Americans for Freedom; and National Conservative Political Action Committee. Leaders and Executive Officers of these groups include key figures who are prominent on the leadership lists of organization after organization—most notably, Jerry Falwell and Senator Jesse Helms.

It's difficult to ignore the subtle racist overtones of the Moral Majority. In March 1965, Falwell gave a sermon at his Thomas Road Baptist Church in which he made the following comment: "I must personally say that I do question the sincerity and non-violent intentions of some civil rights leaders such as Dr. Martin Luther King, Jr., and Mr. James Farmer and others, who are known to have left-wing associations."

Off the record, Falwell took his accusation even further, implying that King and Farmer were unwitting dupes of an international Communist conspiracy—along the same line J. Edgar Hoover was using during the 1960s.

It is a fact of our time that Evangelism has played a significant role in American politics. In 1960, John F. Kennedy chose to deal with the issue of his personal religion directly in a speech he gave at Houston, Texas, and so lay to rest the bugaboo that had haunted Al Smith in the 1928 Presidential election. Kennedy spoke forthrightly about his Catholicism and what he felt it would and would not mean during his own Presidency, then going on to more important issues in his campaign. Fundamentalists who were hoping to use the same whisper tactics against Kennedy that they had used against Al Smith were caught completely off guard by Kennedy's candid confrontation of the issue, and the consequence was that the Democrats won the election.

In the 1964 Presidential election year, the extreme Right took over the Republican National Convention and dictated the party platform, the Fundamentalists sensing that their time for political action was at hand. Although Republicans lost in the Presidential election itself, Fundamentalists began a systematic examination of the voting records of senators and representatives over the next twelve years, and targeted certain key political figures who seemed to be too liberal or left or soft on Communism to suit the tastes of people like Jerry Falwell.

After the scandal of Watergate drove Richard Nixon from office, the 1976 Presidential election loomed as an opportunity for Fundamentalists to gain power in the White House. But the Democratic candidate, Jimmy Carter, beat the Fundamentalists at their own game by announcing early in his campaign that he was, of all things, a born-again Christian. During a speech at Winston-Salem in the North Carolina primary, Carter acknowledged: "I recognized for the first time that I had lacked something very precious—a complete commitment to Christ, a presence of the Holy Spirit in my life in a more profound and personal way."

No Fundamentalist could have said it any better, and Carter had robbed the religious issue from the extreme Right. However, Jimmy Carter may have carried his candor a bit too far in a 1976 *Playboy* interview in which he confessed to harboring lascivious thoughts: "I've committed adultery in my heart many times—something that God recognizes I will do, and God forgives me for it."

Fundamentalists tried to make something out of this remark, but Carter's obvious sincerity was unassailable: Carter won the Presidency in 1976, and the Fundamentalists were back to trying to sabotage Congressional elections during off years.

In 1978 there was a loose coalition of right-wing groups that was able to defeat two United States Senators, Thomas McIntyre of New Hampshire and Dick Clark of Iowa. And then in 1980, at the Republican National Convention in Detroit, it looked like the Evangelical Right was finally coming into its own. As one preacher put it, "We're running for everything from dogcatcher to Senator."

As a spin-off of the Reagan landslide victory in 1980, Jerry Falwell's

Moral Majority movement was able to reap all sorts of political benefits: it forced the FCC and the IRS to back off from challenges to all tax-exempt religious organizations, and it also introduced a Christian Voice rating system on all political candidates based on their voting records in order to mobilize grass roots American voters. The code of "minimum moral standards to evaluate political candidates" included the following questions:

> Do you agree that this country was founded on a belief in God and the moral principles of the Bible?
> Do you consider that this country has been departing from those principles and needs to return to them?

The questionnaire went on to pump for capital punishment for capital offenses, and voluntary prayer in public schools, and any candidate who did not give the appropriate answers was so noted when Christian Voice reported to potential voters.

At about this time, Jerry Falwell announced his own intentions in a fierce piece of jingoism which was included in a Moral Majority mailing piece:

> DECLARATION OF WAR: Be it known that the Old-Time Gospel Hour hereby declares war against the evils threatening America during the 1980s . . . In God's name we vow to fight against the following evils: legalized abortion, pornography, homosexuality, socialism, the deterioration of the home and family . . .

And so on: one gets the nagging feeling one has heard all this before, in the same indignant tone of voice, with the same posture of outraged sensibilities. But if one wanted it put in a cruder way, Senator Jesse Helms of North Carolina was sending out his own letter to his constituency at this time, saying the same thing in different words: "Because your tax dollars are being used to pay for grade school courses that teach our children that *cannabalim* [sic], *wife swapping*, and the *murder* of infants and the elderly are acceptable behavior . . ."

And Jesse Helms took the battle to the floor of the United States Senate: in response to the 1962 Supreme Court ruling that struck down mandatory prayer in public schools, Helms introduced a bill to prohibit federal courts from ever hearing any case that involved school prayer.

It was, in effect, a gag ruling to make it impossible for any federal court to rule on the issue, ever again.

Jerry Falwell's own positions are expressed in his 1980 book, *Listen, America!* in which he advances his views on myriad moral issues. Falwell begins by asserting that according to the Gallup polls, there are more than 60 million people in America who profess to be born-again Christians; then he goes on to equate Christianity with free enterprise Capitalism:

> The free enterprise system is clearly outlined in the Book of Proverbs in the Bible. Jesus Christ made it clear that the work ethic was a part of His plan for man. Ownership in business is biblical. Ambitious and successful business management is clearly outlined as a part of God's plan for His people.

Falwell says it was this kind of thinking that was behind the founding of America: ". . . the goal of the framers of the Constitution was to govern the United States of America under God's laws . . . Our Founding Fathers most certainly did not intend the separation of God and government."

It's this kind of certainty of seeing into the minds of our Founding Fathers, while ignoring contradictory evidence, that makes Fundamentalism so appealing: who could possibly doubt that Jerry Falwell knows what Jefferson, Madison, Hamilton, and Jay had intended, without even having to read the Federalist Papers?

After equating God's laws with the American Constitution, Jerry Falwell goes on to deplore the moral decay that is all around us today in America. With a breathtaking assertion that seems to see right into the mind of God, Falwell asserts: "If God doesn't judge America, He will have to apologize to Sodom and Gomorrah."

Falwell justifies his sweeping pronouncements by showing how exercised he is over the effect of moral decay on today's young people: "They have learned to disrespect the family as God has established it. They have been educated in a public school system that is permeated with secular humanism."

Falwell claims this loss of family values has been spawned by secular humanism, and is the chief reason behind the drug culture today. He says it also accounts for the widespread Socialism, welfare abuses, and a lot of other evils. The only hope for America, according to Falwell, is Fundamentalism, and he gives a strict statement of what this entails:

A thorough study of the Bible will show that it is indeed the inerrant Word of the living God. The Bible is absolutely infallible, without error in all matters pertaining to faith and practice, as well as in areas such as geography, science, history, etc.

As we noted earlier, look out for that "etc."—it leaves the door wide open for Falwell to claim the Bible is also absolutely infallible in all matters relating to gardening, cooking, sewing, city planning, quantum mechanics, space travel, and subway systems.

The extension of this kind of simplistic thinking is a delusional euphoria where wishes are king: "In heaven we'll all be thirty-three, have perfect bodies, no more pain and suffering, no more dying, no more sickness, God himself will wipe away all our tears and there'll be no more lying."

As for secular humanism, Jerry Falwell sees it as an authentic menace to our society with its godless rejection of all supernaturalism: "It even advocates the right to commit suicide and recognizes evolution as a source of man's existence . . . Humanism promotes the socialization of all humanity into a world commune."

According to Falwell, this abominable wickedness got its start in American schools and universities:

Since World War II, there has been a continuing infiltration of Socialism onto the campus of our major colleges and universities. As the Bible and prayer were removed, they were replaced with courses reflecting the philosophy of humanism. It is no wonder that as we review the 1970s, we find radicals and revolutionaries on our campus who plundered and defamed their colleges and universities in the name of academic freedom.

Falwell claims the time is getting late and we must build up our national defenses immediately. Like a Pentagon general, he has all the overkill statistics at his fingertips:

Ten years ago we could have destroyed much of the population of the Soviet Union had we desired to fire our missiles. The sad fact is that today the Soviet Union would kill 135 million to 160 million Americans, and the United States would kill only 3 to 5 per cent of the Soviets because of their antiballistic missiles and their civil defense. Few people today know that we do not have one antiballistic missile. We once had

$5.1 billion worth of them, but Ted Kennedy led a fight in the Senate and had them dismantled and removed.

One has to pinch oneself to be reminded that this is a Christian minister who is lamenting the "sad fact" that we cannot kill as many millions of Russians as they can kill of us. It is so vindictively militarist, how can it possibly call itself a religion of the teachings of Jesus? And not only is Falwell eager to kill off more Russians than they can kill of us, he is also filled with vitriol against certain United States Senators who may have led the way towards total world disarmament. And Falwell's tone, as usual, is so totalitarian in its arrogance as to wipe away the possibility of debate in a free democracy.

And yet this man who seems to be going against the heart and soul of the teachings of Jesus is the same man who keeps insisting on the inerrancy of the Bible. And this man who seems out to stifle the possibility of debate in a free democracy through the invocation of a revealed religion is the same man who keeps insisting that he knows what our Founding Fathers intended when they shaped our Constitution.

The appalling narrow-mindedness of this man's religious and political opinions makes it almost a relief when he changes the subject and begins to wax wroth on the dangers of pornography:

> A thriving new industry floods into the nation's homes through pornographic literature and television programs. Film producers and magazine writers now exploit innocent little children in an attempt to make money from child pornography. It is a fact that more than 20 million sex magazines are sold at our American newsstands every year. The United States will soon be the pornographic capital of the world with 780 X-rated theatres.

Falwell doesn't stop with child pornography; he goes right on to assail rock music as equally immoral: "Satan worship and the occult are often the topics of rock songs. [A song] In a Rolling Stones record of a few years ago, "Goat's Head Soup" was reported to have been taped live at a voodoo ritual . . ."

One wonders who was doing the reporting on this gossipy bit of behind-the-scenes scuttlebutt. Falwell himself reports on a surprising encounter he had with a rock concert audience in Seattle, Washington, after he had left a prayer meeting and gone with his chorale to the site of the concert: "There I witnessed one of the most horrifying scenes I think I will ever see. Thousands of young men and women were lying on the floor engaged in every filthy act imaginable." Falwell adds as an afterthought: "That night I could not sleep."

Regaining his composure, Jerry Falwell singles out Jimi Hendrix, David Bowie, and Alice Cooper for special contempt, and he warns: "The Bible states that the pleasures of sin are but for a season. Young people cannot live in discos."

But all of Jerry Falwell's shock and disdain for the debauchery and corruption of contemporary society is nothing compared to his absolute loathing of homosexuality:

> The sin of homosexuality is so grievous, so abominable in the sight of God, that He destroyed the cities of Sodom and Gomorrah because of this terrible sin . . . Jesus Christ loves every man and woman, including homosexuals and lesbians. Only He has the power to forgive and cleanse people guilty of this terrible sin. But this does not mean that we should accept their perversion as something normal . . . Heterosexuality was created by God and is endorsed by God.

At this point, Falwell takes another solemn public vow:

> With God as my witness, I pledge that I will continue to expose the sin of homosexuality to the people of this nation. I believe that the massive homosexual revolution is always a symptom of a nation coming under the judgment of God . . . Please remember, homosexuals do not reproduce! They recruit! And many of them are out after my children and your children . . .

Falwell is strenuously opposed to any form of legalized abortion and to the Supreme Court ruling that grants the right to abortion during the first trimester of pregnancy and in the last two trimesters for reasons of health. Falwell supports the National Association for Repeal of Abortion Laws, and he vigorously opposed Ronald Reagan's nomination of Sandra Day O'Connor to the Supreme Court, not because she is a woman but because she once voted in favor of legalized abortion.

Falwell bases his entire argument on the defense of the American family:

There is a vicious assault upon the American family. More television programs depict homes of divorced or of single parents than depict the traditional family. Nearly every major family-theme TV program openly justifies divorce, homosexuality, and adultery.

One wonders how Falwell can infer "a vicious assault" when TV programs are simply depicting the way things are in America today. Perhaps Falwell would advocate doctoring these shows and programming "the traditional family" the way Falwell thinks it ought to be? One hears an echo of Savonarola stacking up his Pyramid of Vanities for the bonfire, in his brief Florentine Theocracy.

Jerry Falwell seems to be most articulate in his attack on Women's Rights, and specifically with the views of Betty Friedan of NOW and Gloria Steinem of *Ms* magazine:

Many women have never accepted their God-given roles. They live in disobedience to God's laws and have promoted their godless philosophy throughout our society. God Almighty created men and women biologically different and with differing needs and roles. He made men and women to complement each other and to love each other . . . a definite violation of holy Scripture, ERA defies the mandate that "the husband is the head of the wife, even as Christ is the head of the church."

Some readers may feel that Falwell's views are laughable, but other readers may be wondering just how dangerous this sort of Fundamentalist thinking might be and to what extent it could grow into a totally uncontrollable political force in America.

The distinguished historian Arthur M. Schlesinger, Jr., in his book *The Cycles of American History* (1986), is inclined to see Jerry Falwell and his Moral Majority as one more periodic swing of Fundamentalist thought in a historical process that has been occurring in America once every generation:

The Moral Majority, in its efforts to dictate private behavior, is a reenactment of the fundamentalist movement that sixty years ago imposed prohibition on a hapless country and tried to expel Darwin from Tennessee classrooms. The twenties were the heyday of Billy Sunday, Aimee Semple McPherson, and the types that Sinclair Lewis celebrated in *Elmer Gantry*. The next great outburst of evangelical moralism came thirty years later, when Norman Vincent Peale and Billy Graham in the 1950s appointed themselves the nation's moral arbiters.

Indeed, there are strong signs now that the Moral Majority has already begun to run into massive reaction against its methods and mentality. In a September 1981 debate Senator Barry Goldwater entered an angry speech into the *Congressional Record* on what it meant to be a true conservative:

> In the past couple years, I have seen many news items that referred to the moral majority, pro-life, and other religious groups as "the new right" and the "new conservativism." And I can say with conviction that the religious issues of these groups have little or nothing to do with conservative or liberal politics.
>
> And I'm frankly sick and tired of the political preachers across this country telling me as a citizen that if I want to be a moral person, I must believe in "A," "B," "C," and "D." Just who do they think they are? And from where do they presume to claim the right to dictate their moral beliefs to me?
>
> And I am even more angry as a legislator who must endure the threats of every religious group who thinks it has some God-granted right to control my vote on every roll call in the Senate. I am warning them today: I will fight every step of the way if they try to dictate their moral convictions to all Americans in the name of "conservatism."

Senator Edward Kennedy made a similar statement: "We must not permit our principles to be swept aside by the negativism of the new right—or by those who dare to call themselves the Moral Majority."

Senator Mark Hatfield, known for his strong religious convictions, made a sober and realistic appraisal of Jerry Falwell's followers:

> They talk about the evils of abortion and the rights of the unborn, but I hear too little about the post-natal child . . . They talk about the need for prayers in the schools; but there is nothing to stop voluntary prayers right now. And if they get the right to mandatory prayers, whose prayers should they be? They talk about taking the life of an unborn fetus as if that's murder, and then they go on to champion capital punishment and encourage killing on a global scale through the arms race.

And in September 1986, speaking before an audience of students at Meredith College in North Carolina, ex-President Jimmy Carter was even more to the point when he spoke of Jerry Falwell: "In a very Christian way, as far as I'm concerned, he can go to Hell."

The reaction against Falwell and his Moral Majority ran even more deeply among leading theologians and academics across the country. William Sloane Coffin, former minister of Riverside Church in New York, commented:

> The Bible is something like a mirror: if an ass peers in, you can't expect an apostle to peer out . . . I think deep down, [Falwell] is shallow. His biblical positions are not sound biblical study. *Anybody* who has done any *real* Bible study knows you can't come up with those conclusions from the Bible. I think what he calls a simple moral issue is very complex. It is very rare to get a Christian position. You get Christians believing different things.

Richard John Neuhaus, Lutheran pastor and contributor to *Worldview*, commented on the Moral Majority:

> Its leaders are profoundly immature. They don't really understand the ethical and philosophical tradition of democracy or how to bring about change in a pluralistic society.

A. Bartlett Giametti, President of Yale University, had this to say to the entering freshman class in 1981:

> A self-proclaimed "Moral Majority" and its satellite or client groups, cunning in the use of a native blend of old intimidation and new technology, threaten the values I have named. Angry at change, rigid in the application of chauvinistic slogans, absolutistic in morality, they threaten through political pressure or public denunciation whoever dares to disagree with their authoritarian positions. Using television, direct mail, and economic boycott, they would sweep before them anyone who holds a different opinion.
>
> From the maw of this "morality" come those who presume to know what justice for all is; come those who presume to know which books are fit to read, which television programs are fit to watch, which textbooks will serve for all the young; come spilling those who presume to know what God alone knows, which is when human life begins. From the maw of this "morality" rise the tax-exempt Savonarolas who believe they, and they alone, possess the truth. There is no debate, no discussion, no

dissent. They know. There is only one set of overarching political and spiritual and social beliefs; whatever view does not conform to these views is by definition relativistic, negative, secular, immoral, against the family, anti-free enterprise, un-American. What nonsense.

And in September 1981, Timothy S. Healy, S.J., President of Georgetown University, had this to say: "If we stretch any revelation to cover items like treaties with Taiwan, and the Panama Canal, we make a mad world where the things of God and the things of man are confused."

Partly as a consequence of these powerful academic and theological and political rebukes, and partly because Jerry Falwell himself began to sense that his Moral Majority movement may have overreached itself, Falwell began to back away from his position as self-appointed spokesman of the New Christian Right. In a September 1985 interview with Cal Thomas in the *Washington Post*, Falwell said:

> I'm not going to get involved anymore in campaigns as I have in the past. I may speak out on particular issues and a candidate or two from time to time, but as far as getting into another Reagan thing and sticking my neck out, I'm not going to do that for anybody else, because it is too polarizing to unbelievers . . . I will no longer allow in my pulpit anything but a minuscule amount of politics. We are going back to where we were before Moral Majority when we had a clear purpose, but did not have a major emphasis on politics.

It sounds like Prospero at the end of Shakespeare's *Tempest*, vowing to break his staff, bury it certain fathoms in the earth, and deeper than did ever plummet sound, he'll drown his book.

But no sooner had Jerry Falwell made the above statement forswearing any further embroilment in political matters, than he received a phone call from Jim Bakker to come to the aid of the embattled *PTL Club*. And before one could say "Moral Majority," Falwell was deeply enmeshed in another awesome power struggle, this time a "Holy War" of colossal proportions for the heart and soul and TV sets of American Protestantism. That struggle is discussed elsewhere in this book and its outcome is still uncertain.

What is important to us here is that Jerry Falwell, disclaimers notwithstanding, seems born for the fray and is never satisfied unless he is acting out some kind of adversarial combat situation. And as we implied at the beginning of this chapter, this strong predilection may have more to do with his own feuding ancestry than it has to do with his Fundamentalist theology.

Jerry Falwell's jousting at moral decay in America may be reminiscent of Don Quixote's tilting at windmills, but the significant thing is that such antics have served Falwell well in his own ministry. Head of the 22,000-member Thomas Road Baptist Church, Chancellor of the 7,500-student Liberty Baptist University, head of the Liberty Broadcasting Network, Jerry Falwell has an empire that logged a gross revenue of $84 million in 1986, and Falwell himself received a fixed income of $100,000 annually plus $5,000 for outside speaking engagements.

Not bad for a man who began his ministry in an abandoned Donald Duck bottling plant, and who affected the course of American politics more than his Puritan forebears would have dared to imagine.

There is one later event to note in the career of Jerry Falwell, something that will go down for all time in this nation's Constitutional history.

In March 1984, *Hustler* Magazine Publisher Larry Flynt ran a full page parody ad spoofing celebrities who tell about "their first time" to sell products. Flynt pictured Jerry Falwell telling about his own "first time."

Jerry Falwell immediately filed a $45 million damage suit in Roanoke, Virginia, charging Larry Flynt and *Hustler* with libel, invasion of privacy, and intentional infliction of emotional distress. Falwell lost on the libel and invasion of privacy charges, but the jury ruled in his favor on the claim of emotional distress, awarding him $200,000.

The Fourth Circuit U.S. Court of Appeals upheld the award, but on February 24, 1988, the United States Supreme Court, in a rare 8-0 unanimous decision, ruled in favor of Larry Flynt and *Hustler* Magazine and threw out the $200,000 award. It was a landmark decision that significantly expanded the Constitution's First Amendment protection of parody and satire of public figures under the guarantee of freedom of speech.

Chapter 14

WHY IN AMERICA?

WE BEGAN BY DEFINING Evangelism as any conversionary activity that tries to effect an authentic change in someone from one state of thinking and feeling to another. The question we have to face here is: why should America be so peculiarly disposed to this phenomenon?

We know Americans are deeply committed to the idea of religion: recent polls show that over 95% of Americans believe in a personal God of some sort, and some form of life after death. And as we've seen in this book, Evangelism has accounted for some of the most profound social and political revolutions in America, such as the Civil Rights Movement of the 1960s led by Martin Luther King, Jr. We've also seen that Evangelism has accounted for some of the most ludicrous and despicable errors in American history, such as the Salem Witch Trials and the catastrophe of Jonestown.

The question is, why should America find itself so uniquely blessed and cursed with this curious thing called Evangelism? Note that Evangelism does not preoccupy the cultural life of other countries in Europe, Asia, Africa, Latin America, or any of the emerging Third World nations, the way it does in America. Nor does one find a solid tradition of Evangelism in England, France, Spain, Germany, Italy, or the Middle East. When we asked the American actress Inessa Balashova, who was born and raised in Moscow, whether there was any tradition of Evangelism in Russia, she answered: "No no, no Evangelism. Purges and revolutions and genocide, yes. But never Evangelism. We have always been too intelligent for that."

Then why does America have such an amazing incidence of in-

215

digenous Evangelism? To answer that question, we have to go back to the nineteenth century and look to an extraordinary Frenchman who came to live in America from 1831–1840 and then published his impressions of the American character and its institutions in a remarkable book, *La Démocratie en Amérique* or *Democracy in America*, published 1835–1840.

Alexis de Tocqueville (1805–1859) begins his study of America by noting that religion is the underlying basis of everyday life:

> There is hardly any human action, however particular it may be, that does not originate in some very general idea men have conceived of the Deity, of his relation to mankind, of the nature of their own souls, and of their duties to their fellow creatures. Nor can anything prevent these ideas from being the common spring from which all the rest emanate.

But de Tocqueville knows that while men need a clear idea of religion in order to live their daily lives, they nevertheless are usually too busy to create these religious ideas for themselves: "Fixed ideas about God and human nature are indispensable to the daily practice of men's lives; but the practice of their lives prevents them from acquiring these ideas."

De Tocqueville describes the deep need for religion in a free society, and he observes that the more free one is, the more jealous that person will be of his religious liberty: "For my own part, I doubt whether man can ever support at the same time complete religious independence and entire political freedom. And I am inclined to think that if faith be wanting in him, he must be subject; and if he be free, he must believe."

De Tocqueville finds this split between political and religious liberty exists in America preeminently, where men tend to live in the here and now:

> In the Middle Ages the clergy spoke of nothing but a future state; they hardly cared to prove that a sincere Christian may be a happy man here below. But the American preachers are constantly referring to the earth, and it is only with difficulty that they can divert their attention from it.

This is a clear prophecy of the self-help religions of the twentieth century, the Positive Thinking of Norman Vincent Peale and the

Possibility Thinking of Robert Schuller, which offer to show men how they can use their faith to work secular miracles with their marriages and their bank accounts.

De Tocqueville also predicts the multitude of sects and cults that will spring up in America during the twentieth century, and the strong need of Americans for a pervasive Evangelism:

> Here and there in the midst of American society you meet with men full of a fanatical and almost wild spiritualism, which hardly exists in Europe. From time to time strange sects arise which endeavor to strike out extraordinary paths to eternal happiness. Religious insanity is very common in the United States.

There it is!—"Religious insanity is very common in the United States." That statement was written in the 1830s by a Frenchman visiting America, and he already saw that Evangelism would continue to flourish in America into the twentieth century. It had to continue, there was no other alternative because, as de Tocqueville says, there is a deep underlying anxiety in this great land of opportunity: "In America I saw the freest and most enlightened men placed in the happiest circumstances that the world affords; it seemed to me as if a cloud habitually hung upon their brow, and I thought them serious and almost sad, even in their pleasures."

The reason that Americans have such a deep need for Evangelism, then, is that they already have such an Evangelical fervor towards the material things in their lives: "It is strange to see with what feverish ardor the Americans pursue their own welfare, and to watch the vague dread that constantly torments them lest they should not have chosen the shortest path which may lead to it."

This explains that curious conjunction of industrial and financial giants like John D. Rockefeller, Andrew Carnegie, Cyrus McCormick, Marshall Field, J. P. Morgan, and William Randolph Hearst, with outstanding modern Evangelists like Dwight L. Moody, Billy Sunday, Billy Graham, and Oral Roberts. It is because, although these two groups may seem to be pursuing completely different objectives, they all share the same underlying Evangelical zeal and singlemindedness. It's just that the first group directs its Evangelical energies to acquiring and manipulating worldly goods, while the second group directs its Evangelism towards an ongoing cultivation of spiritual goods. No wonder both groups recognize themselves in each other, in spite of their seemingly disparate vocations, as if they were blood brothers. Because in a very real sense, they are: they both share the same "feverish ardor" that de Tocqueville speaks of.

De Tocqueville lays the blame for the deep underlying anxiety in America on the blinding materialism that is all around us:

> A native of the United States clings to this world's goods as if he were certain never to die; and he is so hasty in grasping at all within his reach that one would suppose he was constantly afraid of not living long enough to enjoy them. He clutches everything, he holds nothing fast, but soon loosens his grasp to pursue fresh gratifications.

De Tocqueville seems to be describing America as a modern Tower of Babel, with its citizens hopelessly frantic in their obsessions. And if this sounds like the familiar indictment of America that Evangelists have been hurling at us for generations, we should remind ourselves that this is not an Evangelist who is speaking here but a dispassionate French observer, interested only in describing accurately what he sees:

> At first sight there is something surprising in this strange unrest of so many unhappy men, restless in the midst of abundance. The spectacle itself, however, is as old as the world; the novelty is to see a whole people furnish an exemplification of it.

Seventy-five years later another European visitor would have similar things to say about the "strange unrest" to be found among "so many unhappy men" in America. Sigmund Freud came to this country in 1909 to deliver a series of lectures at Clark University in Worcester, Massachusetts, and he perceived the American culture as "anal-acquisitive" and he saw no remedy for the frantic pace which characterized the life-style of most Americans. "America is a mistake," he commented, "A gigantic mistake, it is true, but none the less a mistake."

Alexis de Tocqueville reaches the same conclusion in *Democracy in America*—that there is no remedy for the curse that besets Americans:

> Materialism, among all nations, is a dangerous disease of the human mind; but it is more especially to be dreaded among a democratic people because it readily amalgamates with that vice which is most familiar to the heart under such circumstances.

De Tocqueville's observations are an extraordinary insight into the malaise of the American character, and they are also an amazing anticipation of the widespread prevalence and scope of Evangelism in America in the twentieth century. All we need to do now is break down the several reasons in our American experience that make Evangelism such an indigenous and inevitable phenomenon.

Following are seven major reasons for the prevalence of Evangelism in America. Each of these reasons has already been suggested in the course of this book, and in all likelihood all seven of these reasons will be functioning simultaneously around us at any given time.

Here are the seven major reasons:

Materialism. America is the most affluent and technologically proficient nation in the history of the world; yet, as de Tocqueville points out, this material prosperity has endowed Americans with a peculiar curse: the maddening pace of daily life in America which often precludes any genuine original thought about our spiritual destiny.

Henry David Thoreau (1817–1862) described this terrible plight of modern Americans caught up in the wilderness of a willy-nilly materialism, in his great book *Walden* (1854):

The mass of men lead lives of quiet desperation. What is called resignation is confirmed desperation. From the desperate city you go into the desperate country, and have to console yourself with the bravery of minks and muskrats. A stereotyped but unconscious despair is concealed even under what are called the games and amusements of mankind. There is no play in them, for this comes after work. But it is a characteristic of wisdom not to do desperate things.

And as R. H. Tawney points out in his book *Religion and the Rise of Capitalism,* the overwhelming pressure of economic interests in a capitalist society too often impinges on the need to develop and sustain a deeply felt and consistent personal religion.

Hence our desperate need for Evangelists in America, because they can offer us solace for our desperation as they offer us ready-made programs for our spiritual destiny.

Politics. America has survived as a Constitutional Republic for over 200 years, and in no other nation on earth is individual liberty so jealously guarded or the individual's right to redress so scrupulously espoused, as in our Declaration of Independence and our Constitution with its Bill of Rights.

Yet the continuing survival of our democracy is dependent on an extraordinary vigilance: from the first Constitutional Conventions through Watergate and the Iranscam hearings, America has always had to be committed to the most scrupulous vigil of continuous self-examination.

Thomas Jefferson described this need for vigilance in a portrait he wrote of George Washington in 1814. Jefferson said Washington considered the American government as a noble experiment which had absolutely no guarantee that it would work:

> He has often declared to me that he considered our new Constitution as an experiment on the practicality of republican government and with what dose of liberty man could be trusted for his own good; that he was determined the experiment should have a fair trial, and would lose the last drop of his blood in support of it.

Abraham Lincoln also implied in his Gettysburg Address that there would continue to be critical circumstances which would always test whether "this nation, or any nation so conceived and so dedicated, could long endure."

Such a state of perpetual concern over the preservation of our personal and civil liberties exacerbates the anxieties of the average citizen to such an extent that evangelists are needed as an anodyne. Evangelists are also able to capitalize on this chronic state of vigilance by connecting it with another kind of vigilance that we should also be exercising towards another dimension of our experience. This vigilance is best expressed in the first Letter of Peter Chapter 5:

> 8 Be sober, be vigilant; because your adversary the devil, as a roaring lion, walketh about, seeking whom he may devour:
> 9 Whom resist stedfast in the faith . . .

Evangelists can then take upon themselves this task of vigilance on behalf of their followers, and thus save their followers from the individual self-examination that would otherwise be required of them.

Puritanism and Protestantism. America is the most populous Protestant nation on earth, and it has a solid grounding in early Puritan thought and values. But the essence of both Protestantism and Puritanism is in reaction to historical structures and forms of the more traditional Christian dogma and practice.

What could be more reactionary than the anger of Martin Luther in the following comment on the Catholic Mass, in his *Table Talk* of 1569:

> The Mass is the greatest blasphemy of God, and the highest idolatry upon earth, an abomination the like of which has never been in Christendom since the time of the Apostles.

Yet this anger of Martin Luther is no more zealous than the anger that Jimmy Swaggart displays when he goes to work on Roman Catholicism during one of his Revival programs, or the anger that Jerry Falwell displays when he attacks the Supreme Court decision on abortion.

Protestantism is at heart a protest religion, and it is no wonder modern Protestantism has continued as a reactionary attitude rather than as a viable theology in its own right. This explains why there are so many visible Evangelists ready to decry the wrongs they see all around them, yet so few Protestant theologians who are able to provide new forms and doctrines to meet the needs of a changing world.

The Protestant experience has tended to disperse into a multiplicity of cults, sects, and denominations ever since its inception, and it has never been able to achieve a truly univocal response to the crucial issues of our contemporary life.

Hence the need for Evangelists to compensate for the conspicuous lack of any adequate Protestant theology, by continually citing the inerrancy of the Bible. According to these Evangelists, if the Bible is literally the Word of God, then there is no need for any further theology. Fundamentalism is the only authoritative overview of life that one might ever need.

Immigration. America has traditionally been the melting pot for dislocated nationalities and ethnic groups: an excerpt from the poem "New Colossus" by Emma Lazarus is carved on our Statue of Liberty and sets forth this ideal with grim eloquence:

> Give me your tired, your poor,
> Your huddled masses yearning to breathe free,
> The wretched refuse of your teeming shore,
> Send these, the homeless, tempest-tossed, to me . . .

Admirable as this melting pot ideal may be, it nonetheless tended to create a vague sense of displacement among a majority of Americans who found themselves living next to neighbors who were raised in some totally alien language and culture. These circumstances quicken the hunger for some common faith and experience where the divergences of background and values might come together and be reconciled in one single shared belief.

Up to the Johnson Act of 1921, unrestricted and unlimited immigration to the United States included the unskilled and illiterate, and it excluded only Asians, extreme indigents, the retarded, and prostitutes. In the early part of the twentieth century, there was an annual average immigration of one million persons per year. The high incidence of Catholic and Jewish immigrants to America occasioned a strong coalescence of Protestant Fundamentalist groups, and the more extreme reaction to this immigrant population took the form of the predominantly white Protestant Ku Klux Klan.

Two other immigrant groups deserve special mention for their relationship to Evangelism. The first was a radical form of reverse immigration, when Native American Indians were forcibly relocated onto reservations as white European settlers tricked them out of their ancestral lands and made fraudulent bargains such as the sale of Manhattan Island for twenty-four dollars. As if to assuage the guilt of the white man, early Puritans like John Eliot set out to convert these Indians to Christianity using an Algonquin translation of the Bible; he actually set up "Praying Indian Towns" for early Indian converts to live and work in. This was probably the first example of American Evangelism, practiced on a proud people who had been displaced from their own Indian roots.

The second immigrant group was the product of one of the most brutal and cruel of all migrations in human history: the African Slave Trade. Hapless blacks who were forced into bondage and servitude found a psychological haven in the white man's Evangelical gospel religion: the black slave could identify mightily with Biblical events which told of wholesale dislocations such as "when Israel was in Egypt land," and he also found a promise of redemption in the New Testament salvation as the only hope on earth. Evangelism was the only recourse for these lost souls who had been so painfully deracinated from their own culture and homeland.

The melting pot was indeed a crucible of violent and disparate ingredients so that even the middle class felt discomfited by the continual reminder of alien elements in its midst. Only the Evangelist in America could seem to offer an abode where all souls could be welcomed home and feel reunited in one common, shared community of faith.

Science. One of the most significant reasons for the prevalence of Evangelism in America is the rapid growth of science in our time. As someone once commented, "Science is the true religion of the twentieth century," and the fear of this godless transplantation has kept religion itself in an almost continuous reaction against almost every major scientific breakthrough of the last hundred years, as witness the Fundamentalist flurry and fury over what John Scopes was teaching to his high school biology class in Dayton, Tennessee, in 1925.

Yet the irony is that with contemporary scientific technology extending into digital printing, laser recording, cable television and holograph photography, American Evangelism has made a curious accommodation to these advances in mass communication. Televangelists will use the full range of satellite and cable television networking to broadcast their Revival programs, and they will also use computer technology to track their mass mailings on color-coded cards so they can tabulate the freewill gift offerings that come in, while denouncing the secular humanism and science that created all these miraculous technologies.

It is true that science has created a cultural nightmare for us today: the computer chip has rendered each individual into a display face statistic, allowing instant recall of all his vital records, from psychiatric history to credit ratings. And while advocates of science can point to the astonishing success of our Space Program which put a man on the moon and launched space probes of planets, critics of science can point out that the flip side of this technology is the deployment of over 50,000 nuclear warheads over every part of the earth. We may have made it possible to explore our own solar system, but we have also created the potential for our own push-button apocalypse.

It is not so much the fruits of science which are disquieting to religionists, as it is the underlying assumption of godlessness which seems to underlie so much modern technology. No less a figure than Albert Einstein was one of the last theoretical physicists who insisted it would be possible to reconcile science with some semblance of an unseen order in the universe. In his debate with Werner Heisenberg over the Uncertainty Principle, Einstein claimed he could devise a Unified Field Theory which would join together the principles of gravity, electromagnetism, and the stronger and weaker forces of the universe. Einstein argued, "I shall never believe that God plays dice with the world."

But by the time of his death, Einstein had not succeeded in formulating his Unified Field Theory, and Heisenberg claimed he had not been able to do it because it simply could not be done. The universe, Heisenberg claimed, had no underlying unity to anything and had to be approached through the Uncertainty Principle, which posits randomness and chance happenings as a key to unlocking the mysteries of the cosmos.

And that appears to be the drift of most modern American scientific thought. As John B. S. Haldane commented in *Possible Worlds and Other Papers* (1928): "My suspicion is that the universe is not only queerer than we suppose, but queerer than we can suppose."

To be sure, there have been brave attempts to reconcile modern physics with religion: most notably by Eddington, Sherrington, C. S. Lewis, and the Catholic paleontologist Teilhard de Chardin in *The Divine Milieu*. Sir James Jeans has also tried to create a philosophical world-view that could keep free will as an option in the midst of scientific determinism that governs atoms and photons that are predictable *en masse* but not necessarily in their singular movements.

But whatever reconciliation may be possible between physics and faith, the grim truth is that science offers us no hope of any afterlife nor any promise of salvation and redemption here on earth, and it certainly does not posit any moral ordering of the universe. Therefore Evangelism has rushed in to fill this enormous void created by an agnostic Scientism. To counter the cold and soulless claims of science, Evangelism offers a world view based on faith, hope, and charity. This is no mean proposal, and it is no wonder Evangelism has had a huge response to this offer.

Communism. Hand in hand with the agnosticism of science, the atheism of Marxist Communism has haunted every God-fearing Evangelist in our time.

From its origins with Karl Marx (1818–1883) and his major work *Das Kapital* (1867), world Communism has seen itself as a radical criticism of all Capitalist systems and has announced an international movement to supplant all other political economies with the Marxist one. Marx diagnosed the ills of our modern world as coming from the unfair Capitalistic means of production which were kept in the hands of the few, and the distribution of goods and services which did not make a fair allotment to the many. Marx advocated the remedy of abolishing all private property, setting up state-owned and state-operated industries, and creating a society "from each according to his abilities and to each according to his needs."

Religion, for Marx, was an opiate of the masses and should go the way of private property. And since the 1917 Russian Revolution, religion has played only a token role in the Soviet Union and has certainly not been a vital factor in the ongoing life of that nation.

By mid-century there was the spectre of a godless communist takeover of the entire world. Nikita Khrushchev said it bluntly to the West: "We will bury you."

The systematic Soviet expansion in Western Europe, the strategic importance of Communist China influencing events in Korea and Vietnam, and the more recent Communist aggressions in Afghanistan and infiltration of Central America—all these events have exacerbated American Fundamentalist fears of a Marxist world order which would deny the freedom of worship to all people under a Communist regime.

Evangelists in America have mounted major campaigns to inform and alarm their congregations of the dangers of world Communism. The ironic thing is that these same American Evangelists have unconsciously transformed themselves into such veritable tycoons of accumulated wealth and power, they look for all the world like walking emblems of Capitalism.

Even so, Evangelists have seen themselves as essential in their Crusade of warning Americans as to what the Communist menace might mean to the American way of life.

Entertainment. America has created a number of unique forms of popular mass entertainment. From the earliest Mississippi River Show Boats to the vaudeville circuits. From silent slapstick comedies of Charlie Chaplin, Buster Keaton, and Mack Sennett's Keystone Kops, to original Broadway musical comedy shows such as *Oklahoma!*, *West Side Story*, and *A Chorus Line*, through MGM technicolor musicals with Fred Astaire, Judy Garland, and Gene Kelly, America has always had a genius for Show Biz of every kind and variety.

Europe has nothing to compare with the American Jazz of Charlie Parker, Duke Ellington, or Charlie Mingus, or the ragtime of Scott Joplin; Asia cannot offer any equivalent of the crooning of Bing Crosby or Frank Sinatra, or the folk rock of Woody Guthrie, Bob Dylan, or Paul Simon; or the pre-recorded VCR music cassettes of Michael Jackson or Madonna.

We saw Mark Twain's report on the unique form of rough frontier entertainment of early nineteenth century Camp Meetings and Tent Revivals, and we also saw H. L. Mencken's report on the mesmerizing power of early twentieth century regional Evangelists. Surely this American Evangelism is as indigenous an art form/entertainment as soft-shoe, burlesque, or the breakaway tap routines of a good banjo minstrel show.

With the advent of television, American Evangelism has taken its place as one more uniquely American form of entertainment. Regardless of whether anyone out there in the TV audience believes one word of what Jimmy Swaggart may be saying, millions of people will still watch his Revival program for the sheer entertainment value of the show: there is the excellent choral singing, and Jimmy Swaggart's playing at the organ, and then the sight of Swaggart himself as he lopes and prowls around the stage, getting himself worked up into a frenzy of energy so he can erupt in a crescendo of rapture. Theology aside, it's a damned good show.

And after all, in the absence of sensational historical occasions such as public whippings, beheadings, hangings, and burnings at the stake in the town square, what better spectacle is there than the sight of a few thousand total strangers brought face to face with their eternal damnation in the hellfire of brimstone?

These seven reasons for the prevalence of Evangelism in America —the curse of materialism, the vigilance required in democratic politics, the reactionary nature of Protestantism, the immigration patterns in America, the sudden acceleration of modern science, the perceived menace of international Communism, and the sheer entertainment value of Evangelism—are the most persuasive factors explaining why we as a people have always been peculiarly susceptible to the power and appeal of Evangelists. And as we said, these seven strong forces are probably all functioning simultaneously on various subliminal levels at any given time, to make this phenomenon of Evangelism seem to be absolutely natural and inevitable in America.

At the same time, these seven reasons do not explain why so many hundreds of thousands of Americans so willingly donate hundreds of millions of dollars every year to these Evangelists, sometimes dipping into their hard-earned life savings and even imperiling their subsistence, based on fixed Social Security checks. What is it that accounts for such a bottom-line response to the crass television pitches for freewill gift offerings?

Surveys reveal there are about five million regular donors to specific Evangelists in America, most being women between the ages of fifty and seventy-five. Seventy-one seems to be the median age for making a contribution to a Televangelist.

The explanation shouldn't be hard to find, as we've already characterized materialism in America as a disease of the mind that seems to be hellbent on blowing itself up. De Tocqueville and Freud reinforced the widely held theory that America, as a culture, is inherently vacant and valueless; Thoreau said it best when he wrote, "The mass of men lead lives of quiet desperation."

This being so, what better panacea for the suffering organism than the strong unconscious wish to make everything all right somehow, by mailing off a substantial contribution to some charismatic Evangelist? It gives one a momentary glow of peace and joy, and the spiritual high may be a temporary respite from the rest of one's existential anxieties.

It's a very human attribute to want to endow some monument or institution as a lasting legacy of one's own life experience. And if one is alone, or somehow aging past any hope of meaningful reconciliation with one's own past, one may well feel disenfranchised of any communication or relevance with one's family, or schools, or former associates. What, then, could be more natural than to make a legacy, endowment, or bequest to some Evangelist who professes to be doing so many Good Works? That legacy would take the form of a freewill gift offering to the ongoing Crusade of the Evangelist—a simple enough deed. One sends off a check in an envelope to the address given on the TV screen, and in a few days one gets back a computer-signed "personal" letter from this very Evangelist, thanking the generous donor for helping to do God's work.

Of course it's a sad commentary on the world we live in, but then sadness is nothing new in human history. American Evangelists have just hit on a new way of packaging and marketing it.

Chapter 15

WHAT THEOLOGY FOR OUR POST-MODERN ERA?

ORIGINATING IN THE EARLY Paleolithic period before 8000 B.C., at sites around Altamira, Lascaux, Gargas and other locations scattered within modern France, Germany, Spain, Russia, and northern Italy, there are drawings on the walls and ceilings of caves. These drawings are awesome and immense images, skillfully executed figures of horses, bison, mammoths, deer, bears, and fish, as well as silhouettes of hands, tools, and weapons—all of them colored with black manganese and red and white ocher and iron oxide, with accurate proportional details, with highly stylized lines and masterful shading effects.

No one knows why these images were painted on the walls and ceilings of these caves. Could they be exercises in sympathetic magic, part of a religious ritual to make it easier for prehistoric man to go out and kill his prey? Or were these early cavemen trying to tell someone something about their own lives? Were they trying to make some kind of statement about their precarious life and death situation here on earth?

If they were indeed trying to make such a statement, then that would make these early cave dwellers the first Evangelists in human history.

Precisely what these first Evangelists may have been trying to convey has been completely obscured in time. The images they painted on their walls and ceilings show remarkable and persuasive technique and artistry, yet the fact remains that their message is unfathomable. And the same thing may be said of many other Evangelical attempts throughout human history: remarkable and persuasive technique and artistry, but no really coherent or tenable underlying message that might help us cope with our own human condition.

What is our human condition?

Victor Hugo once summed it up this way: *"Les hommes sont tous condamnés à mort avec des susis indéfinis."* ("Men are all under sentence of death with an indefinite reprieve.")

That's a pretty stark description of our lot, and our problem is how we can adjust to such a view of mortality without committing suicide or succumbing to insanity. The truth is that our human condition has always been grim, life-threatening, and desperate for as long as anyone can remember: there have always been plagues, famines, floods, earthquakes, droughts, and invasions by barbaric hordes.

And there have always been Evangelists who were ready and willing to come up with some kind of answer to our desperate stalemate situation. Sometimes, like the early cave dwellers, the technique and artistry of these Evangelists was remarkable and persuasive, but unless the underlying message was coherent and tenable, the results were usually futile.

Psalm 127 says this succinctly:

1 Except the Lord build the house, they labour in vain that build it: except the Lord keep the city, the watchman waketh but in vain.

That is to say, without the authentic presence of some underlying truth, any Evangelist is foredoomed to failure, and the absence of a coherent and tenable theology will render any Evangelism an exercise in futility.

One can think of many such Evangelisms in history: Machiavelli's teachings in *The Prince*, and the philosophical underpinnings of the French Revolution. There are remarkable and persuasive technique and artistry in these works but they were accompanied by an overwhelming failure of underlying message and theology, and the results were catastrophic.

Surely the most disastrous Evangelism of our modern world was the Third Reich of Adolf Hitler (1889–1945), who created and implemented many of the modern techniques of mass Evangelism. Hitler outlined these Evangelical techniques in his autobiography *Mein Kampf*, which sold over 6 million copies by 1940. Hitler writes:

The power which has always started the greatest religious and political avalanches in history rolling has from time immemorial been the magic power of the spoken word and that alone . . . The broad masses of the people can be moved only by the power of speech. All great movements are popular movements, volcanic eruptions of human passions and emotional sentiments, stirred either by the cruel Goddess of Distress or by the firebrand of the word hurled among the masses; they are not the lemonade-like outpourings of the literary aesthetes and drawing-room heroes.

This is not bad as an assessment of the most powerful and persuasive techniques of Evangelism. Hitler's 1934 Nuremberg Nazi Party Rally was one of the most carefully orchestrated Revival Meetings in history: the entire event was a masterpiece of irony, eloquence, wiliness and hysteria, which built to a fever pitch of frenzy. The whole spectacle was brilliantly documented on film by Leni Riefenstahl in *Triumph of the Will*, one of the great propaganda instruments of all time.

George Orwell, the author of *1984*, pinpointed Adolf Hitler's Evangelical appeal in a 1940 review of *Mein Kampf*:

> Hitler has grasped the falsity of the hedonistic attitude toward life. Nearly all western thought since the last war, certainly all "progressive" thought, has assumed tacitly that human beings desire nothing beyond ease, security, and avoidance of pain. In such a view of life there is no room, for instance, for patriotism and the military virtues. Hitler knows that human beings don't only want comfort, safety, short working-hours, hygiene, birth-control and, in general, common sense; they also, at least intermittently, want struggle and self-sacrifice, not to mention drums, flags, and loyalty parades. Whereas Socialism and even capitalism have said to people "I offer you a good time," Hitler has said to them "I offer you struggle, danger, and death," and as a result a whole nation flings itself at his feet.

Of course, Hitler did not rely entirely on drums, flags, and loyalty parades: he took no chances with a purely Evangelical approach. He made sure there was also a strong ambience of fear and terror to insure total obedience to his particular ideology. Willa Appel writes in *Cults in America*:

> One element in the "breaking" of the German population was disorientation. An atmosphere of uncertainty and fear was deliberately created so as to impress upon the average citizen that nothing was as it had been and that no one was safe any longer. Surprise was manipulated to this end: arrests took place in the middle of the night, rumors

about concentration camps were circulated, and important members of society, in particular the once sacrosanct aristocracy, were abruptly denounced. The effect of this policy, as the German theologian Paul Tillich described it, was the "feeling that our existence was being changed." It bred an atmosphere of permanent insecurity, which debilitated those subjected to it and thus allowed the Reich to flourish.

This is an excellent example of powerful Evangelical techniques in action, with no coherent or tenable theology behind them. Hitler's political ideology was a weird twist of Darwinian theory about the survival of the culturally fittest: a master race which claims its own *Lebensraum*, or living space—"soil exists for the people which possess the force to take it . . . what is refused to amicable methods, it is up to the first to take."

Hitler also had the idiosyncratic notion that blood mix and the resultant drop in racial level were the sole causes of the death of old cultures: men do not die because wars are lost so much as they die because of the loss of bloodstream purity. "All who are not of good race in this world are chaff." Hitler put this simplistic idea into practice with his "final solution" of the Jewish question during the Holocaust, although Hitler himself was canny enough never to sign or initial any documents which might implicate him directly with the extermination camps: he had a genius for delegating the gruesome consequences of his empty theories to be carried out by others in the details of their execution.

Simplistic ideas usually lead to despicable results in this world. One may have a genius for Evangelical techniques; yet, if the underlying message is not coherent and tenable, the consequences will be devastating. Hitler's Evangelism ended in the death camps of Auschwitz, Dachau, Buchenwald, and Treblinka. "Except the Lord build the house, they labour in vain that build it: except the Lord keep the city, the watchman waketh but in vain."

Before we flatter ourselves that we could not be capable of such a self-destructive Evangelism in America, we should remind ourselves the Ku Klux Klan has been just such a despicable exercise in futility, with no authentic theology underlying its techniques and methods.

The following is the most comprehensive statement of the Klan's ideology, set down in the early 1980s. It is a bewildering hash of segregationism, anti-Catholicism, and disavowal of the United States Supreme Court:

We the Klan believe in God and the tenets of the Christian religion, and that a Godless nation cannot long prosper. We, the Klan, will never allow our blood bought liberties to be crucified on a Roman cross; nor will we yield to the integration of white and Negro races in schools or anywhere else. We will follow the teaching of the Bible and not the unwise and one-sided ruling of the U. S. Supreme Court which is not in keeping with the Constitution of the United States of America.

Like the Nazis, the Klan created nightmare circumstances to execute its Evangelism, to disorient and break down the Black and Catholic population through the systematic practice of terror and surprise.

First formed during the Reconstruction Period following the American Civil War, the Ku Klux Klan was begun in Pulaski, Tennessee, in 1867 as "The Invisible Empire of the South," also known as "The Knights of the White Camellia." Early members wore sheets and pillowcases not only to protect their anonymity but also to arouse superstitious panic at the sight of white-hooded knights riding on horseback and carrying flaming torches. It was similar to Nazi arrests that took place in the middle of the night, only these night-riders of the Klan always reverted to their middle-class personae the next day and pretended they didn't know anything about the "Klan."

The immediate object of Klan activity was to keep the "nigra" in his place and prevent him from ever using the ballot; it incidentally went out of its way to harass immigrant Catholics wherever they got out of line. Although the Klan was legally disbanded in 1869, its activities continued illicitly, which only added to the terror. Over the course of several decades, thousands of innocent Blacks were whipped, beaten, lynched, tarred and feathered, and burned alive by Klan members, and rarely did any of these cases ever come to indictment. In the 1920s the Klan became active in state politics and helped to elect governors in Oregon and Oklahoma, and in 1924 the Klan almost took over the entire state of Indiana.

Like Hitler, the Klan had no coherent or tenable ideology underlying its Evangelism, so it conducted its furtive terrorism just as certain radical left-wing guerrilla groups do in the present day, and we will probably see more examples of sabotage and terrorism in our cities over the next few decades. It is in the nature of these runaway political Evangelisms to wreak havoc with as much secrecy and cowardice as possible, since there is no underlying principle or philosophy worth maintaining in the light of day.

The problem for us is to try to locate a coherent and tenable theology that may be appropriate for our post-modern era, to see if it is possible to create an Evangelism that might be adequate to our time. To do this, we will have to examine modern Christianity and see where it has failed to provide us with a theology that is sane, sufficient, and satisfactory for our world.

One of the most astute critics of modern Christianity, Soren Kierkegaard (1813–1855) challenged the hypocrisy and pietism of the Lutheran Officialdom of his time. Living in Denmark and using pseudonyms to preserve his anonymity, Kierkegaard published book after book in which he laid the foundations of modern Existential thought.

Kierkegaard's distrust of abstract concepts and his passionate belief in the individual's power of choice, as well as his awareness of the element of risk that must accompany any personal faith—these themes are all developed in Kierkegaard's major works: *Fear and Trembling; The Concept of Dread; The Sickness unto Death; Stages on Life's Way; The Present Age;* and *Purity of Heart Is to Will One Thing.*

Kierkegaard's ideas of radical Christianity involved a "leap of faith" and a "teleological suspension of the ethical" that bypassed the conventional moral order when one's faith called on one to respond to a higher religious imperative. Kierkegaard gave the example of Abraham, who was called on to transgress the conventional moral order by showing his willingness to sacrifice his son Isaac because the angel of the Lord commanded it of him. This, for Kierkegaard, was a sufficient circumstance to rise above one's notions of right and wrong, and do whatever one's God required.

Kierkegaard may seem to be the antithesis of the modern Evangelist in his wariness of crowds, mass emotion, and mob psychology: he had a special suspicion of newspapers and any form of media exploitation. This was because Kierkegaard insisted the chief danger of our modern world was that the crucial dialogue between man and God was being continuously interrupted, and he wanted to restore the urgency of conversion in the life of the solitary individual soul. Kierkegaard's whole emphasis was in returning the human spirit to its own sources of inspiration; he quoted Proverbs Chapter 5 to illustrate this point:

15   Drink waters out of thine own cistern, and running waters out of thine own well.

Kierkegaard was fearless in his denunciation of the hollow forms and Phariseeism of modern Christianity, which tend to lure an individual further away from himself instead of allowing him to remain centered in himself. Christianity was becoming a hostage of the newly rising middle class, with its self-serving shibboleths of smug righteousness and its obsession in always looking good up front. Kierkegaard had contempt for this desecration of the teachings of Jesus and he called on the solitary individual to renew his confrontation with the living God.

Another critic of modern Christianity who had an enormous impact on contemporary thought was Friedrich Nietzsche (1844–1900), who began writing his major work, *Thus Spake Zarathustra*, in Rapallo, Italy, during the winter of 1883, privately published in 1885.

In the first part of *Zarathustra*, Nietzsche's Zoroastrian prophet makes a startling pronouncement: "But when Zarathustra was alone he spoke thus to his heart: 'Could it be possible? This old saint in the forest has not yet heard anything of this, that *God is dead!*' "

This single statement gave rise to the "God is dead" theology of the twentieth century, and it also went a long way towards enforcing a horrified Fundamentalist reaction against what looked like Nietzsche's outright assertion of atheism. Actually it was no such thing: Nietzsche was simply out to overthrow the superannuated God of the age-old Judeo-Christian theology, that archaic artifice that was supposed to have ordered the world according to certain quaint symmetrical principles. Nietzsche knew that science was seeing through these outmoded forms, and he wanted to replace the lifeless fossil of the Biblical God with a living presence, a reckless and chaotic Dionysian Creator who could not be contained in any Church or Temple. Zarathustra was calling on all men to return to their primordial fertility and find joy in their own energies as they realized their innate Will to Power. To be sure, Nietzsche probably could have agreed whole-heartedly with the revolutionary statement of Jesus in John Chapter 4:

24   God is a Spirit; and they that worship him must worship him in
     spirit and in truth.

But to hammer home his point, Nietzsche had to assume the role of ruthless iconoclast, smashing as many false idols as he could: thus Nietzsche proclaimed himself unremittingly anti-Christian in his sentiments about "that Nazarene," and he announced he would rather be a pagan than a papist: "I am a disciple of the philosopher Dionysos, and I would sooner be a satyr than a saint."

The irony of all this is that so many contemporary Evangelists pretend to be offended by Nietzsche, while they assimilate his Will to Power in their practice of amassing gargantuan empires—and in their endless frenzy of preaching, these same Evangelists more closely resemble the sexual intensity of Dionysos than they do the serenity of Jesus.

Another critic of modern Christianity is the Russian novelist Fyodor Dostoyevski (1821–1886), whose *Brothers Karamazov* contains the monumentally disturbing "Grand Inquisitor" section.

Ivan Karamazov has created a poem about how Christ returns to Seville in Spain in the sixteenth century during the height of the Inquisition, and instead of being welcomed as the Second Coming, Christ is arrested and thrown into prison by the Catholic Church. That evening, the Grand Inquisitor visits Christ in his cell and tells him why Christ's message has failed in this world:

> You promised them bread from heaven, but, I repeat again, can it compare with earthly bread in the eyes of the weak, always vicious and always ignoble race of man? And if for the sake of the bread from heaven thousands and tens of thousands will follow you, what is to become of the millions and scores of thousands of millions of creatures who will not have the strength to give up the earthly bread for the bread of heaven?
>
> Man, so long as he remains free, has no more constant and agonizing anxiety than to find as quickly as possible someone to worship. But man seeks to worship only what is incontestable, so incontestable, indeed, that all men at once agree to worship it all together. For the chief concern of those miserable creatures is not only to find something that I or someone else can worship, but to find something that all believe in and worship, and the absolutely essential thing is that they should do so *all together.*
>
> I tell you man has no more agonizing anxiety than to find someone to whom he can hand over with all speed the gift of freedom with which the unhappy creature is born.

In this "Grand Inquisitor" scene Dostoyevski argues that the aims of the Catholic Church and, indeed, historical Christianity itself have been diametrically opposed to the original teachings of Jesus. Judging the nature of man to be antithetical to the demands of freedom, Christianity has created a slave religion that serves man's earthly hunger instead of his spiritual need. It is a devastating attack on the foundations of Christianity and calls into question the theology underlying two thousand years of Christian practice.

The last critic of modern Christianity we will examine here is Sigmund Freud (1856–1939). We will discuss Freud's contribution of classical psychoanalysis in the Afterword of this book, but right now we have to deal with Freud's serious criticism of religion in the modern world, as outlined in his book *The Future of an Illusion*.

Freud begins by tracing the psychic origin of all religions, and he makes a severe indictment of Karl Marx's irreligious *Das Kapital*:

> It has become clear that civilization cannot consist primarily or solely in wealth itself and the means of acquiring it and the arrangements for its distribution; for these things are threatened by the rebelliousness and destructive mania of the participants in civilization.

He then turns to religion itself and sees that it is an even worse option than irreligion: "Civilization runs a greater risk if we maintain our present attitude to religion than if we give it up." In fact, Freud is for beginning with education—no "prayers in public schools," but exactly the opposite: "Perhaps there is a treasure to be dug up capable of enriching civilization and that is worth making the experiment of an irreligious education."

Freud's proposal is an entirely new approach based on an acknowledgement of things as they are: "Men cannot remain children forever; they must in the end go out into 'hostile life.' We may call this *education to reality*."

Freud's vision is of a civilization devoted to the conscious mind trying to make sense out of objective reality. He argues that since this has never been done before in the history of man, we might as well consider giving it a try:

> The voice of the intellect is a soft one, but it does not rest until it has gained a hearing. Finally, after a countless succession of rebuffs, it succeeds. This is one of the few points on which one may be optimistic about the future of mankind, but it is in itself a point of no small importance . . . In the long run nothing can withstand reason and experience, and the contradiction which religion offers to both is all too palpable.

Hence Freud's title: *The Future of an Illusion*. One might agree that the history of religion has been every bit as illusory and self-serving as Freud claims it to be, yet even so one would have a hard time accounting for those few authentic presences which historical religion has produced: men and women who were neither illusory nor obsessional but rather reality-oriented persons like Augustine, Francis, Teresa of Avila, Martin Luther, Pascal, Albert Schweitzer, Mahatma Gandhi, Malcolm X, and Martin Luther King, Jr.—for the sake of these persons, at least, we would have to think twice before dismissing historical religion altogether. And on the other hand one should also point out that such an attempt as Freud is proposing, to substitute an irreligious rationality and experience for historical religion could have its own disastrous results, as George Orwell and Aldous Huxley tried to prophesy when they envisioned a fascistic Scientism which manipulated the horrendous worlds of *1984* and *Brave New World.*

All four of these critics claim that modern Christianity has failed us: Kierkegaard attacks the hypocrisy of middle-class Official Religion; Nietzsche advocates the overthrow of Judeo-Christianity and opts for a return to Dionysian earth religion; Dostoyevski indicts historical Christianity for misgauging the nature of man; and Freud asserts civilization itself would be better off with an irreligious rather than a religious culture and education.

These are strong voices and they coincide with our own bewildering experience of the twentieth century: Americans have had to live through the catastrophe of the Great Depression and the shock of two World Wars, as well as several undeclared wars that were unprecedented in scope, savagery, and senselessness. Gradually the realization has begun to sink in on us that the real world out there is an ethical shambles: over 100 million human beings have been killed in military action alone in this century, and the killing is still going on.

Modern man is beginning to sense he is a godforsaken animal who can no longer go along with Robert Browning's sanguine line, "God's in his heaven, all's right with the world."

After the Holocaust, after Buchenwald, Dachau, Auschwitz, Treblinka, and Bergen Belsen; after Hiroshima, Nagasaki, Korea, and Vietnam—modern man is beginning to feel that maybe God is not in his heaven and maybe man himself is nothing but a monstrous absurdity, a nightmare monument to the meaninglessness of existence. Modern man may also be starting to realize that the real mainsprings of human behavior, the great shaping forces of life itself, are hidden away in some secret abyss that is far beyond the reach of reason: for the unconscious is by definition quite a curious absurdity and it can only be dimly glimpsed through the weird logic of dreams.

Add to all this absurdity and meaninglessness the possibility of a ruinous nuclear war or a worldwide epidemic of AIDS, and our contemporary world looks more and more idiotic. Albert Einstein felt this way when he was first told of our dropping an atomic bomb on a civilian population. In horror and astonishment, Einstein tried to alert all the nations on earth to the menace of an imminent nuclear conflagration: "The unleashed power of the atom has changed everything except our modes of thinking, and thus we drift towards unparalleled catastrophe."

Is it at all likely that we can change our modes of thinking? Most modern Americans have outgrown the delusional Hollywood way of seeing the world, as if a vicarious love affair with Doris Day, Rock Hudson, or Marilyn Monroe could ever be the source of enduring values. Yet these same Americans realize they must face the chaos they have made without the stability or guidance of any traditional assumptions or assurances, and they do not know where to turn.

Like the rest of the modern world, Americans feel they have been betrayed because they are no longer able to draw inspiration from the same fountains that they used to drink from: in this twentieth century, those fountains seem to be hopelessly contaminated. The archetypal poem of the modern era is T. S. Eliot's *The Waste Land* (1922) with its world of hollow men and desperately bored and infertile women, "a heap of broken images" that are shored against their own ruins. And the archetypal play of the modern era is Samuel Beckett's *Waiting For Godot*, which presents man as suffering from a contagion of sadness, a hopelessly lost soul dumbstruck from the breakdown of language and logic, who can only make loud shouts out of a joyless void.

No wonder art in our modern world has become fractured and cubist, and literature preoccupied with stark metaphors, stoic jokes, oblique parables, and farces of abandonment. As the European playwright Eugene Ionesco writes: "Cut off from his religious, metaphysical and transcendental roots, man is lost; all his actions become senseless, absurd and useless."

The German philosopher Martin Heidegger states it as a dire indictment of the modern world in his book *Poetry, Language and Thought*:

Night is falling . . . The era is defined by the god's failure to arrive, by the "default of God" . . . The default of God means that no god any longer gathers men and things unto himself, visibly and unequivocally, and by such gathering disposes the world's history and man's sojourn on it . . . It has already grown so destitute, it can no longer discern the default of God as a default . . . At this night's midnight, the destitution of the time is greatest. Then the destitute time is no longer able to experience its own destitution . . .

Man stares at what the explosion of the atomic bomb could bring with it. He does not see that the atom bomb and its explosion are the mere final emissions of what has long since taken place, has already happened.

And in his 1957 Nobel Acceptance Speech, the French writer Albert Camus spoke for a generation of Europeans who had experienced the living hell of this century in their own lifetime:

For more than twenty years of an insane history, hopelessly lost like all the men of my generation in the convulsions of time, I have been supported by one thing: by the hidden feeling that to write today was an honour because this activity was a commitment—and a commitment not only to write. Specifically, in view of my powers and my state of being, it was a commitment to bear, together with all those who were living through the same history, the misery and the hope we shared. These men, who were born at the beginning of the First World War, who were twenty when Hitler came to power and the first revolutionary trials were beginning, who were then confronted as a completion of their education with the Spanish Civil War, the Second World War, the world of concentration camps, a Europe of torture and prisons— the men must today rear their sons and create their works in a world threatened by nuclear destruction. Nobody, I think, can ask them to be optimists. And I even think that we should understand—without ceasing to fight it—the error of those who in an excess of despair have asserted their right to dishonour and have rushed into the nihilism of the era. But the fact remains that most of us, in my country and in Europe, have refused this nihilism and have engaged upon a quest for legitimacy. They have had to forge for themselves an art of living in times of catastrophe in order to be born a second time and to fight openly against the instinct of death at work in our history.

What kind of theology is possible for our post-modern era?

There is the "crisis theology" of Karl Barth, Nicolai Berdyaev, Rudolph Otto, Martin Buber—even Paul Tillich, Erich Fromm, and

Thomas Merton—theologians who have refused, like Albert Camus, to sidestep the awful implications of our time.

As one contemporary theologian, Harvey Cox of the Harvard Divinity School, commented:

> When the disclosure of what happened at Auschwitz did not lessen the modern world's capacity for mass slaughter, and the realization of what took place at Hiroshima did not evoke a shrinking back from the making of more nuclear weapons, something began to change. Growing numbers of people began to regard the modern logos not as something one tried to weave religion back into but as a world view which was itself fatally flawed. The modern mind became not the audience but the problem.

Another leading theologian of our time, Reinhold Niebuhr, writing in *Christianity and Crisis* back in 1941, anticipated our present era with its Evangelical Christianity which, Niebuhr insisted, was an anachronism because "its uncomplex message was particularly relevant to frontier conditions." Faced now with the ambiguity and complexity of the modern era, Niebuhr hinted that Evangelical Christianity may no longer be relevant:

> We do not believe that the Christian faith as expressed in the New Testament and as interpreted in historic Christianity, both Catholic and Protestant, implies the confidence that evil and injustice in history can be overcome by such simple methods as are currently equated with Christianity.

This inadequacy on the part of contemporary Christian thought may help us to understand the prevalence of Evangelism in America. Confronted with moral issues we can neither avoid nor ignore, and unable to find any rational or theological basis of dealing with these issues, the temptation to submerge ourselves in a mindless Salvationism may be enticing. Furthermore, after the deaths of Paul Tillich and Reinhold Niebuhr, modern American Protestantism began to resemble one of those black holes in space which has no substance in itself but has to eat the light of nearby luminosities. There is an almost total absence of theological understructure to Evangelism in America except for their often-cited reliance on the inerrancy of the Bible.

Yet if we examine this claim of Biblical inerrancy once and for all, we find ourselves in an even worse quagmire. What kind of coherent and tenable theology are we supposed to derive from a book which contains such disparate elements as Ecclesiastes and Revelations, the Epistles of Paul and the Song of Solomon? Of all the major primal source books of religion—the Upanishads, the Tao Te Ching, the Bhagavad Gita, the Koran, the Talmud—this Bible is the most eclectic of any text that has ever spawned a major world religion. This is not to impugn the majesty of the Bible—it is in all likelihood the single greatest book ever written, albeit the most irritating and erratic as well as the most lyrical and exalted account of our human condition here on this planet earth.

But from a theological point of view, this Bible is filled with so many discrepancies, one can find virtually anything one wants to find in it. If someone is a pacifist, he can find strong arguments for non-violence in the Sermon on the Mount; if someone is a hawk, he can find strong arguments for militancy in the Books of Samuel, Kings, and Chronicles. One can also find in this Bible, if he cares to look hard enough, evidences of agnosticism, atheism, polytheism, cannibalism, incest, parricide, polygamy, and just about anything else you can think of.

It does no good to say, as the Fundamentalists do, that you have to know how to read this Bible as the gradual unfolding of a Revelation, that it is a succession of Covenants, each one superseding the previous one. This insistence that there is a "correct way" of reading the Bible only exacerbates the problem and takes away our power of reasonable inquiry to figure out what the whole thing is all about. And it might drive highly intelligent men like Christopher Marlowe to ditch the whole thing altogether and dismiss the Bible as "filthily written."

One of the chief features of the Bible is that despite its many inconsistencies and discrepancies, it is so powerfully moving and persuasively written that one can turn to the letters of Paul with a perfect contempt for the man's narrow biases and gross distortions of the teachings of Jesus, and still be perfectly charmed by Paul's inspired writing in Romans, Ephesians, or Corinthians. In a similar manner, one can be ready to despise any of the televangelists on sight; yet, when one tunes them in, one is surprised at how powerful and persuasive they can be, in spite of the fact that they have no underlying theology to speak of.

It's enough to boggle the mind, but it also irritates a lot of people. Carroll Terrell, the world's foremost Ezra Pound scholar and Emeritus

Professor of English at the University of Maine at Orono, comments in issue 33 of *The New York Quarterly*:

> Christ was angry a lot of times. It's perfectly all right to be angry, and I get more angry than most people at these religious con men, Falwell and Swaggart, and whatever their names are. Maybe Swaggart can be justified, he may be ignorant. He went to the 8th grade or something, but that Robertson, he has a Yale degree. He knows better. Bleeding millions of dollars out of people. So I get angry at these "holier than thou" Baptists and their hell . . .

This impatience and anger at simplistic Evangelists and their pious racketeering may actually mask a much deeper impatience with modern Protestant theology itself, for not coming up with any adequate response to the problem of evil in our time.

But then in the entire history of Judeo-Christian thought there has been only one really adequate response to the problem of evil and that is contained in what is probably the oldest book in the Bible, the Book of Job.

Job complains to God about his sufferings, the loss of his family and all his worldly goods, together with the physical pain he experiences when his body breaks out in boils. And beyond his complaining, Job wants to have some explanation for these evils that are being visited on him: he needs to be assured that in spite of all his pain he still lives in a moral universe.

God answers Job out of the whirlwind and demands what right Job has to be challenging God about the nature of the universe. It is, to be sure, a begging of the question, but it does reduce Job to a humility which seems to be requisite for his eventual redemption.

The awful truth is that there may be no adequate answer to the problem of evil and meaninglessness, at least not in our lifetime. And that means there may be no lasting or satisfactory theology for our post-modern era, except for a lowering of our pride and the acceptance of a humility that may be requisite for our own eventual redemption.

For the first time in human history, our science has shown us that our earth is an insignificant speck that is floating along in a cosmic ocean of expanding galaxies. Our earth keeps turning in its socket like an old eyeball that is staring out at the night sky, and it sees stars far in the darkness—stars and stars and stars. And our earth wonders what are those stars, those tiny brightnesses of light that seem to be so alive with life? But there is no answer from that cold ocean space out there, no word, only a winking like the winking of blind eyes.

This is the profound humility we feel in the eighth Psalm:

3 When I consider the heavens, the work of thy fingers, the moon and the stars, which thou hast ordained,

4 What is man, that thou art mindful of him, or the son of man, that thou visitest him?

And we get the same sense of humility in that line of Pascal in his *Pensées*: *"Le silence éternel de ces espaces infinis m'effraie."* ("The eternal silence of these infinite spaces terrifies me.") (206)

We know there are some 10^{20} stars out there within the range of our strongest telescopes, and there is probably an infinity of stars beyond those stars. And one cannot keep from speculating about these night skies and wondering if there may be other forms of life or spirit out there. And could any of those possible worlds ever know or care anything about what we may be going through down here on our planet earth?

We know that here on earth our ultimate destiny is to deal with our past, present, and future with as much clarity and insight as we are capable of. And we know that in the next few decades we will probably face the staggering prophesies of worldwide famine on an unprecedented scale, with hundreds of millions of people starving to death. Paul Ehrlich sets down the simple acceleration rate of world population in his book *The Population Bomb*:

6000 B.C.	5 million people
A.D. 1650	500 million people
A.D. 1850	2 billion people
1980s	5 billion people

The reader can take it from there. It doesn't take much imagination to foresee what cataclysms of famine or exhaustion of resources, global nuclear conflagration, or pandemic AIDS scourge may be lying in wait for us.

We have to say it: God help us. Even though we do not know what God we may be praying to anymore, and even though the only theology we have been able to find for our post-modern era is the soul-searing humility of Job—even so, we still have to pray for the grace to pray.

Afterword

TOWARDS A NEW
EVANGELISM

Now THAT WE have examined the background and practice of Evangelism in America, we may be getting a little bit impatient with the limited range and scope of all our contemporary Evangelists.

Because we already know the whole scenario by heart, whether it's Jimmy Swaggart, Jerry Falwell, Billy Graham, Oral Roberts, or Jim Bakker: they all preach a terrifically theatrical message of moral outrage and cosmic doomsday, and they're also awfully good at simulating a Dionysian frenzy, rapture, and sincerity onstage; and then they all want us to receive Jesus and send in our freewill gift offering to support their television ministries.

And if we've already made up our minds that we're not going to opt for any of these illogical, outdated, or exotic types of Evangelical pitches that are being directed at us, then perhaps we may wonder if it might be possible to sketch out some radically different types of Evangelism that might be able to satisfy our deepest needs more directly and honestly.

Following are a few unorthodox forms of Evangelism which have been going on around us for some time, although they have not been seen as "Evangelical." If we look to see what sort of conversionary changes are involved in these unusual movements, we may be able to encounter some possibilities for a new Evangelism in the future.

Alcoholics Anonymous can be called Evangelical because of its phenomenal record of converting behavior patterns in people, from drunkenness to a life of sobriety. A.A. was begun by two businessmen who downplay their own role in the organization: Bill Wilson and a man known simply as "Dr. Bob." One of these two founders of A.A. suffered delirium tremens and hospitalization before he came up with the simple twelve-step program that governs all A.A. groups.

There is a spirit of selflessness in the concept and administration of Alcoholics Anonymous which prompted Aldous Huxley to call its founders "among the great social architects of our time." There are chapters of A.A. in virtually every major city of America, with membership and attendance at meetings entirely voluntary and under the cloak of anonymity.

The following statement by one active A.A. member was given to us for publication in this book under the promise of anonymity:

> I have been surrounded by alcoholism my entire life. My parents, my brother, and all of my friends abused alcohol and usually drugs. Almost anyone I had any social contact with did. My behavior did not seem to deviate from what, in my world, had always been the norm.
>
> I was aware that I was in pain; suffering from a self-destructive compulsion that was making me more and more isolated—taking me farther from reality. My day-to-day tasks had grown to unbearable challenges. Human interaction served only to make me more aware of my acute isolation and intensified my hopelessness. I had no way to bridge the gap between reality and the horrible place where I lived in my mind. Perhaps the most terrifying aspect of my alcoholism was coming to the realization that I had lost, or was losing, everything I once valued, including my values themselves. I was caught in a downward spiral and had no idea why, or how to make it stop. I perceived drinking as providing me with the only solace in a world that had no place for me. The worse things became, the more I drank.
>
> I had been abusing drugs and alcohol for ten years, from the ages of 13 to 23, when I joined A.A. In the beginning, they told me simply, "Don't drink, and go to meetings." "Bring the body and the mind will follow." "Keep it simple." "Take it easy." Gradually, I began to grow again. They taught me how to take care of myself, to avoid becoming too hungry, angry, lonely or tired. Not to beat myself up. And not to pick up a drink or a drug one day at a time. People gave me their phone numbers in case I needed to talk to someone and suggested I get a sponsor—someone to guide me through the "program," with whom I could let down my defenses and discuss my fears more openly.
>
> Though the A.A. program is relatively easy to follow, achieving sobriety has been difficult . . .

Another movement that has been going on around us for some time is the Peace Corps, first proposed by President John F. Kennedy in 1960. Over the last three decades, the Peace Corps has been sending American citizens into Third World developing nations in Asia, Africa, and Central and South America, where they help to improve the social and economic conditions, and try to bring about better world understanding.

Following are journal entries by one Peace Corps volunteer, Laura Herbst, who went through a five-day initial Stateside evaluation of her motives followed by a three-month technical and language training program in Togo, French West Africa, where she spent two years living and working in a remote Togolese village as the Women's Community Development Agent:

Arrived in Lomé. Embarrassed. Was received by a noticeable, loud crowd of white people off to one side, projecting their differential presence like the nipple on an aroused breast. Waving their arms, displaying welcome banners, applauding our arrival, while a silent, dignified black people looked on.

Riding in a van to a suburb of Lomé where our hotel is located. Cardboard roadside stands selling, bikeriders endlessly peddling, and people walking, walking and always carrying something—a basket of baguettes, a bundle of cloth, an expression of dignity that does not comprise lips turned falsely upward.

I almost cried. Something struck me as exceedingly beautiful here, exceedingly right—a purity which perhaps we westerners pollute by our very presence. I cannot attribute it to a lack of indulgent affluence, or proximity to earthly processes, but it feels somewhat like a spiritual well-being.

Living in non-Western society for two years confirms that Western civilization is not working as model for majority of humankind—sense that something is amiss in our lives, wrong with the society, unaccountable in our world view.

This pragmatic Evangelism of the Peace Corps may appear to be like the missionary activities of various Church groups who simply work to ameliorate conditions among Third World nations and/or underdeveloped environments. It may also seem to be like some drug-help groups here in the United States, purely humanitarian service groups, or Vista volunteers, coalitions for the homeless, or the more radical sanctuaries for illegal immigrants.

All these agencies, like the Peace Corps and like Alcoholics Anonymous, are direct responses to immediate human need.

Another approach to a new Evangelism is the modern view of the Artist as Priest. This movement found its best expression in the nineteenth century in Walter Pater's insistence on "art for art's sake": the practice of art became an end in and of itself.

It was Paul Cézanne (1830–1906) who first verbalized how modern art could be seen as a sacred vocation, when he said "Art is a priesthood." The German poet Rainer Maria Rilke (1875–1926) went further and claimed art was a more valid form of worship than any of the traditional religions: "How other, future worlds will ripen to God I do not know, but for us art is the way."

One reason underlying the phenomenal worldwide popularity of Vincent van Gogh (1835–1890) is that his life and work were such a clear testament to this religion of art for art's sake. The son of a Dutch pastor, Vincent began his life as an itinerant Evangelist trying to preach the gospel to remote mining outposts. Eventually he wearied of trying to preach the zeal he felt for sunlight, cornfields, and windmills, and he began painting them instead. In his extraordinary letters, Vincent wrote how he felt his work itself was a religious quest: "One does not expect out of life what one has already learned it cannot give. But rather one begins to see more and more clearly that life is only a kind of sowing time, and the harvest is not here."

Other nineteenth century artists embodied this idea of art as a kind of inspired Evangelism. Fyodor Dostoyevski (1821–1881), whose "Grand Inquisitor" section we discussed in the preceding chapter, also felt art was its own religion: "Perhaps the only goal on earth toward which mankind is striving lies in the process of attaining—in other words, in life itself, and not in the thing attained."

In Catholic Ireland, James Joyce (1882–1941) wrote a *non serviam* at the end of his *Portrait of the Artist as a Young Man* in which Joyce consciously renounced his family, his country, and his religion, in favor of the practice of his art:

I will not serve that in which I no longer believe, whether it call itself my home, my fatherland, or my church: and I will try to express myself in some mode of life or art as freely as I can and as wholly as I can, using for my defense the only arms I allow myself to use, silence, exile, and cunning.

Franz Kafka (1883–1924) also insisted that the practice of art for art's sake was a new Evangelism: "Truth, after all, is an affair of the heart. One can get at it only through art."

If the practice of art for art's sake is indeed a new Evangelism, then the artist's own work is analogous to the prayers of a contemplative monk or the mystical vision of some prophet-seer. A Latin maxim hints at this: "*Laborare est orare.*" ("To work is to pray.")

The Irish poet William Butler Yeats (1865–1939) insisted on the sanctity of the artist's work in his poem "Adam's Curse" where he wrote "It's certain there is no fine thing / Since Adam's fall but needs much laboring":

> A line will take us hours maybe;
> Yet if it does not seem a moment's thought,
> Our stitching and unstitching has been naught.
> Better go down upon your marrow-bones
> And scrub a kitchen pavement, or break stones
> Like an old pauper, in all kinds of weather;
> For to articulate sweet sounds together
> Is to work harder than all these, and yet
> Be thought an idler by the noisy set
> Of bankers, schoolmasters, and clergymen
> The martyrs call the world . . .

The French Impressionist painter Henri Matisse (1869–1954) summarized this whole Evangelism of art for art's sake when he said: "Work is heaven."

Of course the movement was not limited to painting or poetry: art for art's sake as a new religion also permeated modern drama so that major reformers like Henrik Ibsen (1828–1906), August Strindberg (1849–1912), and Eugene O'Neill (1888–1953) saw the theatre as a cathedral in which one must sacrifice all one's middle-class notions of "entertainment" and "amusement" for the larger goals of seeing deeply into the human condition. Eugene O'Neill proclaimed this larger purpose when he wrote:

I mean the one true theatre, the age-old theatre, the theatre of the
Greeks and Elizabethans, a theatre that could dare to boast—without
committing a farcical sacrilege—that it is a legitimate descendent of
the first theatre that sprang, by virtue of man's imaginative interpretation
of life, out of his worship of Dionysos. I mean a theatre returned to its
highest and sole significant function as a Temple where the religion of
a poetical interpretation and symbolical celebration of life is commu-
nicated to human beings, starved in spirit by their soul-stifling daily
struggle to exist as masks among the masks of the living!

Art as a modern Evangelism that is pitted against the stultifying and
mindless materialism of our civilization makes each individual artist
a vessel of the living message that is to be given form. And this is in
the best Protestant tradition of Martin Luther, who taught that every
man was a Priest of the Living God.

Another approach to a new Evangelism has its roots in Greek thought,
in the Delphic Oracle's command of *Gnothi seuton*—know thyself.

Self-knowledge for the Greeks was the supreme challenge of life
and one ignored it at one's peril, as Oedipus Rex was to find out to
his chagrin. As far as the Greeks were concerned, the tragic flaw of
Oedipus Rex was not that he had killed his own father and married
his own mother, but that he failed to find out who he really was.

Of course one may well wonder how anyone can ever arrive at any
self-knowledge in this world of shifting shadows and charades. But the
Greeks had devised an effective method of discovering the truth of any
matter by the systematic asking of questions: all Greek philosophy
begins with the asking of the simple question *"Tò ti"*—"what is it"?
And this persistent honest inquiry into all matters was embodied in
the homely figure of Socrates, that querulous gadfly of Athens who
taught that the only sin is ignorance.

Socrates did not pretend to know anything, and therein lay his
special claim to wisdom: he mercilessly baited anyone who made any
pretensions to knowledge of any kind, whether that person were Senator, teacher, or plain citizen, and whether that claim to knowledge
was in the field of politics, education, or virtue. The searing honesty
of Socrates cut through the fog and foolishness of officialdom and
professorial pomp in his own time, and it finally put him on trial for
his own life in 399 B.C.

During that trial, as described for us in Plato's *Apology*, Socrates
still insisted that an enlightened life consisted of an endless questioning:

"I say again that daily to discourse about virtue, and of those other things about which you hear me examining myself and others, is the greatest good of man, and that the unexamined life is not worth living."

The simple act of dialectical questioning is the cornerstone of classical psychoanalysis, which is the science most completely devoted to fulfilling the Delphic Oracle's command to know thyself. Sigmund Freud (1856–1939), like Socrates, developed a simple technique of asking questions continuously: he just shifted the field of inquiry. Whereas Socrates continually cross-examined himself and others as to the nature of reality and the good life, Freud began exploring an entirely new area of awareness in the depths of the unconscious mind.

Freud gives the key to this new approach in the citation he uses for his major work, *The Interpretation of Dreams* (1900), in which he quotes from Virgil's *Aeneid*: *"Flectere sinequeo superos, Acheronta movebo."* ("If I cannot bend the gods above, then I will move the infernal region.")

This single line may mark one of the most significant events in modern thought, once we realize what Freud is saying through Virgil: that if he cannot draw his insight from the heavens overhead, as traditional Judeo-Christian thought has taught us that we ought to do, then Freud will see if he cannot unlock new gods who may be slumbering in the demonic regions of the unconscious mind.

It is a reckless, brazen, and revolutionary adventure Freud is proposing, almost as anti-religious and Dionysian as anything Nietzsche ever came up with in *Thus Spake Zarathustra*. Freud even offers a systematic technique for this descent into the unconscious which modern man has to accomplish: by analyzing our dreams as coded emblems of our secret wishes, Freud shows that dreams are the royal road to the unconscious mind. The American poet W. H. Auden calls this radical new pilgrimage a "technique of unsettlement" as it presupposed the unsettling of all our well-meaning masks, all our social roles and poses, before we can find out what is really going on behind the eyes, inside the mind, far in the darkness of the heart.

Of course our resistance rises up against an exploration of these forbidden areas because we may not like what we see in our own unconscious. After all, it is in this same *Interpretation of Dreams* that Freud first presents us with the dreaded Oedipus Complex, which he insists is the *sine qua non* of all human sexuality: that every man secretly wishes to kill his father and mate with his mother, and every woman secretly wishes to kill her mother and mate with her father.

At this point the reader is probably getting irritated, and wants to turn this page and forget all about it. What kind of Evangelism is this, that says such outrageous things about what we "secretly" wish to do? Kill our fathers? Mate with our mothers? Give us a break!

Indeed, this Oedipus Complex is so offensive to our sensibilities, so ludicrous to our common sense, and so awful to our sense of self-esteem, we will do anything and everything we can think of to refute, ignore, or forget it. Yet the more we live, the more we realize how pervasive our primal feelings are, no matter what disguises or surrogate forms they may take, and we begin to realize we are acting out the same formula in our lives over and over. And that's when we turn back and say maybe there is something to this Oedipus Complex after all.

In fact, Freud's Oedipus Complex may be so far-reaching in its implications, and so deep-seated in its relevance to our own life, it may rival Einstein's ($E = mc^2$) as a universal equation which sums up everything we may hope to know about the physical basis of our human experience here on this planet earth.

Freud went on to write other books which were also guides to the descent inside ourselves: in *Three Contributions towards a Theory of Sexuality*, he advances the premise of Infantile Sexuality, which says children from birth to six are more libidinal and even more sexually knowing than they will ever be in later life. Curiously this premise is still vigorously suppressed and conspicuously lacking in almost all contemporary American behavioral psychology and sociological thought. Freud himself predicted that of all his major ideas—the Oedipus Complex, the Interpretation of Dreams, Infantile Sexuality—it would be this last premise of Infantile Sexuality which would meet with the strongest resistance, especially in America, because we Americans still cling tenaciously to the delusion that children are oblivious to all matters pertaining to human sexuality. Worst of all, we still insist on seeing our own childhood in the light of this delusion, which only reinforces our amnesia of what we were really feeling during those fearful early years.

Freud's *Totem and Taboo* is a remarkable study of clans of persons related by blood and the "magic" they employ to perpetuate their primordial bonding. The book is a useful explanation of the unconscious patterns that are at work in that placid domain of the American family which produces so many lifelong psychic cripples among us.

Freud's later work is disconcerting even for his most enthusiastic followers. We have already discussed the ideas contained in *The Future of an Illusion* and his advocacy of an irreligious education and upbringing. Freud's last book, *Moses and Monotheism*, begins with the hypothesis that Moses was not Jewish but Egyptian, and Moses did not receive the Ten Commandments on Mount Sinai but was murdered there. Freud claims the whole of the Old Testament is the record of the covering over of that murder: as he comments in the book, it is not so difficult to kill someone but it is awfully difficult to cover over the traces of that killing.

At this point the reader probably not only wants to turn this page, he wants to rip it right out of the book! That's how strong the resistance is to these radical ideas that Freud is advancing. We suggest the reader take a deep breath and let us continue on for just a few more pages.

Why would Freud suggest that Moses had been murdered on Mount Sinai? It follows inescapably from his insistence on the Oedipus Complex. In fact, Freud sees parricide underlying almost all religion, history, and art; he once commented that the three greatest works of Western literature were *Oedipus Rex*, *Hamlet*, and *The Brothers Karamazov*, pointing out that it was no accident that all three works focused on parricide as their most prominent underlying theme.

We may dispute this new Evangelism of classical psychoanalysis all we like, but we cannot quarrel with the centrality of Freud in our modern world. Three of our most distinguished poets testify to Freud's significance—the first, W. H. Auden, in his poem "In Memory of Sigmund Freud," describes how the impact of Freud's ideas changed the modern world:

> . . . simply by looking back with no false regrets;
> all he did was to remember
> like the old and be honest like children.
>
> He wasn't clever at all: he merely told
> the unhappy Present to recite the Past
> like a poetry lesson till sooner
> or later it faltered at the time where
>
> long ago the accusations had begun,
> and suddenly knew by whom it had been
>   judged,
> how rich life had been and how silly,
> and was life-forgiven and more humble,

able to approach the Future as a friend
without a wardrobe of excuses, without
a set mask of rectitude or an
embarrassing over-familiar gesture . . .

The second poet, Robert Duncan, describes how Freud opened us up to trust in our own life and work:

After Freud, we are aware that unwittingly we achieve our form . . .
The magnificence of Freud is that he never seeks to cure an individual
of being himself. He seeks only that the individual may come to know
himself, to be aware. It is an underlying faith in Freud that every
"patient" is Man himself, and that every "disease" is his revelation.

The third poet, Robert Lowell, describes Freud in clearly Evangelical terms: "Freud is the man who moves me most . . . Freud seems the only religious teacher . . . What I find about Freud is that he provides the conditions that one must think in . . ."

The Delphic Oracle commanded man to know himself, and Socrates developed the dialectic technique of questioning which insisted that the unexamined life is not worth living. Freud commented, "Self-analysis is a never-ending process that must be continued indefinitely." All these approaches are really the same—the endless examination of one's own life is the only thing that will make one's life worth living.

If the reader has experienced any resistance to the ideas expressed in the last few pages of this book, he can imagine how a Fundamentalist Evangelist would react! No wonder Evangelists decry "secular humanism" with such contempt, and see modern art and literature as a foolish offshoot of pagan idolatry. As for the writings of Sigmund Freud and the practice of classical psychoanalysis—any Fundamentalist worth his salt would condemn the whole thing as an immoral concentration on sexuality and selfhood, and say that it has more kinship with the Devil than it has with Judeo-Christian worship.

Of course, the Fundamentalist would be absolutely correct in his allegations, especially that bit about how Freud has more kinship with the Devil than with Judeo-Christian worship: remember that Freud himself began his *Interpretation of Dreams* with that citation from Virgil, disassociating himself from the heavens overhead and announcing he was going to descend into the demonic regions.

The fact is that in its comparatively brief history, and in spite of the furious storms of controversy which have always enveloped it in this country, psychoanalysis has established itself as a healing agency every bit as efficacious as penicillin or Charismatic faith healing.

The final approach to a new Evangelism we will look at is the practice of Quietism, which espouses a modest contemplation of religion without the intermediate agency of Church or Priest. Quietism is the height of Protestant independence, being a prayerful awareness that is set down in both the Old and New Testaments.

A lifetime of Quietism is implied in the shepherd imagery of the twenty-third Psalm where the lost soul is told it will lie down in green pastures and be led beside the still waters. Quietism underlies the fourth Psalm:

4   Stand in awe, and sin not: commune with your heart upon your bed, and be still.

And again, in Psalm 46:

10 Be still, and know that I am God: I will be exalted among the heathen, I will be exalted in the earth.

In the New Testament, a simple life of Quietism is a constant theme in the teachings of Jesus, especially in the Sermon on the Mount, Matthew Chapter 6:

6   But thou, when thou prayest, enter into thy closet, and when thou hast shut the door, pray to thy Father which is in secret; and thy Father which seeth in secret shall reward thee openly.

28 And why take ye thought for raiment? Consider the lilies of the field, how they grow; they toil not, neither do they spin:
29 And yet I say unto you, That even Solomon in all his glory was not arrayed like one of these.

33 But seek ye first the kingdom of God, and his righteousness; and all these things shall be added unto you.

The practice of Quietism in the modern world began in the seventeenth century with the Spanish priest Miguel Molinos (1640–1696), who advocated the absence of individual will and a withdrawal from all sensory experience in prayer, as set down in his *Spiritual Guide*

(1675). About the same time as Molinos, the French François Fénelon (1651–1715) was called "the apostle of interior inspiration" and developed his Quietist thought along similar lines in *Maximes des Saints* (1697).

A more recent description of the practice of Quietism can be found in the *Letters* of Baron Friedrich von Hugel, a German Catholic living in England. Von Hugel's gentle advice to his niece encouraged her to remain quiet before the ultimate mysteries of life:

> Be silent about great things; let them grow inside you. Never discuss them; discussion is so limiting and distracting. It makes things grow smaller. You think you swallow things when they ought to swallow you. Before all greatness, be silent—in art, in music, in religion: silence.

This simple practice of Quietism is not as easy to achieve as it may appear: it takes a lifetime of inner discipline to remain silent before ultimate mysteries. Quietism may also be precariously misleading, as there is always the danger one may internalize one's psychological problems under the guise of devotional worship, and that may lead to delusion or hallucination.

Of course contemporary Evangelists are every bit as scathing towards Quietism as they are towards art or psychoanalysis, and it's no wonder: Quietists seem so blandly anti-Evangelical in their non-verbalism and their underlying assumption that no one needs to tell anyone anything. Quietists simply go on practicing their meditation on the ultimate mysteries, bypassing conversion, Revivals, Crusades, and all the other accoutrements of contemporary Evangelism.

Even so, Quietism through its very simplicity continues to attract solitary souls in every age who wish to pursue a life of inner discipline and contemplation.

These are a few approaches towards a new Evangelism that may speak to our needs in the immediate future: there are the social rehabilitiation programs such as Alcoholics Anonymous; there are the international assistance programs such as the Peace Corps; there is the Evangelical practice of art for art's sake; there is the self-knowledge to be derived from the continuous practice of the techniques which are taught by classical psychoanalysis; and there is the modest pursuit of the practice of Quietism.

Of course there are other activities and practices which might be included on this list, as approaches to a new Evangelism in the future: there is the practice of jazz, acting, dance, mathematics, filmmaking, or any other creative discipline that draws on one's inner resources as a human being. Martin Luther King, Jr., went so far as to include street cleaners as instruments of God's will.

And there is one last approach to Evangelism, which is probably the most deeply natural and inevitable type of personal conversionary experience. We are thinking of the profound changes one observes taking place inside oneself during the course of living one's life. There are experiential sufferings, conversions, and redemptions that one is hardly aware of during the process of maturation and adaptation in one's lifetime, and these crucial inner events make up one's surest spiritual destiny.

Leo Tolstoy portrays such experiential changes taking place inside the soul of the character of Pierre in the novel, *War and Peace*. During the Napoleonic invasion of Russia, Pierre is arrested as an incendiary by the French in Moscow, and he is sentenced to face a firing squad. While waiting in line to be shot, Pierre witnesses the execution of an eighteen-year-old Russian factory lad who is tied to a post in front of a French musket team of sharpshooters. Pierre sees this young boy shot and then thrown into a large pit where he is buried alive by the French soldiers. And at that instant, Pierre realizes he has lost all faith in life itself, and any hope of ever reclaiming any belief in God is no longer in his own power.

But then a curious thing happens: Pierre is pardoned from his own execution, and instead he is thrown in a dark prison cell where he comes in contact with the simple Russian peasant Platon Karataev, and Pierre witnesses this little man get down on his knees and say prayers for all of humanity and also for the dogs and horses of the world. And in that instant, inexplicably, Pierre experiences a return of his faith in life, and he realizes that his new faith is on foundations now that can never be shaken by anything that ever happens to him again.

Later when Pierre and Platon are forced to go on a death march outside of Moscow, Pierre has to witness the senseless shooting of this saintly peasant Karataev, but even this cruel absurdity does not shake his new faith in the ultimate meaning of life: on the contrary, Pierre has a revelation about the underlying unity of all things in the universe. Tolstoy describes this in Part 13, section 15, of *War and Peace*:

> Life is everything. Life is God. All is changing and moving, and that motion is God. And while there is life, there is the joy of the con-

sciousness of the Godhead. To love life is to love God. The hardest
and the most blessed thing is to love this life in one's sufferings, in
undeserved suffering.

This type of sudden loss and restoration of one's deepest faith in
life is completely inexplicable, and may seem to belong more in the
realm of shock therapy than it does in the annals of Evangelism. Yet
we know these profound inner events are not at all unusual to those
who have had to endure the most crucial tests of life: men who took
part in trench warfare during the First World War, those who suffered
and survived the concentration camp experiences of World War II, or
those who experienced the guerrilla warfare in Korea and Vietnam.
People who have ever gone through radical life experiences know
what sudden shifts of spiritual life are all about, and every woman
who has experienced natural childbirth understands. Ask any of these
people and they will report experiential states of sudden despair and
then restoration of faith which are completely unaccountable. Walt
Whitman testifies to the inexplicable nature of our life, when he tries
to sum up his experiences in the American Civil War in one single
line from *Leaves of Grass*: "I was the man, I suffered, I was there."
There is simply no arguing with this type of existential and experiential witnessing to the profoundly conversionary nature of life itself.
Life is ineluctable, unaccountable, and sacred, and it shapes our human personality in mysterious ways, even beyond our wildest imag-
inings. No Evangelist could ever hope to duplicate the searing power
and the soaring effects of life experience, in bringing about authentic
changes in the human heart.
What we are saying here is that there is more than one way to enter
into the kingdoms of Heaven or Hell; this being so, it seems supremely
arrogant for any Evangelist to claim the human spirit operates according to certain fundamental rules of conversion and redemption.
We are all children of the living God and each man and woman has
his or her truth which has to be realized in its own unique way.
This trust in the experiential powers of life is entirely in accord with
the teachings of Jesus, who insisted that the worship of God was
inextricably bound up with the discovery of one's own spiritual destiny.
In the gospel of John Chapter 8, Jesus thus summarizes the goal of
all true Evangelism:

32   And ye shall know the truth, and the truth shall make you free.

Suggested Reading

Appel, Willa. *Cults in America: Programmed for Paradise.* New York: Henry Holt, 1983.

Ashman, Chuck. *The Gospel According to Billy Graham.* Secaucus, New Jersey: Lyle Stuart, 1977.

Augustine, Saint. *Confessions.* Any edition.

———. *City of God.* Any edition.

Bakker, Tammy. *I Gotta Be Me.* Green Forest, Arkansas: New Leaf Press, 1987.

———. *Run to the Roar.* Green Forest, Arkansas: New Leaf Press, 1987.

Barber, Richard. *The Reign of Chivalry.* New York: St. Martin's Press, 1980.

Bettelheim, Bruno. *The Uses of Enchantment.* New York: Knopf, 1976.

Bradford, Gamaliel. *D.L. Moody: A Worker in Souls.* Chicago: George H. Doran Co., 1927.

Bunyan, John. *Grace Abounding to the Chief of Sinners.* (1666.) Any edition.

———. *The Pilgrim's Progress.* Any edition.

Carlyle, Thomas. *On Heroes, Hero-Worship and the Heroic in History.* Any edition.

Clarke, John Henry. *Marcus Garvey and the Vision of Africa.* New York: Random House, 1974.

Cleaver, Eldridge. *Soul on Ice.* New York: Dell, 1968.

Cowan, Wayne H. *Witness to a Generation: Significant Writings from Christianity and Crisis, 1941–1966.* Indianapolis: Bobbs-Merrill, 1966.

Cox, Harvey. *Religion in the Secular City: Towards a Post-Modern Theology.* New York: Simon & Schuster, 1984.

Eckhart, Meister. *Works.* Any edition.

Edwards, Christopher. *Crazy for God.* Englewood Cliffs, New Jersey: Prentice-Hall, 1979.

Ehrlich, Paul. *The Population Bomb.* New York: Ballantine, 1968.

Emerson, Ralph Waldo. *Essays.* Any edition.

Erasmus. *In Praise of Folly.* Any edition.

Falwell, Jerry. *Listen, America!* New York: Doubleday, 1980.

Fitt, Arthur P. *The Shorter Life of D.L. Moody.* Ringgold, Louisiana: Bible Memory, 1982.

Fox, George. *Journal.* Any edition.

Frady, Marshall. *Billy Graham: A Parable of American Righteousness.* Boston: Little, Brown, 1979.

Francis of Assisi, Saint. *Fioretti.* Any edition.

Frazer, James. *The Golden Bough.* Any edition.

Freud, Sigmund. *The Future of an Illusion.* Any edition.

———. *The History of the Psychoanalytic Movement.* Any edition.

———. *The Interpretation of Dreams.* Any edition.

Gandhi, Mohandas K. *The Story of My Experiments with Truth.* Any edition.

"God and Money." *Time* (cover story), August 3, 1987.

Goldwater, Barry. *The Coming Breakpoint.* New York: Macmillan, 1976.

Hadden, Jeffrey and Charles Swan. *Prime Time Preachers: The Rising Power of Televangelism.* Reading, Massachusetts: Addison-Wesley, 1985.

Harrell, David, Jr. *Oral Roberts: An American Life.* Bloomington, Indiana: Indiana University Press, 1987.

Hitler, Adolf. *Mein Kampf.* Any edition.

Huxley, Aldous. *The Perennial Philosophy.* New York: Harper, 1945.

James, William. *The Varieties of Religious Experience.* Cambridge, Massachusetts: Harvard University Press, 1985.

John of the Cross, Saint. *Works.* Any edition.

Kant, Immanuel. *The Critique of Pure Reason.* Norman Kemp Smith, trans. New York: St. Martin's Press, 1969.

Kierkegaard, Soren. *The Concept of Dread.* Any edition.

———. *Either/Or.* Any edition.

———. *Fear and Trembling.* Any edition.

———. *Purity of Heart Is to Will One Thing.* Any edition.

———. *The Sickness Unto Death.* Any edition.

———. *Stages on Life's Way.* Any edition.

King, Martin Luther, Jr. *Strength to Love.* Philadelphia: Fortress Press, 1981.

Knox, John. *The History of the Reformation in Scotland.* Any edition.

Lewis, C.S. *The Case for Christianity.* New York: Macmillan, 1943.

———. *The Screwtape Letters.* New York: Macmillan, 1982.

Lincoln, Eric. *The Black Muslims in America.* Boston: Beacon Press, 1973.

Master, Roy. *How to Survive Your Parents.* Grants Pass, Oregon: Foundation for Human Understanding, 1982.

Mather, Cotton. *Memorable Providences.* Any edition.

Mehta, Ved. *Mahatma Gandhi and His Apostles.* New York: Viking, 1976.

Mencken, H.L. *A Mencken Chrestomathy.* New York: Knopf, 1946.

Moody, Dwight L. *Moody's Latest Sermons.* Boston: Ogilvie, 1894.

Moody, William Revell. *The Life of Dwight L. Moody.* Old Tappan, New Jersey: Fleming H. Revell, 1900.

Morrison, Samuel Eliot. *The Oxford History of the American People.* New York: Oxford University Press, 1965.

Niebuhr, Reinhold. *Moral Man and Immoral Society.* New York: Scribner's, 1932.

Nietzsche, Friedrich. *Beyond Good and Evil.* Any edition.

———. *The Birth of Tragedy.* Any edition.

———. *Thus Spake Zarathustra.* Any edition.

Oates, Stephen B. *Let the Trumpet Sound: The Life of Martin Luther King, Jr.* New York: Harper & Row, 1982.

Packard, William. *The American Experience.* New York: Barlenmir House, 1979.

———. *Savonarola and the Italian Renaissance.* New York: Bird Girl Press, 1979.

Paine, Thomas. *Common Sense.* Any edition.

———. *The Crisis.* Any edition.

———. *The Rights of Man.* Any edition.

Pascal, Blaise. *Pensées.* Any edition.

———. *The Provincial Letters.* Any edition.

Plato. *The Republic.* Any edition.

Powell, Emma Moody. *Heavenly Destiny.* Chicago: Moody Press, 1943.

Renan, Ernest. *The Life of Jesus.* New York: Modern Library, 1927.

Roberts, Oral. *Miracles of Seed Faith.* Tulsa, Oklahoma: Oral Roberts Evangelistic Association, 1987.

———. *Holy Spirit in the Now.* Tulsa, Oklahoma: Oral Roberts Evangelistic Association, 1987.

Roberts, Richard. *He's the God of a Second Chance!* Tulsa, Oklahoma: Oral Roberts Evangelistic Association, 1987.

Robertson, Pat. *Answers to 200 of Life's Most Probing Questions.* New York: Bantam, 1987.

———. *Beyond Reason: How Miracles Can Change Your Life.* New York: William Morrow, 1985.

———. *Shout it from the Housetops.* Plainfield, New Jersey: Bridge, 1987.

Schuller, Robert. *The Peak to Peek Principle.* New York: Doubleday, 1981.

Schweitzer, Albert. *Aus meinem Leben und Denken. (Out of My Life and Thought.)* Hamburg: F. Meiner, 1975.

———. *The Quest of the Historical Jesus.* W. Montgomery, trans. London: A. & C. Black, 1952.

Siegel, Eli. *Self and World.* New York: Definition Press, 1981.

Smith, Joseph. *The Book of Mormon.* (1830.) Salt Lake City, Utah: Church of Jesus Christ of Latter Day Saints, 1964.

Stark, Rodney. *Religious Movements: Exodus, Genesis, and Numbers.* New York: Paragon House, 1985.

Straub, Gerard Thomas. *Salvation for Sale: An Insider's View of Pat Robertson's Ministry.* Buffalo, New York: Prometheus, 1987.

Swaggart, Jimmy. *Catholicism and Christianity.* Baton Rouge, Louisiana: Jimmy Swaggart Ministries, 1987.

———. *The Pre-Adamic Creation and Evolution.* Baton Rouge, Louisiana: Jimmy Swaggart Ministries, 1987.

———. *To Cross a River.* Baton Rouge, Louisiana: Jimmy Swaggart Ministries, 1987.

Teilhard de Chardin, Pierre. *The Divine Milieu.* New York: Harper & Row, 1954.

Teresa of Avila, Saint. *El Castillo Interior.* Any edition.

———. *Vida.* Any edition.

———. *The Way of Perfection.* Any edition.

Thomas, Cately. *Storming Heaven: Aimee Semple McPherson.* New York: William Morrow, 1970.

Thoreau, Henry. "Civil Disobedience" in *Selected Essays*. Putney, Vermont: Hendricks House, 1973.

———. *Walden*. New York: Modern Library, 1981.

Tocqueville, Alexis de. *Democracy in America*. Any edition.

Tolstoy, Leo. *The Kingdom of God is Within You*. Any edition.

———. *My Confession*. Any edition.

———. *War and Peace*. Any edition.

———. *What Then Are We to Do?* Any edition.

Underhill, Evelyn. *Mysticism*. New York: New American Library, 1954.

U.S. Congress. House. Committee on Foreign Affairs. Staff Investigative Group. *The Assassination of Rep. Leo J. Ryan and the Jonestown, Guyana, Tragedy*. 96th Congress, 1st Sess., May 1979.

von Daniken, Erich. *Chariots of the Gods?* Belfast, Maine: Bern Porter, 1985.

von Hugel, Friedrich. *Letters to a Niece*. Any edition.

———. *The Mystical Element in Religion as Studied in St. Catherine of Genoa and Her Friends*. New York: Gordon Press, 1977.

X, Malcolm. *The Autobiography of Malcolm X*. New York: Grove, 1964.

Young, Perry Dean. *God's Bullies: Native Reflections on Preachers and Politics*. New York: Henry Holt, 1982.

Zaretsky, Irving and Mark Leone. *Religious Movements in Contemporary America*. Princeton, New Jersey: Princeton University Press, 1974.

Index

Abbott, Lyman, 65
abortions, 202, 209–210
Ackerman, Nancy, 74
"Adam's Curse," (Yeats), 248
Addams, Jane, 62
Aeneid (Virgil), 250
Aesthetic Realism, 117–118
African Slave Trade, 222
Age of Reason, 34–35
Age of Reason, The (Paine), 37
Albert, David, 165
Alcoholics Anonymous, 244–245
Alexander VI, Pope, 24–25
Algonquin Bible, 46
Alev, Reginald, 75
Alighieri, Dante, 23. *See also* Dante
Allen, Ethan, 36
American Conservative Union, 203
American Gospel (Gortner), 171, 178
Ames, Richard, 165
Androcles and the Lion (Shaw), 11
Angley, Ernest, 167, 176
Ankerberg, Rev. John, 172
Anthony, Susan B., 61–62
Anti-Evangelism, 178–179
Apostolic Charge, 6–8
Applewhite, Herff, 108
Aristotle, 18–19
Armstrong, Garner Ted, 165
Armstrong, Herbert W., 164–165
Arnold, Matthew, 66
art, as modern Evangelism, 248–249
Artist as Priest, 247–249
Asbury, Francis, 52–53

Astor, John Jacob, 57
Astounding Science Fiction, 109
Auden, W.H., 250, 252–253
Autobiography of Malcolm X, The
    (Little), 130–131

Bach, Johann Sebastian, 100
Bakker, Jim, 69, 164, 166, 170–175;
    Falwell and, 213; Swaggart and,
    195–196
Bakker, Tammy, 166, 171–175
Balashova, Inessa, 215
Baraka, Amiri. *See* Jones, LeRoi
Barber, Richard, 18
Barnett, Donald Lee, 75
Barnum, P.T., 77
Barrows, Cliff, 152, 156, 167
Barth, Karl, 239
Bauer, Bruno, 96
Baur, Ferdinand Christian, 96
Beckett, Samuel, 238
Beecher, Henry Ward, 53, 90–91
Beecher, Lyman, 53
Be Happy You Are Loved (Schuller),
    191
Belli, Melvin, 174
Berdyaev, Nicolai, 239
Bernard of Clairvaux, 17
Bernstein, Leonard, 168–169
Bernstein (Peyser), 168–169
Berrigan, Daniel, 121–122
Berrigan, Philip, 121–122
Bhgavad Gita, 110

Bible, 241–243; higher criticism of, 100
Billy Graham: A Parable of American Righteousness (Frady), 151
Billy Graham Evangelical Association, 154–155
Black Death Plague, 26–27
Black Evangelists, 125–137
Black Liberation movement, 127, 137
Black Muslim movement, 129–135, 136–137
Black Panther Party, 135
Blake, William, 57
"Blue Buildings in the Summer Air, The" (Stevens), 47–48
Bob Jones University, 73, 152
Boleyn, Anne, 32
Bonaparte, Napoleon, 95, 96
Book of Mormon, The (Smith), 63–64
Booth, General William, 104
Botticelli, Sandro, 25
Bourne, Richard, 46
Bradford, Gamaliel, 94
Bradford, Sarah, 125
Brave New World (Huxley), 237
Breslin, Jimmy, 197
Brothers Karamazov (Dostoyevski), 235
Brown, H. Rap, 136
Brown v. Board of Education of Topeka, 143
Browning, Robert, 237
Bruno, Giordano, 32
Bryan, William Jennings, 69–72
Bryant, Anita, 116
Buber, Martin, 239
Bunyan, John, 44–45
Buonarroti, Michelangelo. *See* Michelangelo
Burckhardt, Jacob, 25
Bush, George, 198
Butler, N.M., 102
Butterworth, Eric, 165

Caliph Hakim, 17
Calvin, John, 31

Camp Meetings, 49–52
Camping, Harold, 165
Camus, Albert, 239
Canterbury Tales (Chaucer), 23–24
Carlyle, Thomas, 29
Carmichael, Stokely, 136
Carnegie, Andrew, 57
Carnegie, Dale, 163–164
Carr, Peter, 37–38
Carter, Pres. Jimmy, 204, 211–212
Cartwright, Peter, 53
Catholic Church, Evangelical movements in, 119–122
Catholic Worker, 120, 121
Catonsville Nine, trial of, 121–122
Cézanne, Paul, 247
Chanson de Roland, 16
Chardin, Teilhard de, 224
Charismatic movement, 69, 175–176
Charlemagne, 16
Charles Martel, 16
Charlotte Observer, 171–172
Chaucer, Geoffrey, 17, 23–24
Chrétien de Troyes, 16
Christian Broadcasting Network, 171, 187
Christian Science, 105–106
Christian Socialism, 65
Christian Union, The, 65
Christian Voice, 203, 205
Christianity and Crisis (Niebuhr), 240
Circus of the Sun, The (Lax), 120
Citizens for Freedom, 75
City of Faith Hospital, 181–182
City of God, The (Augustine), 14
"Civil Disobedience," (Thoreau), 138–141
Civilization of the Renaissance in Italy, The (Burckhardt), 25
Clark, Sen. Dick, 204
Clay, Cassius, 134
Cleaver, Eldridge, 135–136
Coffin, William Sloan, 123–134, 212
Cole, Glen, 197
Collins, Jerry, 185
Commager, H.S., 72

Committee for the Survival of a Free
    Congress, 203
Common Sense (Paine), 36
Communism, Evangelism and, 224–
    225
Community Chapel and Bible
    Training Center, 75
Confessions (Augustine), 12–13
Congress of Afrikan People, 136
Connally, John, 151
Conservative Caucus, 203
conversionary experience: Billy
    Graham's, 154; Moody on, 92;
    personal, 256–257; reasons for, 3–4
Copernicus, Nicholas, 27
Copland, Kenneth, 178
Corey, Giles, 47
corruption, levels of in Medieval
    Catholic Church, 22
Cotton, John, 46
Coughlin, Father, 162–163, 170
Counter-Reformation, 31–33
Cox, Harvey, 240
Crisis, The (Paine), 36–37
Critique of Judgment, The (Kant), 35
Critique of Practical Reason, The
    (Kant), 35
Critique of Pure Reason, The (Kant),
    35–36
Cromwell, Oliver, 116
Crouch, Paul, 171
Crucible, The (Miller), 47
Crusades: First, 17; overview of, 17–
    18; reverse Evangelism and, 18–19
Crystal Cathedral, Schuller's, 191
Cults in America (Appel), 113
Cuyler, Theodore, 89
Cycles of American History, The
    (Schlesinger), 210–211

Dante, 18
Darrow, Clarence, 69–72
Darwin, Charles, 56
Das Kapital (Marx), 224, 236
Davies, Samuel, 48
Day, Dorothy, 120–121

Day of Discovery, 177
Decameron (Boccaccio), 27
DeHaan, Richard and Martin, 177
Deism, 35, 36, 41–42
De Libero Arbitro (Augustine), 14–15
Democracy in America (de
    Tocqueville), 216–218
De Rerum Natura (Lucretius), 20
Descartes, René, 35
dialectical questioning, self-knowledge
    and, 250–254
Dialogues (Plato), 27
Dianetics, 109
Dickens, Charles, 57
Diet of Worms, 29–30
Discour de la Méthode, Le (Descartes),
    35
*Disputatio pro Declaratione Virtutis
    Indulgentiarum* (Luther), 29
"Disputation for the Clarification of
    the Power of Indulgences, The"
    (Luther), 29
Divine, Father, 126–127
Divine Comedy (Dante), 23
Divine Milieu, The (de Chardin), 224
Dix, Dorothea, 62
"Dr. Bob," 245
Dostoyevski, Fyodor, 235–236, 247
"Dover Beach," (Arnold), 66
Duffus, on Moody, 78
Duncan, Robert, 253
Durst, David, 122
Dutchman (Jones), 136
Dwight, Timothy, 53
*Dynamics of Change, Religious
    Movements: Genesis, Exodus and
    Numbers*, 108

Eastern thought, Fundamentalism
    and, 110–113
*Ecomium Moriae. See Praise of Folly,
    The*
Eddy, Mary Baker, 105–106
Edison, Thomas Alva, 58
Edwards, Jonathan, 48–49
Ehrlich, Paul, 243

Eichenberg, Fritz, 120
Eikenkroetter, Frederick J. II
  ("Reverend Ike"), 127
Einstein, Albert, 223–224, 238
Eisenhower, Pres. Dwight D., 145–
  146
El Greco, 31
Eliot, Rev. John, 46
Eliot, T.S., 238
Elmer Gantry (Lewis), 101
Emancipation Proclamation, 125
Emerson, Ralph Waldo, 59–60
Endicott, John, 45–46
Enquiry into the Nature and Causes
  of the Wealth of Nations (Smith),
  56
Entertainment, Evangelism and, 225–
  226
Epistles: as stumbling blocks, 11;
  themes of, 10–11
Equal Rights Amendment (ERA),
  189, 190
Erasmus of Rotterdam, 25
Erhard, Werner, 109–110
EST, 109–110
euangelion (glad tidings), 2
Evangel, derivation of, 2
Evangelical Christianity, major
  movements in, 175–176
Evangelical Council for Financial
  Accountability, 155
Evangelical groups, partial listing of,
  108
Evangelical Protestantism, 65–66
Evangelical Reform movements, 61–
  66
Evangelism: America's deep need for,
  217–218; Crusades and militant,
  17, 19–20; definition of, 215; goal
  of, 257; hypocrisy of Christian, 20–
  21; Medieval chivalry and, 16–17;
  radical, 60–66; reasons for
  prevalence of, 219–227; reverse,
  18–20; role of in politics, 203–205;
  seeds of radical, 4–8; towards a
  new, 244–257; true fruits of, 8–9;
  working definition of, 1. See also
  Protestant Evangelism

Evangelists: black, 125–137; female,
  177. See also radio evangelists;
  television evangelists
Evers, Medgar, 133
Evolution: and Scopes trial, 69–72;
  theory of and Fundamentalism, 68

faith healing: hypnosis and, 184–185;
  Roberts on, 182–184
Falwell, Jerry, 69, 200–214; influence
  of Fuller on, 163, 167; and PTL
  scandal, 172–175
Fard, W.D., 129–130
Farmer, James, 203
Farrakhan, Louis, 134
Faubus, Gov. Orval, 145
Faustus, Doctor, 28
Fénelon, François, 255
Finney, Charles, 53
Florida Bible Institute and Seminary,
  152
Flynt, Larry, 214
Ford, Henry, 57
Fortunatus, 14
Fosdick, Harry Emerson, 101
Foundation for Human
  Understanding, 165–166
Fox, George, 43–44
Frady, Marshall, 151, 155, 157–158
Franklin, Benjamin, 58
Frazer, James, 12, 52
free association, cathartic method of,
  185
Frelinghuysen, Theodorus, 48
frenzy, phenomenon of, 167–170
Freud, Sigmund: on American
  culture, 218; and cathartic method
  of free association, 184–185;
  classical psychoanalysis and, 250–
  254; criticism of religion of, 236–
  237
Fricke, Henry Clay, 57
Friedan, Betty, 210
Fromm, Erich, 239
Fundamentalism: American, 67–76;
  Christian, 67–69; doctrine of, 67;
  higher Bible criticism and, 100;

Muslim, 131; as political force, 73–76
Fundamentalists: educational institutions of, 73; and 1928 election, 72–73; Social Gospel and, 158
Fundamentalists Anonymous, 179
Fuller, Charles E., 163
Future of an Illusion (Freud), 236, 252

Galileo Galilei, 32–33
Gandhi, Mahatma, 138, 140–142
Gardner, Martin, 186
Garvey, Marcus Aurelius, 127–128
"geek," 168
Giametti, A. Bartlett, 212–213
Gibbon, Edward, 16
Gibran, Kahlil, 110
Ginsberg, Allen, 108
Gladden, Washington, 65
"glossolalia," 69
Gnothi seuton (know thyself), 249
"God is dead" theology, 234
Goethe, J.W., 3
Goethe: The Story of a Man (Lewisohn), 3
Gogh, Vincent van, 247
Golden Bough, The (Frazer), 12, 52
Goldwater, Sen. Barry, 211
Gorman, Marvin, 195
Gortner, Marjoe: on Angley, 176; as critic, 178; on Falwell, 200–201; on Humbard, 176; on Roberts, 182; on Robertson, 186–187; on Schuller, 192–193; on Swaggart, 194–195
Grace Abounding to the Chief of Sinners (Bunyan), 45
Graham, Billy, 151–161; crusades of, 155–158; as *ex officio* minister, 155, 159–160; influence of Fuller on, 163, 167; vs. issues of day, 158–160; on Martin Luther King, Jr., 158
Graham, Rev. Sylvester, 64
Great Awakening movement, 48–49

Gregory IX, Pope, 19
Guccione, Bob, 195

Hadden, Jeffrey, 166, 174–175
Hahn, Jessica, 172
Haldane, John B.S., 224
Ham, Mordecai, 152
Hare Krishna, 111–113
Harrison, "Uncle" Henry, 171
Hatfield, Sen. Mark, 211
Healy, Timothy S., S.J., 213
Hearst, William Randolph, 153
Heidegger, Martin, 238–239
Heindel, Max, 64
Heisenberg, Walter, 223–224
Helms, Sen. Jesse, 203, 205–206
Henry VIII, King of England, 32
Herod, 4
Herzl, Theodore, 119
Historical and Biographical Papers: Sketches from the Life of Mary Baker Eddy and the History of Christian Science, 105–106
History of the Jews (Josephus), 96–97
History of the Reformation of Religion Within the Realm of Scotland (Knox), 31
Hitler, Adolf, 168, 229–230
Holocaust, 231
"Holy Wars," 195, 213
homosexuality, 209
Hoover, Herbert, 72
Hoover, J. Edgar, 146, 148–149, 203
Hope, Bob, 159
"Hot Afternoons Have Been in Montana," (Siegel), 117–118
Hour of Power, 191
How To Survive Your Parents (Masters), 166
How to Win Friends and Influence People (Carnegie), 163–164
Hubbard, David, 174
Hubbard, L. Ron, 108–109
Huckleberry Finn (Twain), 49–51
Hugel, Baron Friedrich von, 255
Hugo, Victor, 229
Humbard, Rex, 167, 176

Hus, Jan, 26
Hustler magazine, 214
Huxley, Aldous, 108, 237, 245

Ibsen, Henrik, 248
Ignatius de Loyola, 31
immigration, Evangelism and, 221–
   222
Index Librorum Prohibitorium, 31
indulgences, selling of, 23–24, 28
Infantile Sexuality, 251
In His Steps (Sheldon), 65
"In Memory of Sigmund Freud,"
   (Auden), 252–253
Innocent IV, Pope, 19
Inquisition, 19–20
Interpretation of Dreams, The (Freud),
   250, 251
Ionesco, Eugene, 238
Irwin, James, 108
It Is Written, 176

Jackson, Jesse, 136
Jacobs, Rep. Andrew, 186
James, William, 3
Janway, Cecil, 196
Jefferson, Thomas, 37–38, 220
Jehovah's Witnesses, 64, 106–107
Jesuits. *See* Society of Jesus
Jimmy Swaggart Bible College, 73,
   194
Jimmy Swaggart Evangelistic
   Association, 194
John the Baptist, 5
John XXIII, Pope, 119–120
John Paul II, Pope, 120
Johnson, Pres. Lyndon, 148
Johnson, Mordecai, 143
Johnson Act of 1921, 222
Jones, Rev. Jim, 113–115
Jones, LeRoi, 136–137
"Jonestown," 113–115
Josephus, 96–97
Journal (Fox), 44
Journals (Woolman), 44

Joyce, James, 247
Jubilee, 120

Kafka, Franz, 248
Kant, Immanuel, 35–36
Keats, John, 11
Kennedy, Sen. Edward, 211
Kennedy, James, 178
Kennedy, Pres. John F., 148, 203–
   204
Ker, W.P., 15
Khrushchev, Nikita, 225
Kierkegaard, Soren, 233–234
Kimball, Edward, 78–79
Kinchlow, Ben, 187
King, Coretta, 148
King, Martin Luther, Jr., 138–150,
   158, 203
Kingdom of God Is Within You, The
   (Tolstoy), 141
Knox, John, 31
Ku Klux Klan, 231–232
Kuhlman, Katharine, 177
Kurtz, Paul, 179

La Démocratie en Amerique (de
   Tocqueville), 216–218
Lancelot, 16
La Valley, Tammy Faye. *See* Bakker,
   Tammy
Lax, Robert, 120
Lazarus, Emma, 221
Leary, Timothy, 108
Leaves of Grass (Whitman), 61, 257
Lee, Mother Ann, 64
Leo X, Pope, 29
Letters (von Hugel), 255
Letters to a Young Poet (Rilke), 1
Lewis, C.S., 224
Lewis, Sinclair, 101
Lewisohn, Ludwig, 3
Liberty Broadcasting Network, 203
Liberty University, 73, 202
Life, 153
Life Is Worth Living, 170

Life of Jesus, The (Heinrich), 95–96
Life of Jesus, The (Renan), 96
Like It Is (TV), 136
Lincoln, Abraham, 125–126, 220
Listen, America! (Falwell), 206
Little, Rev. Earl, 130
Little, Malcolm, 130–132. *See also*
    Malcolm X
Little, Philbert, 131–132
Loisy, Abbé, 96
"London" (Blake), 57
London Saturday Review, 88
Longinus, 16
Lowell, Robert, 54–55, 253
LSD, use of, 108
Luce, Henry, 153
Lucretius, 20
Luther, Martin, and Protestant
    Reformation, 22–33

Macaulay, T.B., 44
McCloskey, Rep. Pete, 186
McGready, James, 49
McIntyre, Sen. Thomas, 204
McPherson, Aimee Semple, 101,
    102–104
Magellan, Ferdinand, 27
Mahomet, 15–16
Major Barbara (Shaw), 104
Malcolm X, 130–135
Manicheanism, 14
Marlowe, Christopher, 241
Marx, Karl, 224–225
Masters, Roy, 165–166
Materialism, Evangelism and, 219
Mather, Cotton, 45
Matisse, Henri, 248
Maurin, Peter, 120
Maximes des Saints (Fenelon), 255
Mein Kampf (Hitler), 229–230
Melancthon, Philip, 26
Melville, Herman, 60–61
*Memorable Providences Relating to
    Witchcraft and Possessions*
    (Mather), 46
Mencken, H.L.: as anti-evangelist,

178; on Fundamentalists, 203; on
    McPherson, 102–103; on
    Puritanism, 54; on Scopes' trial,
    70–72
Merton, Thomas, 120, 240
Mesmer, Franz, 64
"Methodist Society," 53
Michelangelo, 24
Miller, Arthur, 47
Miller, William, 64, 106
Milton, John, 45
Mitchell, John D., 103–104
Moby Dick (Melville), 60
Molinos, Miguel, 254–255
Montgomery bus boycott, 144
Moody, Dwight Lyman, 73, 77–94
Moody Bible Institute, 73, 93
Moorehouse, Henry, 80–81
Moral Majority, 202
More, Thomas, 32
Morgan, J. Pierpont, 57
Morison, Samuel Eliot, 15, 43
Mormons, as radical Evangelists,
    63–64
Morris, Samuel, 126
Moses and Monotheism (Freud), 252
Mother Angelica, 177
Mott, Lucretia, 61
Move That Mountain (Bakker), 171
Muhammad Ali, 134
Muhammad, Elijah, 129–130, 132,
    133
Murphee, Debra, 197
music, sacred, 54
Muslim religion, 16
Muste, A.J., 143
My Confession (Tolstoy), 140

Nation, Carrie, 62
National Association for Repeal of
    Abortion Laws, 209
National Conservative Political Action
    Committee, 203
Neuhaus, Richard John, 212
Neo-Pentecostal movement, 189. *See
    also* charismatic movement

Nettles, Bonnie, 108
"New Colossus," (Lazarus), 221
New York Herald Tribune, 168
New York Review of Books, 186
New York Quarterly (magazine), 136–137, 242
New York Times, 74
Newsweek, 151, 160–161
Nicolai Copernici de Hypothesibus Motuum Coelestium a se Constitutis Commentariolus (Copernicus), 27
Niebuhr, Reinhold, 143, 158, 240
Nietzsche, Friedrich, 234–235
1984 (Orwell), 237
"Ninety and the Nine, The," 80
Noel, Jeannette, 121
Noble, Gil, 136
Northfield Schools, 93–94
Notes of a Dead Lecturer (Jones), 136
Noyes, John H., 64

O'Connor, Sandra Day, 209
Oedipus Complex, 250–252
Ogilvie, Lloyd, 177
O'Hair, Madalyn Murray, 116–117
Old Fashioned Revival Hour, The, 163, 200
Old Time Gospel Hour, The, 163, 200
Olford, Stephen, 153
Oliver Twist (Dickens), 57
Oneida Community, 64
O'Neill, Eugene, 248–249
On Heroes, Hero-Worship and the Heroic in History (Carlyle), 29
Oral Roberts University, 73, 181
Origin of Species, The (Darwin), 56
Ormiston, Kenneth, 102
Ortega, Pres. Daniel (Nicaragua), 123
Orwell, George, 237
Otto, Rudolph, 239
Our Country (Strong), 65
Out of My Life and Thought (Schweitzer), 98
Oxford Bible (Scofield), 7
Oxford History of the American People (Morison), 43

Pabhopda, A.C. Bhaktivedanta Swami, 111
Packard, Elizabeth Parsons Ware, 63
Paine, Thomas, 36–37
Paradise Lost (Milton), 45
Paradise Regained (Milton), 45
Parks, Rosa, 144
Pascal, Blaise, 38–41
Pater, Walter, 247
Paul, 10–11
Paulus, Heinrich, 95–96
Peace Corps, 246–247
Peace Mission Movement, 126
Peace of Mind through Possibility Thinking (Schuller), 191
Peak to Peek Principle, The (Schuller), 191
Peale, Norman Vincent, 163–164
Pelagianism, 14, 163–164
Pensées, Les [Thoughts] (Pascal), 38–41, 243
Pentecostal movement, 69, 175–176
People for the American Way, 74
Perspective, 189
Peter Popoff Evangelical Association, 179
Peyser, Joan, 168–169
Pilgrim's Progress, The (Bunyan), 45
Pincus, Dion, 134
Pius XII, Pope, 119
Plain Truth magazine, 165
Poetry, Language and Thought (Heidegger), 238–239
Politics, Evangelism and, 219–220
polygamy, 64
Popoff, Peter, 179
Population Bomb, The (Ehrlich), 243
pornography, 208
Portrait of the Artist as a Young Man (Joyce), 247–248
Positive Prayers for Power-Filled Living (Schuller), 191
"Possibility Thinking," 191–193
Possible Worlds and Other Papers (Haldane), 224
Powell, Rep. Adam Clayton, 127
Power of Positive Thinking, The (Peale), 163

Praise of Folly, The (Erasmus), 25–26
predestination, doctrine of, 31
Pressler, Paul, 73
Price, K.C., 127
Prince, The (Machiavelli), 229
printing press, invention of, 26
Prophet, The (Gibran), 110
Protestant Evangelism, growth of, 34–42
Protestant Reformation, 22–33
Protestantism: problem for modern, 58; Puritanism and, 220–221. *See also* Protestant Evangelism; Protestant Reformation
Provincial Letters (Pascal), 38
psychoanalysis, Freud and classical, 250–254
PTL Network, 171–175
Ptolemy, 27
Puritanism: and Great Awakening, 43–55; Protestantism and, 220–221
"Pyramid of Vanities," 24

"Quaker," 43
Quakers, 43–44
Quest for the Historical Jesus, The (Schweitzer), 98–99
Quietism, 254–255

Rabelais, 24
radio evangelists, 162–166
Rajneech, Bhagwan Shree, 111
Randi, James, 178–179
Randolph, A. Philip, 147
Rauschenbush, Walter, 65
Reach Out for a New Life (Schuller), 191
Reagan, Ronald, 75–76, 204–205
Reason: The Only Oracle of Man (Allen) . . . *A Compendious System of Natural Religion*, 36
Reign of Chivalry, The (Barber), 18
Reimarus, Hermann, 95
religion, objective definition of, 3
Religion and the Rise of Capitalism (Tawney), 219

Renan, Ernest, 96
Republic (Plato), 14, 91
Revell, Emma, 79
Revival Meetings, 86–87; financing of, 93; Mencken on, 70; Moody on, 90
Revolution, The, 62
Rights of Man, The (Paine), 37
Rilke, Rainer Maria, 1, 247
Rimbaud, Arthur, 3–4
Rise and Fall of the Third Reich, The (Shirer), 30
Roberts, Oral, 69, 164, 181–186
Robertson, Pat, 74, 164, 167, 171, 175, 186–191, 198
Robeson, Paul, 128–129
rock music, 208–209
Rockefeller, John D., 57
Roe v. Wade, 202
Roosevelt, Franklin D., 72
Rosenkreuz, Christian, 64
Rosicrucian movement, 64
Roundtable, 203
Rowlatt Act, 141
Russell, Charles Taze, 106
Ryan, Leo J., 115
Ryle, Gilbert, 35

St. Augustine, 12–15, 164
Salem Witch Trials, 46–48
Salvation Army, 104
Sane-Freeze, 124
Sankey, Ira, 79–80, 86, 90
Saul of Tarsus, 9–10. *See also* Paul
Savonarola, Girolamo, 24–25
Schlesinger, Arthur M., Jr., 210–211
Schuller, Robert, 164, 167, 191–194
Schweitzer, Albert, 95, 98–100
Science, Evangelism and, 223–224
Science and Health with a Key to the Scriptures (Eddy), 105
Scientism, 237
Scientology, 109
Scofield, C.I., 7
Scopes, John, 69–72
Scott, Gene, 177
Second Awakening, 49–52

Second Coming of Jesus, 202
Secret Kingdom, The (Robertson), 190
"secular humanists," 69, 73, 74, 207
Seeds of Contemplation (Merton), 120
Self and World, 118
self-knowledge, as Evangelism, 249–254
"Self-Reliance" (Emerson), 59–60
Sermon on the Mount, 8
700 Club, 171, 187, 189
Seventh Day Adventists, 64
Seven Storey Mountain (Merton), 120
Sewell, Samuel, 47
Shakers, 64
Shaw, George Bernard, 11, 104
Shea, George Beverly, 152
Sheen, Bishop Fulton J., 170
Sheffer, Stuart, 51, 169–170
Sheldon, Charles M., 65
Shirer, William L., 30
Shout It From the Housetops (Robertson), 189
Siegel, Eli, 117–118
"Sinners in the Hands of an Angry God," (Edwards), 48, 53–54
Six Years with God: Life Inside Reverend Jim Jones's People's Temple (Jones), 114
Smith, Adam, 56
Smith, Al, 72–73, 203–204
Smith, Joseph, 63–64
Smuts, Jan Christian, 141
Social Gospel, 65–66, 158
Society of Jesus, 31
Socrates, 249–250
"sola scriptura," principle of, 30
Soul On Ice (Cleaver), 135
Spin magazine, 195
Spiritual Guide (Molinos), 254–255
Spock, Dr. Benjamin, 123
Stanton, Elizabeth C., 61
Steinem, Gloria, 210
Stevens, Wallace, 47–48
stichomancy, practice of, 13
Stone, Lucy, 61
Story of My Experiments with Truth, The (Gandhi), 140

Stoughton, William, 47
Stowe, Harriet Beecher, 53
strappado, 20
Strength to Love (King), 148
Strindberg, August, 248
Strong, Josiah, 65
Sukhdeo, Dr. Hardat, 113
Summa Theologica (Aquinas), 18–19
Sunday, Billy, 101–102
Susskind, David, 117
Swaggart, Jimmy, 69, 164, 167, 194–198
Swedenborg, Emanuel, 64

Tabernacle Sketches, 88
Tawney, R.H., 219
Tetzel, Johann, 28
televangelists, local, 177–178. *See also* television evangelists
television evangelists, 166–180
Templeton, Charles, 153–154
Tennent, Gilbert, 48
Tent Revival, 51–52
Terrell, Claude, 241–242
"thamaturgists," 4
theocracy: Florence, 24–25; Geneva, 31–32; Jonestown as, 115; Muslim, 131; in Salem, 45–46, 47; in Utah, 64
Thomas, Cal, 213
Thomas Aquinas, 18–19
Thomson, Virgil, on Bernstein, 168
Thoreau, Henry David, 61, 219; "Civil Disobedience," 138–141
Three Contributions towards a Theory of Sexuality (Freud), 251
Thus Spake Zarathustra (Nietzsche), 234
Tillich, Paul, 239, 240
Tilton, Robert, 177–178
Time, 153; on King, 145; on Roberts' claims, 185–186; on Robertson, 189
Tolstoy, Leo, 138–140, 256–257
Tocqueville, Alexis de, 216–219
To Tell the World, 176

Totem and Taboo (Freud), 251
Transcendentalist movement, 58–61
transubstantiation, doctrine of, 26
Trinity Broadcasting System, 171
Tubman, Harriet, 125
Twain, Mark, 49–52
Twenty Years at Hull House
    (Addams), 62

UFO cult, 108
ultra-Fundamentalists, 75
Uncertainty Principle, 223–224
Uncle Tom's Cabin (Stowe), 53
Unified Field Theory, 223
Urban II, Pope, 17, 19

Van Gordner, Paul, 177
Vandeman, George, 176–177
Varieties of Religious Experience, The
    (James), 3, 44
Veronese, 31

Waiting for Godot (Beckett), 238
Walden (Thoreau), 61, 219
Wallis, Roy, 108
War and Peace (Tolstoy), 256–257
Washington Post, 213
Waste Land, The (Eliot), 238
Watch Tower, 106
Watergate, 159–160
Wesley, Charles, 53, 54
What Then Must We Do? (Tolstoy),
    140
White Jacket (Melville), 60–61

Whitefield, George, 48–49
Whitman, Walt, 61, 257
Wieland, C.M., 95, 96
Wiesel, Elie, 118–119
Wilkins, Roy, 147
Willard, Frances, 62
Williams, Roger, 45
Wilson, Bill, 245
Wilson, Grady, 152
Wilson, Pres. Woodrow, 89–90
Winchell, Walter, 109
Wolfenbüttel Fragments (Reimarus),
    95
Wolsey, Cardinal, 32
Women's Christian Temperance
    Union (W.C.T.U.), 62, 102
Woman's Rights Movement, 61–62,
    210
Woolman, John, 44
World Tomorrow, The, 164–165, 177
Wycliffe, John, 26

Yao, Richard, 179
Yeats, William Butler, 248
*You Can Become the Person You
    Want To Be* (Schuller), 191
Young, Andrew, 136
Young, Brigham, 64
Young Americans for Freedom, 203

Zalkan, Barbara Singer, 118
Zionism, Jewish, 118–119
*Zion's Watch Tower and Herald of
    Christ's Presence*, 106. See also
    Watchtower
Zwingli, Ulrich, 26